JAMES

MERCY TRIUMPHS

BETH MOORE

with articles by

MELISSA MOORE FITZPATRICK

LifeWay Press®
Nashville, Tennessee

Published by LifeWay Press®

ISBN 978-1-4158-7171-3
Item 005459784

Dewey decimal classification: 227.91
Subject headings: BIBLE. N.T. JAMES—STUDY \ CHRISTIAN LIFE \
INTERPERSONAL RELATIONS

To order additional copies of this resource, write to LifeWay Church Resources Customer Service; One LifeWay Plaza; Nashville, TN 37234-0113; fax (615) 251-5933; phone (800) 458-2772; e-mail *orderentry@lifeway.com;* order online at *www.lifeway.com;* or visit the LifeWay Christian Store serving you.

Printed in the United States of America

Leadership and Adult Publishing
LifeWay Church Resources
One LifeWay Plaza
Nashville, TN 37234-0175

Dedication

To my big sister, Gay—

You are a hero to me. Onward together
to the finish line! Jesus is so worthy.

I love you deeply.

Melissa's Acknowledgements

I'd like to recognize New Testament scholars who spend years working with the Greek text of James and composing journal articles, commentaries, and monographs for simple folks like us to consult. Without proper words, I also thank Mom for taking a massive risk by allowing me to compose articles for this project. On demoralizing days when writing a mere paragraph felt daunting to me, she affirmed me. She taught me how to compose an outline and helped me survive the vexing editorial process. My respect for her has greatly increased through my minor involvement in this project, not least because she writes circles around me. I've learned how isolating and lonely writing can be, and I'm amazed by how happily engaged she has remained with our family despite years of cycling in and out of writing projects. I cherish the time I've spent learning closely from her during this project.

CONTENTS

ABOUT THE AUTHORS

Beth Moore has written best-selling Bible studies on the Patriarchs, Esther, Moses, Paul, Isaiah, Daniel, John, David, and Jesus. *Breaking Free, Praying God's Word,* and *When Godly People Do Ungodly Things* have all focused on the battle Satan is waging against Christians. *Believing God, Loving Well,* and *Living Beyond Yourself* have focused on how Christians can live triumphantly in today's world. *Stepping Up* explores worship and invites us to reach a new level of relationship and intimacy with God.

Beth and her husband, Keith, are devoted to the local church and have the privilege of attending Bayou City Fellowship in Houston, Texas, where their son-in-law, Curtis Jones, pastors. Beth believes that her calling is Bible literacy: guiding believers to love and live God's Word. Beth has a passion for Christ, a passion for Bible study, and a passion to see Christians living the lives Christ intended.

Beth loves the Lord, loves to laugh, and loves to be with His people. Her life is full of activity, but one commitment remains constant: Counting all things but loss for the excellence of knowing Christ Jesus, the Lord (see Phil. 3:8).

NEXT LEVEL ARTICLES BY

Melissa Moore Fitzpatrick has served as research assistant to Beth Moore since earning her M.A. in Biblical Exegesis from Wheaton College in 2007. She has since received her Th.M. in New Testament from Columbia Theological Seminary. She resides in Houston, Texas, with her husband, Colin. They are happy members of Bayou City Fellowship where her brother-in-law, Curtis Jones, pastors and her best friend and sister, Amanda, is her favorite pastor's wife.

ABOUT THE STUDY

James: Mercy Triumphs is designed for both interactive personal study and group discussion. Here are a few suggestions for making your time with the study more meaningful.

First, to enhance your learning and application of Scripture, the study is written in an interactive format. I encourage you to complete all of the written work in your workbook. This isn't just fill in the blanks. The interactive questions represent the very places where we'd look together in Scripture as we shared a cup of French roast coffee together. Please don't let the word *homework* scare you. The Holy Spirit uses your efforts as you respond to the activities in your own words.

Second, to enhance your group time together, you'll find five Principal Questions and five Personal Discussion questions each week. The Principal Questions alert you to look for information as you study and prepare group discussion. They are shaded like this:

This is a Principal Question. Principal means of chief importance.

Your small group will likely discuss the Principal Questions when you meet each week. In addition to the Principal Questions, you will find Personal Discussion segments identified by a colored bar like this:

This is a Personal Discussion Question designed for personal sharing.

These learning activities help you personally apply the material by relating the events to your own life. Your small group will allow time for you to share about your Personal Discussion responses, but you will not be required to share unless you so desire. Oh, how I wish I could be personally present with you each week, but this format provides the most personal contact possible until the time when we can share a cup of coffee. Then I'll look forward to listening to you as you have graciously listened to me through all these studies.

Finally, I need to add a personal request. You will see in a couple of places in the videos that I used the term *social justice*, regarding James' passion for the poor and disenfranchised. Later a reader alerted me about current political uses of that phrase. In this Bible study, please divorce the term from any and all political stands. Our intention is to teach the Book of James and its many themes. Among them is his clear and blunt call to a faith that shows itself through Christians serving the poor, the widowed, and the orphaned. You will discover we ultimately adopt the term *social mercy.* I certainly do not want us to be sidetracked with political issues. I pray that you will gain as much from this journey as I have. Thank you for the privilege to serve you.

INTRODUCTION

I am elated to have you along for this journey into the life and Book of James! This may be our first series together and, if so, I pray with all of my heart that this in-depth study and others like it will fan a lifelong flame in your heart for God's Word. Perhaps we've studied together before and, if so, I'm thrilled to tell you in advance that this one earned its own place in my heart. Each series from *A Woman's Heart: God's Dwelling Place* to this one has been used of God to accomplish a distinctive and lasting work. The mention of each name stirs up the remembrance of that prevailing revelation.

I won't tell you in advance what God worked in my life through this journey because the fun of it for me is to process the material along the way with you. When I penned week 1, day 1, for instance, I had no clearer idea where we were headed than you do now. When you get to difficult material, you will see that I am struggling through it, too. When you're convicted, you can know that my stomach is turning upside down as well. I love the uncertainty of what's ahead as long as I'm in the security of God's hands. It's like taking a winding highway for the very first time in a convertible. I want to feel the wind in my face. If you do, too, we're going to make good traveling partners.

This time God placed the idea on my heart to offer you options. Goodness knows we need a few of those amid frantic schedules and demanding roles. You get to choose your own level of participation.

Level 1: ***Participating in the video sessions only.*** Through the years I've watched women drop out of weekly Bible study because they couldn't keep up with the homework. Don't think for a moment that, if you can't do all of it, you're better off doing none of it. A shorter time in Scripture is far better than none at all. Watch the video sessions even if you can't get your homework assignments accomplished. You have LifeWay's blessing to copy the viewer guides for this purpose.

Level 2: Participating in the video sessions + ***doing the weekly homework assignments.*** Moving up to level 2 where you meet with God on the pages of Scripture numerous times each week exponentially increases your experience. When you turn the last page, you will truly know the Book of James and feel acquainted with the man who wrote it. If you've got the stamina to do the homework (and you do!), you've got it in you to view the sessions. Keep in mind that many of the larger themes are addressed in the sessions, so try your hardest to view the coinciding ones at the end of each week of homework.

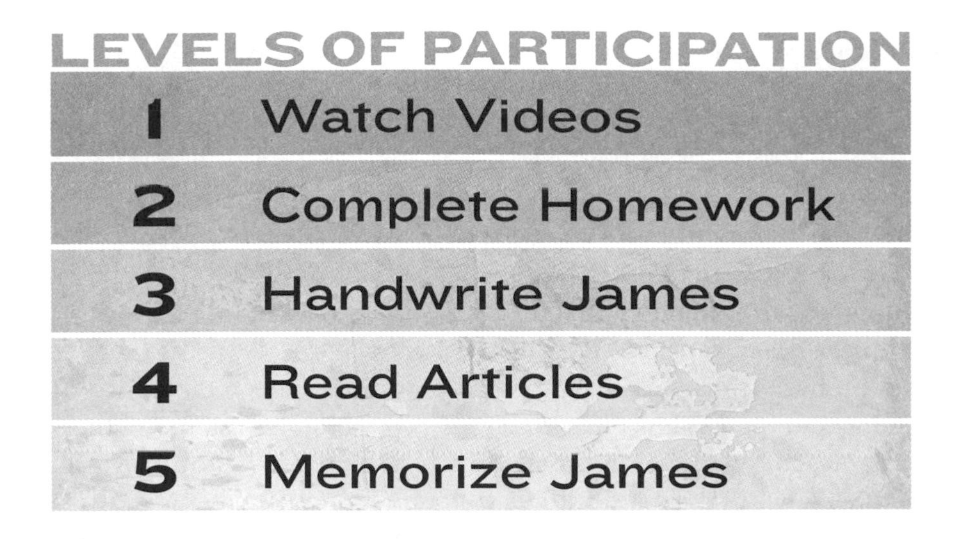

Level 3: Participating in the video sessions + doing the weekly homework assignments + *handwriting the Book of James.* I'm really excited about this level! For the first time in my nearly 20 years of writing Bible studies, we've arrived at a book of the Bible short enough to invite this exercise. The first and last weeks of this series focus on the life of James. In weeks 2 through 6, we'll study the actual Book of James. Each time we come to a new segment of James' epistle, I will ask you to read it then handwrite it in the back of your member book on pages designed for this exercise. If you don't choose level 3, you'll simply read the portion and, I pray, without a hint of self-condemnation. This option is simply available for those who want to take the next step to retain what they're learning.

Level 4: Participating in the video sessions + doing the weekly homework assignments + handwriting the Book of James + *reading "The Next Level with Melissa."* You might say I'm particularly partial to this level since I'm her mother. I say that with a grin but, while that's true, the real reason we incorporated this level is because you—or women like you—asked for it. Many women have written me after a series and asked how they could go even deeper in the material.

By that time, I've usually given them all I have to offer or, at the very least, all that the time and space allotment allowed. Woodrow Wilson once said, "I not only use all the brains I have but all I can borrow." Good advice, if you ask me; so this time around, I've borrowed my daughter Melissa's brain. And it's a big one. She has far surpassed her mother in formal theological training and the use of original languages, so I've asked her to bring a more academic approach to several of our concepts each week. Please keep in mind that her portions are options and that, stylistically, they are exactly what I asked of her.

Melissa and I know up front that neither of our writings will suit everyone's tastes, but we partner this time with a deep and sincere desire to serve you more fully. I would gladly have added her name to the cover, but she asked that I refrain. My daughter Amanda is almost always involved in the Bible study process as my first reader and editor. This time around she had her hands full with my beloved grandchildren. You can know that she joins Melissa and me in serving you through this series as your number one intercessor. We wrote and she prayed.

Level 5: Participating in the video sessions + doing the weekly homework assignments + handwriting the Book of James + reading "The Next Level with Melissa" + ***memorizing the Book of James.*** Trying to picture some of your faces almost has me tickled. But don't blame me. Remember all those women who kept asking for more? Blame them. Beloved, if you commit to all five of these levels, the Book of James will live in the marrow of your bones—probably for the rest of your life. You'll find a short tutorial in the DVD bonus material that may help you if you're interested in this level. Needless to say, we're not recommending that anyone try to memorize the whole book in the seven short weeks of this series. In the tutorial, I suggest a chapter a month for a total of five months, but the best recommendation is whatever works! Because God led me to take this challenge, I've recited the five chapters aloud more times than I can count in the process of writing this study. The exercise continues to bless me beyond what I could have imagined. Think about it! Pray about it! Then, some of you, do it!

OK, Sister, which level seems the most doable for you right now?

1 2 3 4 5

I'm asking you up front because I'd like to challenge you to go one level above what seems reasonably attainable. If you're willing, stretch yourself one more level! If you're pretty sure you can reach level 1, try stretching yourself into level 2 and see what happens. All you overachievers, keep in mind that higher levels and harder work won't make God love you any more than He already does. Nor will memorizing the whole book make us superior to someone else who can barely manage a few sessions. We are secure in Christ and acceptable to God through Him.

We have nothing to lose here but much Scripture to gain if we're game for a challenge.

Do only what BLESSES and not what burdens.

I'd like to say one last thing to you. I believe in experiences like this. I believe in Bible studies and God-centered books. I believe He can use them to alter a path. In the beginning stages of writing this series, a dimension of my life became so hard and had gone on for so long that I felt I could no longer bear it. I wanted to quit in the worst way. In the midst of it, I read a book. It doesn't matter which one it was because God can use anything He wants. I bawled at the end of it. Bawled till the tears were dripping off my nose and into my lap. Bawled until my lungs felt fluish and hot. The book talked about having the courage to live under strain and pain to be part of a better story. A larger story. It said not to wimp out. That only pain can bring about change. And, as a writer, not to be satisfied with writing a life I'm not willing to live. You're wondering what's new about that. But, then again, you know better than that. A subject doesn't have to be new. It just has to speak to the predicament you're in right now.

I'm humbled beyond expression to be your servant.

Jesus, Giver of Life and Lover of our souls, speak!

With deep affection,

Beth

Have the courage to live under strain and pain to be part of a better story. A larger story. Don't wimp out.

viewer guide | session one

I Corinthians 15:1-8

Our journey with James does not begin in the letter he wrote but with a plan God wrote. Part of God's infinite genius appears in how such humanness can play into the divine story.

"Then He appeared to James" (I Cor. 15:7).

1. ________ ____________ to those who ___________ to see Him most.

Consider several we know by name from this and other accounts.

John 7:1-9

"Jesus' brothers said to him" (v. 3, NIV) is one of two quotes attributed to or involving Jesus' brothers in the Gospels. Consider recent events in John 6:60-66.

The only other direct quote from Christ's collective natural family is Mark 3:21 (NIV), "They said, 'He is out of his mind.' "

2. James enters the ________ as an ______________.

3. Jesus radically ____________________ the idea of ____________.

   Consider what seems to be the progression:

____________ Family → Family + __________ → Disciples – __________ → ________ Family → ____________ Family

John 2:12 | Mark 3:31-35 | John 19:25-27 | Acts 1:12-14

1 Corinthians 15:9-10

4. By the __________ of God __________ became what __________ became.

"without effect"—Greek *kenos* (pronounced "kay-NAHS")—
"__________, vain, ineffective, ________________ … The basic meaning of this word is empty, lacking content, or ______________."

5. The power of the ______________________ means that nothing but the __________ is meant to be ___________.

WEEK ONE

A MAN CALLED JAMES

Day One

ALL IN THE FAMILY

FLASH FORWARD

"When the time came to completion, God sent His Son, born of a woman, born under the law, to redeem those under the law, so that we might receive adoption as sons." Galatians 4:4-5

A new era had come, the time for which all time existed. Yet, for the most part, life lapped at the shores of the Sea of Galilee just as it had before the great terror. A handful of years earlier, a crazed King Herod ordered the slaughter of all the baby boys in Bethlehem. By the time the decree was issued, an angel of the Lord had already appeared to Joseph in a dream and told him to make haste to Egypt with Mary and the child born to her of the Holy Spirit.

Don't suppose these kinds of dreams became a habit. Joseph had received a grand total of two. But by now he knew better than to doze back off and think about it in the morning.

Nothing was going as planned. Most Jewish men didn't live like this. They knew what to expect. The only thing they needed to know was what their fathers knew. Their trade was his trade. Their home was his home. The key decisions in life were dictated in advance by those very same fathers. Dad chose the bride in a business transaction with all the romance of a bank loan. Custom suffocated spontaneity from the very moment a Jewish boy gasped his first breath of air. That's not to say life wasn't good, but it was rarely unexpected.

The moment Joseph learned that the woman pledged to him was expecting, normalcy sprouted wings and flew like a raven to the wilderness. Suddenly the unexpected became all this carpenter could expect. If the angel of the Lord had not specified Egypt as their place of escape, the thought would have been appalling. He'd never imagine the cries of the world's oppressed rising to Heaven again from Egypt—this time through the wails of a toddler destined to be the Deliverer. No, nothing was going as planned.

Joseph may have become one of the rare men of history who thought going to sleep was his best option when he needed direction. Night after night brought no word; then, when he probably wondered if they'd been banished to the badlands, the angel of the Lord appeared to him in a dream for a third time. "Get up! Take the child and His mother and go to the land of Israel." Why don't you complete the rest of the quote from Matthew 2:20 in the margin?

"... because those who ...

Continue the line of thought by reading Matthew 2:21-23. Where did the young family settle and why?

Many would ultimately live because the One humanity sought would die.

Matthew 2:22 recorded yet another dream. If you didn't know better, you might think getting divine messages in your sleep had something to do with the name. Joseph designated dreamers in both Testaments.

Some of the dreams of the new era's Joseph were more like nightmares. Can you imagine the agony and irony a set of parents felt knowing that many died while the child Herod sought lived? They could not yet have comprehended that many would ultimately live because the One humanity sought would die. Then again, perhaps this was the meaning of the strange words of Simeon on the temple grounds when he beheld the infant Jesus.

Read Luke 2:34-35. Put yourself in Mary's sandals. What impact would Simeon's words have on you?

A sword will pierce our own soul, too. By the time Joseph and his family finally settled in Nazareth, he and Mary probably concluded that the sword piercing her soul had already sliced through her heart and done its damage. It had ripped them from their families and terrorized them with infanticide. It had bloodied their heels like a mad wolf chasing them all the way to Egypt, and it had turned home into hiding. *Finally*, perhaps they thought. They'd found their new normal. Thinking the worst is behind us is the better of two options, and for a while Mary and Joseph would have been right.

The Lord Himself will give you a sign: The virgin will conceive, have a son, and name him Immanuel.
ISAIAH 7:14

Scripture politely tells us that Joseph "had no union with her until she gave birth to a son" (Matt. 1:25, NIV). The young woman plucked from the pages of obscurity became the sign Isaiah 7:14 foretold, "The virgin will conceive, have a son, and name him Immanuel." Matthew 1:23 translates the name for us in a way that could take the perceptive among us to our faces or at least to our feet. "'Immanuel'—which means, 'God with us'" (NIV).

Behold the gospel. Good news at its best.

Those of us with appetites whetted by tell-all TV may regret that the Bible has manners. It often holds its tongue. We don't know how long the couple waited to be together, and even to suggest that we imagine exceeds good taste. This is not the couple for our romantic notions, and even those who don't lean toward perpetual virginity don't want to talk about it. So, let's not. We can, however, talk about the outcome if we're willing.

Read Matthew 13:55-56 and record the minimum number of children under Mary and Joseph's roof: _____.

Since Jesus was conceived of the Holy Spirit and did not share the same father, we can call them half siblings. Infant mortality rates were high in those days and only about half of the population lived past childhood, so there may have originally been more than seven children born to this household.[1] Matthew's Gospel tells us Jesus had "sisters," but we don't know how many, and we don't know their names.

The brothers, however, have the benefit of being both numbered and named. List them here in the order given.

Circle the first one.

So, there you have it: your introduction to the protagonist who will accompany and instruct us for the next seven weeks. Meet James, the half brother of Jesus Christ. You can't really know someone unless you know something about that person's beginnings. We know something about James' background from Jesus' beginnings. We can fairly safely assume that James was the second in the birth order of sons because he is listed first in the grouping as ancient literature was apt to convey.

Maybe I'm wrong, but I picture a person's life story differently according to the size of their family of origin. My co-worker, Evangeline, came from a family of 10 children. I can't think of her under the same lamp as another co-worker, Kimberly, who was an only child. One is not better. It's just bigger. Bigger families mean smaller houses, not by square feet necessarily but by sheer elbow room. In the days of Jesus and James, bigger families in smaller houses meant that meals, chores, and play mostly took place outdoors. When night fell, the sleeping quarters were skintight, and it's safe to say that, if Joseph snored, the whole family lay awake.

I also tend to think that people are shaped by the size of their towns of origin. Scott Korb, author of *Life in Year One*, suggests we picture Nazareth with a population of around 400 in the first century.[2] The roads were unpaved and public buildings were few. The houses were all one story, made of mud and stones, and topped with thatched roofs.

The windows of the small dwellings were usually high "allowing for light and ventilation but keeping passersby from peering in on you asleep on another straw mat." As Korb writes, "You would grind your flour, cook, and eat in the courtyard."[3] Neighbors often ate together in those adjoining courtyards, a fact that sounds fun to a sanguine like me, as long as we're eating on paper plates. They didn't, however. "Everyone used limestone or chalk cups, mugs, bowls, and storage vessels—known to us as Herodian stoneware."[4]

Low carb was not in the dietary vocabulary of the residents of Nazareth in the first century. Bread ate up about 70 percent of their daily calories so, by all means, go ahead and picture Jesus and James often breaking bread together and maybe several times a day.[5] It was so much a part of their diet that the word *lehem,* Hebrew for *bread,* became a common colloquialism for food in general.[6] It's not unlike the way we use the term *coke.* My girls and I often go "get a coke"; but when we order, they get Dr. Peppers and I get a cherry limeade. Everybody understands what we mean. That's how the Israelites were about bread when Jesus and James grew up.

Keep in mind as we draw this word picture of their young lives, we're only comparing their surroundings and circumstances and not their character or calling. One was the son of Joseph. The other was the Son of God.

Don't jump to the conclusion that these small-town boys never tasted city life.

What does Luke 2:41 tell you about the travel lives of Mary and Joseph's family?

This was only one of three feasts of the Lord that Jewish men were required to attend in Jerusalem. They didn't have to bring their entire families, but many did. Most families made all three trips annually. Go ahead and read the verses that follow in Luke 2:42-52.

Based on the information offered in verse 44, how on earth could these two parents have traveled an entire day without realizing their 12-year-old son was missing?

Welcome to life in the first century. They lived en masse, ate with the neighbors, and traveled in caravans. While no home is perfect, there was one in Nazareth that housed a boy who was. We can't really know James until we see him growing up beside the ray of sunlight beaming through that high window on the face of Jesus. What a strange way to live.

In closing our first lesson of the series, briefly describe your young life in the margin by including the size of your family, your town, and the foods you regularly ate. Share these biographical facts as a way of getting to know your small group when you meet for session 2. I'm so glad you came along. They will be too. May God make His Word a holy fascination to us and a flame leaping upward to its sacred source. Our God is an all-consuming fire.

Day Two
RESURRECTION POWER

FLASH FORWARD

"All these were continually united in prayer, along with the women, including Mary the mother of Jesus, and His brothers." Acts 1:14

If you think you've had a multifarious tie with a relative, I offer you James with Jesus. Their relationship was complicated. Let's give them that. None of us wants our closest sibling, half or otherwise, to grow up and leave us. The most complicated part is when they grow up and leave us before they've actually left home. That sense of having grown apart while we're still together is harder than being forced apart by miles while we're otherwise still close.

Jesus was exceptional. Yes, utterly perfect and morally flawless, but few of those around Him could wrap their minds around such a holy anomaly. Unshakably exceptional would have been characteristic enough, in the spirit of Luke 2:35, to reveal the thoughts of many hearts. Though we know Christ's perfections through the unshakable lens of Scripture, let's try to grasp them from the rickety top of a stepladder peeking through a window into their home.

Only two verses forthrightly describe the growth of Jesus in the Gospel of Luke. The first one is in the context of His childhood, of all unfathomable things. The second one is in the context of His growth into manhood. Look up both of these and list their descriptions of Jesus.

Luke 2:40

Luke 2:52

Exactly how does a younger child follow that up? In a legalistic world where being wholly spiritual meant being largely unlikable, Jesus possessed the favor of God and man. You can have a relationship with the most loving, gracious, accepting person on earth and still be jealous of him. That Jesus was already beginning to shift His familial identity is obvious from Luke 2:48-50.

How did the various people in the scene respond to Jesus?

See? Complicated. Astonished, anxious, and upset in the aftermath, Mary was still touched in the secret chamber of her heart where she clutched life's dearest treasures. Sometimes we can know something is right, wonderful, and as it should be yet still be pierced by it. We still feel the tearing away. Strong love includes a possessiveness, and one could not possess Jesus, no matter how close to His side. He was already wholly owned—heart, soul, and mind—by His Heavenly Father.

Younger siblings have accused their older brothers and sisters of playing God, but Jesus wasn't playing.

If Jesus jarred the mind of Mary and Joseph, who'd both been prepared by angels for His arrival and upbringing, imagine younger children thrown into the most complex family mix in human history. Younger siblings throughout time have accused their older brothers and sisters of playing God, but Jesus wasn't playing. And oddly, they weren't believing. Not the brothers anyway. John 7:5 says, "even his own brothers did not believe in him" (NIV).

We ask ourselves how Christ's brothers could possibly have disbelieved. Because timing was critical in the unfolding of the gospel, Jesus may not have made Himself fully known to those beyond the tightest inner circle. To Mary's eagerness to expose His miracle-working power at the wedding in Cana, Jesus responded: "Dear woman … My time has not yet come" (John 2:4, NIV). By the time Jesus went public, His brothers might have been so defensive over His independence that their hearts were hardened.

Why hardened? Describe the event recorded in Mark 3:31-35.

Picture yourself as a sibling in a similar situation. You're trying to get to your brother, but a crowd stands between you. You play the family card, but the door turns to concrete. Please don't miss the part when the crowd tells Jesus His family is outside looking for Him. Picture how public this scene is.

Now, choose four words that might well describe your reaction if you were one of those siblings:

Two words keep nagging at me: poor Mary. Is anybody else thinking that? We moms find ourselves sandwiched between our family members like salami in grilled rye. We love all of them. We want them to get along. If not for their sakes, do it for ours. My mom used to threaten a nervous breakdown if we five kids didn't stop it. I always pictured that it would come on all the sudden like a heart attack and she'd just break on down from one joint to the next like a collapsing deck of cards.

Refereeing is exhausting and uglier in the home than on the court. Can't you hear the sound of a whistle in Luke 2:48 when Jesus was 12 and footloose in Jerusalem? "Son, why have You treated us like this? Your father and I have been anxiously searching for You." Not a single word from Joseph is recorded in that scene. Maybe Mary was talking for him. I try a similar tactic: me getting mad for him might temper him getting mad at him.

A lot of baggage gets stuffed into a family trunk until it finally pops open under the pressure. Often in families we don't get the luxury of one clearly-definable feeling. As much as we wish we could at times, we often can't just decide not to like someone and write him off. Usually we love him even when we don't like him.

I'm not forcing these feelings on the other children of Mary. I just want us to imagine the family dynamics later when Jesus was arrested, beaten almost beyond recognition, and publicly crucified. The horror and the rush of love, regret, fury, and blame must have been unbearable. Then He "was raised on the third day according to the Scriptures, and … he appeared to Peter, and then to the Twelve. After that, he appeared to more than five hundred of the brothers at the same time. … Then he appeared to James" (1 Cor. 15:4-7, NIV).

That's where our journey begins. We don't know where they were standing or what they were doing. We know one thing from this inference: they were alone—just the two of them. Jesus and James.

In the remainder of our lesson, we're going to look in chronological order at the next two scenes that involve James either by name or as one of the brothers of Jesus. Look at each context with the complexities we've suggested and with the inferred impact of that private meeting. First, read Acts 1:4-15.

How do we know James was in the scene?

How recently must James have seen the resurrected Christ? Just make an educated guess within so many days or weeks for the sake of establishing how new he was on the believing scene. (Hint: read Acts 1:3.)

The power of the resurrection trumps the power of the past if we're willing to let it. Gathering in that upstairs room with some of the very ones Jesus earlier called His real family, they could have posed for a poster with the caption "awkward." But this was no place for something so ridiculously narcissistic. When, like a laser, the call of Christ sears a hole through your self-protectiveness, you go wherever He leads whether or not you feel like you fit. How will we ever press onward through the hot winds from hell if we can't even get past awkward?

When the call of Christ sears a hole through your self-protectiveness, you go wherever He leads whether or not you feel like you fit.

What do you think would have made James feel awkward about joining the apostolic group after his previous disbelief?

Describe a time when you faced feeling awkward, battling with doing what God was calling you to do.

Oh, that we'll find fresh courage in this journey to take our places in history alongside those who sought Jesus at the cost of fitting in.

One more scene and we close. Turn to Acts 12 and find the account of Peter's imprisonment when fiery trials were blistering the feet of those early Christ followers. To give you an idea of the time line, glance back to Acts 11:26.

What name had recently tagged those followers?

Now, read Acts 12:1-2. Who had been killed?

- ☐ Herod, the enemy of the church
- ☐ John, the brother of James
- ☐ James, the brother of John
- ☐ Stephen, the first of the martyrs

Read Acts 12:3-17. (You've got to love Rhoda here.) In verse 17 where our protagonist is mentioned, what instruction did Peter give concerning "James and the brothers"?

What range of elements might have been involved in their account to James and the brothers "about this" (NIV)? Think broadly and list possibilities here.

Now, imagine James getting the news from all angles. Maybe his thoughts went something like: *This thing we're doing is deadly. Terrifying. I feel sick. I feel exhilarated. He said not to fear those who can only kill the body. Think past the pain. What about our families? What does all this mean? I feel like hoards of demons have been unleashed on us. There are angels. Real, live angels—and some of them appear in beams of brilliant light. We may be captured, but we may be rescued. We may see horrors, but we may see wonders. We may lose our heads, but we cannot lose our souls. The stakes are up. The fire is lit. It's time to live like those who cannot die.*

Welcome to the life of those called Christians.

Day Three
THE LORD'S BROTHER

FLASH FORWARD

"I didn't see any of the other apostles except James, the Lord's brother." Galatians 1:19

The English clergyman John Donne penned words centuries ago that many of us know by heart. "No Man is an *Island*, entire of itself; every man is a piece of the *Continent*, a part of the main."[7] The apostle Paul might have put it more like this: "No man is a body, entire of itself; every man is a piece, a part of the main." To be exact, Paul wrote: "The body is a unit, though it is made up of many parts; and though all its parts are many, they form one body. So it is with Christ" (1 Cor. 12:12, NIV). If we really want to get to know James, we're wise to know as much as we can about his relationship to his contemporaries in the early work of the gospel. They did not operate alone. In fact, as God would have it, the work of each was incomplete without the other.

Take James and the apostle Paul, for instance. Each was necessary to the gospel work despite our endless attempts to stick the two of them in a boxing ring and demand they duke it out. Today we'll read about their first encounter, and we'll have to be satisfied with seeing the meeting from Paul's point of view. Most of us probably feel that we're better acquainted with him anyway. By sheer volume in the canon, it's little wonder. The stack of inspired Scripture written by or about Paul towers over that of James.

So, for the sake of familiarity, we're going to let Paul further introduce James to us today as long as you make one promise: that you'll keep in mind the roles were completely reversed in the early Jerusalem church. Indeed, James helped introduce the former persecutor. Paul, not James, was the newcomer when we see their lives intersect.

Forgive the redundancy, but who came first? □ James □ Paul
OK, now don't forget it.

Read Galatians 1:11-24. What is this passage about?

We have before us what scholar Scot McKnight calls a "biographical reconstruction." I'll let him explain. "The first thing a convert does is tell his or her own biography in a new way. A basic reorientation is like this: what mattered most before no longer matters; what did not matter before is now central."[8]

I'll take a stab at it to help clarify. We tell a life story in the light of a life-changing event that not only sheds light on the future but also on the past. For instance, once God threw me into the world of women's ministry, my background of childhood abuse was no longer just something Satan orchestrated. It became something God redeemed and used. It dramatically changed how I saw the outcome of certain events. Paul was doing this and more in his "biographical reconstruction." He was not only sharing his story but also making the case that his preaching came from none other than Jesus Himself (see v. 12). He wasn't just parroting others.

Before we get to the snippet of Paul's story involving James, let's behold some of the power of his remarkable testimony in Galatians 1. Let's build a time line and document the events chronologically from the information offered. Don't stress over getting the events spaced out in perfect ratio because we don't have all those facts. Just get them all down in order and label them. Make sure to document his involvement with James. Here's a start and a finish. You fill in the rest.

Conversion

On to Syria & Cilicia

Reread Galatians 1:22-24. The chief goal of every testimony is summed up beautifully in verse 24. What does it say?

This glorious result is not only for our conversion stories. What does Matthew 5:14-16 say about the purpose of our works?

Now, let's go back to the Galatians segment. According to Galatians 1:18, why did Paul make the trip in the first place?

Let your imagination fly for a moment. What would we give to watch a reality show from these 15 days? This was the intersection of two of the most influential minds in Christendom. We can't even fathom how the New Testament would look apart from their stories and callings. Peter and Paul can also pose next to each other on poster boards as Exhibits A and B for the drastically different forms our conversions can take.

Scripture tells us they got "acquainted" (NIV), but goodness knows the way two men get to know each other compared to two women could be planets apart. They may have needed 15 days to our 5. As rabbis are at times apt to do, they might have also enjoyed some spirited debates.

List three conversations you picture Peter and Paul possibly having during these 15 days.

This is the point where Paul's testimony throws a rope around James, drags him into the picture, and then seems to forget he's there. Glance back at verse 19.

How was James distinguished from the others called apostles in the New Testament? "I didn't see any of the other apostles except James, ______________________."

I want to bang my fist on the table and demand more than this, don't you? We want to know what they said and how they looked when they said it. We wish we had all the pieces of the James puzzle from the time of his conversion past his acquaintance with Paul, but we don't. Here's what we can surmise, however, based on the conclusion of our previous lesson in Acts 12:17 and our present preoccupation with Galatians 1:18-19.

After his saving encounter with the resurrected Christ, James must have resided in Jerusalem and ended up working alongside Peter. In the early years of Christianity, Peter was the unchallenged leader of the budding church in and around Jerusalem. This position shifted to James, however, and Acts 12:17 probably best explains why.

According to this verse, what did Peter do immediately after he instructed the band of prayer warriors to "tell James and the brothers about this" (NIV)?

You are very likely looking at the moment of Peter's temporary departure from Jerusalem and when James began to take the lead position among the converts there. Don't jump to the conclusion that Peter left for a while because he was a coward. He hightailed it out of Jerusalem for at least two very good reasons. The first one is because he had good sense. King Herod would have surely killed him just as he did the brother of John, leaving Peter's work unfinished. The second reason is the sum of all reasons: the sovereignty of God.

According to Acts 11:19-21, what happened as a direct result of the persecution?

Amazing, isn't it? The very thing meant to stamp out the fires of Christianity only kicked the coals across the land and set a parched forest ablaze. Imagine how often Satan has to reconsider his schemes in light of how they could backfire on him. In the meantime, he enlists blame and accusation as his coconspirators, and under his subtle influence the people of God often turn on one another rather than rally in unity against our real enemy.

This is where the triangular story of Peter, James, and Paul turns upside down onto its tip. The very persecution that sought to dog Peter and James to their bloody deaths was fueled by the fanaticism of people like the old Paul. Only a few chapters earlier in the Acts account, "Saul was still breathing threats and murder against the disciples of the Lord. He went to the high priest and requested letters from him to the synagogues in Damascus, so that if he found any men or women who belonged to the Way, he might bring them as prisoners to Jerusalem" (Acts 9:1-2). In Galatians 1:13, Paul said it for himself: "You have heard about my former course of life in Judaism, how beyond all measure I persecuted the church of God and laid it waste."[9]

Do we think we have a few strikes against our relationships with other servants of God? Do we think the work of God is only accomplished when we're riding tandem with our personal favorites? Do we believe we always have to see it the same to do ministry together? Has "the kindness and love of God our Savior" not "appeared" to us all (Titus 3:4, NIV)? Have we not all denied Him at one time or another?

Describe a time when you grappled with some of these questions and tell what happened.

Picture Paul, Peter, and James all under the same roof at one point or another, staring at each other and sometimes perhaps blankly. Yes, they had much in common, but we could argue that each of their theologies would have been considerably simpler, lines cleaner apart from the others. What three lives could have told more different stories of Christ's redemption? Just when we think we've got it all figured out, God sends along a person who rips a hole in our belief system that only Jesus can fill.

As we conclude today's lesson, reflect on the time line we drew from Paul's testimony. Choose a period of years in your own life that proved very strategic in your journey toward Christ or with Him. Comprise a time line of your own on an extra sheet of paper and label it accordingly. It will remind you how faithful and intentional your God has been toward you. If you're participating with a small group, be ready to share it as a means of giving your testimony. Please go do the extra work because it will return to you in blessing! You are loved, dear Sister.

LEVEL 4

The **NEXT LEVEL** with Melissa

JAMES & THE NAZIRITE VOW

Many scholars have linked James, the brother of Jesus, with the Nazirite vow.[1] You may already be familiar with the contents of the vow, but if not, you may want to peruse Numbers 6:1-21 where the terms are set out. Baruch A. Levine notes:

> The underlying concept of Nazirite devotion, in all of its forms, is that of surrender and renunciation, perceived as ways of drawing nearer to God so as to partake of his power; or to put it differently, so as to become an instrument of divine power. The goal of the Nazirite could be defined as the attainment of holiness.[2]

The basic sense of the Hebrew noun rendered "Nazirite" is "consecrated one."[3] The most well-known Nazirite in the Bible is Samson, who was dedicated to God by his mother as a Nazirite even before he was born. Samson credited his exceptional strength to one of the symbols of the Nazirite vow, his hair that had never been cut since birth (see Judg. 16:17).

Judges 16:19 says that Samson's strength left him when Delilah shaved off the seven locks of his hair, and verse 20 takes the connection even further by linking the dedicated hair with the strength of the Lord. When the hair was cut, Samson could no longer shake himself free from chains, and when it began to grow back he was able bring an entire temple down on himself and the Philistines (see Judg. 16:23-31).

We find support for James' association with the Nazirite vow both within the New Testament and beyond. Hegesippus, a Christian historiographer in the second century, notes, that among other things from which James abstained, that he did not drink wine or cut the hair on his head. These elements form two of the primary features of the Nazirite vow.

Of course we cannot verify that Hegesippus passed down accurate information, but the link is noteworthy. Interestingly enough, in Acts 21:17-26, we also find James associated with the vow when, among other things, he suggests that the apostle Paul pay for the expenses of four men, presumably among the Christians in Jerusalem, who have taken a vow and must have their heads shaved.

While James himself does not explicitly take the vow of the Nazirite in the New Testament, his association with the four men who have taken the vow in Acts 21 is extremely intriguing. At the very least, the text shows us that the early Jewish Christians under James' headship were still associated with the Temple, even after Christ's resurrection.

At the very least, the text shows us that the **early Jewish Christians** under James' headship **were still associated with the Temple**, even after Christ's resurrection.

Day Four
THREE PILLARS

FLASH FORWARD

"When James, Cephas, and John, recognized as pillars, acknowledged the grace that had been given to me, they gave the right hand of fellowship to me and Barnabas, agreeing that we should go to the Gentiles and they to the circumcised." Galatians 2:9

Melissa and I had so many eye-openers concerning James, the person, as we dug through the mound of research for this series. I pray you will have the same experience. I only knew a few basics about him going into this journey, and most of them were shaded by his earlier rejection of Jesus as Messiah. Don't get me wrong. I've been a big fan of the Book of James for years, but in retrospect, I don't believe I sufficiently connected it with the man God inspired to write it.

What I discovered in the process of preparation for this study dramatically shaped how I then gleaned from the five-chapter book called by his name. I want us to know the same James the early church knew.

We caught the quickest glimpse of James from Galatians 1 in our previous lesson. We learned that Paul spent some time with him during the trip to Jerusalem where he spent 15 days getting acquainted with Peter. Let's return to the pages of Galatians where we'll find another brief mention of James from the pen of the apostle Paul but this time one with far broader implications. Please review your context, read Galatians 2:1-10, and complete the following.

How much later did the apostle Paul return to Jerusalem?

Who went with him? Circle the correct answers.

Silas Timothy Titus Barnabas John Mark

Share each detail about Titus offered to us in this segment:

In Paul's view, what appeared to be at stake? (See vv. 4-5.)

Obviously from the tone of this portion of Scripture, a wrestling match of the religious sort was taking place. Nothing's muddier.

One of the things I'm sure you noted about Titus is that he was Greek or what the Bible often calls a Gentile.

Glance at Ephesians 2:11-14 for insight regarding the role of circumcision in the differences between people. What was the effect of circumcision?

Part of the tug-of-war in the early church was over whether men coming into the faith from the Gentile world should be circumcised. Remember, Christianity's family tree sprouted from all Jewish roots, so the answer was not quite as simple as it seems centuries later.

For reasons much clearer in retrospect, Paul adamantly maintained that Gentiles not be bound to Jewish laws with their newfound Christianity. After all the rejection he'd suffered from his own people, Paul also might have felt a particular loyalty and protectiveness toward the ones who'd received his ministry with open arms. (See Gal. 2:9.) He believed Jewish Christians were snatching up the new Gentile converts who'd just gained their freedom from darkness and shoving them into the overcrowded prison of legalism. Don't miss the force of Paul's commitment to the issue in light of the risks it incurred.

Read Galatians 5:11 (and add verse 12, if you dare). What did Paul suggest?

The climactic point of the controversy will occupy our thoughts tomorrow, so push pause on the issue until then. Shift your attentions back to Galatians 2:8, and read it again.

God only knows how many effective ministries have disintegrated into irrelevance over addiction to comparison. We talk as those who believe God is omnipotent and omnipresent, but we often act as if He can only work through one person, one method, or one kind of ministry at a time. If we don't refuse ourselves the indulgence, we can lapse into the mentality of a spoiled child who thinks that, if God shows you favor, He must hate me.

On the other hand, we can do our level best not to compare ourselves with those of similar gifting or calling, and others will leap forward to do it for us. Stand back and watch how many observers will try to nudge you into a competition with someone who fills a similar slot. The idea is that anything comparable is automatically competitive.

Remember that at one time you were Gentiles in the flesh—called "the uncircumcised" by those called "the circumcised," which is done in the flesh by human hands. At that time you were without the Messiah, excluded from the citizenship of Israel, and foreigners to the covenants of the promise, without hope and without God in the world. But now in Christ Jesus, you who were far away have been brought near by the blood of the Messiah. For He is our peace, who made both groups one and tore down the dividing wall of hostility.

EPHESIANS 2:11-14

God's way of reaching the big, needy world is to enlist every one of us to do our parts in love and humility, variety and diversity.

In this celebrity culture in which so many scramble for their five minutes in the spotlight, even we followers of Christ can easily fall to the temptation to rewrite 2 Timothy 1:6 from "fan into flame the gift of God, which is in you" (NIV) into "fan into fame the gift of God, which is in you." What a tragedy, and what a colossal waste of time. Let's be crucified to pride and comparison. There's a big, needy world out there, and God's way of reaching it is to enlist every one of us to do our parts in love and humility, variety and diversity. Savor Eugene Peterson's translation of Galatians 5:25-26.

> Since this is the kind of life we have chosen, the life of the Spirit, let us make sure that we do not just hold it as an idea in our heads or a sentiment in our hearts, but work out its implications in every detail of our lives. That means we will not compare ourselves with each other as if one of us were better and another worse. We have far more interesting things to do with our lives. Each of us is an original (Message).

If this line of thought speaks to you about a specific comparison trap you've been in, please look at this rewording of Galatians 2:8 and fill in the following blanks with invisible ink before God. "God, who is at work in the ministry of ________________ as a servant to ____________________________, is also at work in my ministry as a servant to __________________________."

Into what comparison trap do you most often fall? Why?

Now, search Galatians 2:1-10 again. In what context does James, our protagonist, show up in these verses?

What do you think Paul meant by "pillars"?

The terminology was as common a term drawn from Greek architecture as it is from our own use today. It was a metaphor used for someone serving as a column sturdy enough to lend support to a large structure. The Talmud refers to the patriarchs Abraham, Isaac, and Jacob as the three pillars of Israel.[10] Paul may well have seen James, Peter, and John (in that order) as the Abraham, Isaac, and Jacob of the early church. Imagine the ramifications of those kinds of sacred parallels.

That's our James, by the way. We're so accustomed to the grouping of Peter, James, and John in the Gospels where James refers to John's blood brother that we'd tend to assume his identity here.

Based on Galatians 1:18 and 2:1, at least how many years had passed in the gospel movement?

James, the brother of the apostle John, was martyred early on. The pillar here is James, "the Lord's brother" (Gal. 1:19).

Please let this fact sink deeply into your perceptions, shading and shaping everything we study from this point forward: James skyrocketed to a place of tremendous prominence in the early church. He bounced from doubter to leader in a mind-spinning flash of time. Facts like these ought to flood our faith over the certainty of Christ's resurrection. Before we jump to the conclusion that James' status was solely due to his brotherly bond, consider this: All of the brothers came to believe in Jesus as the Christ by the time they met in the upper room in Acts 1:14. Yet only one emerged as a leader and, far more impressively, one of three "pillars."

Glance back at Galatians 2:9. What did the pillars give Paul and Barnabas when they "acknowledged" (HCSB) or "recognized" (NIV) the grace given to Paul?

This wasn't the handshake of a greeting. It was the handshake of an agreement. In this context, it signified a mutual blessing of sorts and a bond to serve the same Lord in two vastly different but equally crucial directions. OK, one last thing.

Look at Galatians 2:10. What was all they asked?

Promise not to forget that! The request of the three pillars—that Paul and Barnabas remember the poor—plants a seed of thought that will produce a very significant harvest later in our series. It had paramount importance to James and weighs heavily in the Book of the Bible he was inspired to write.

I've learned so much today. Have you? I'm so glad you've come along. The thought occurs to me over and over when I'm writing a series that I cannot imagine studying with the same depth if I were on my own. You keep me on my toes, and I'm so grateful to God for you. See you tomorrow!

The **NEXT LEVEL** with Melissa

JERUSALEM COUNCIL, PART ONE

In day 5, you will look at Acts 15, a chapter important enough in James' life that we need to spend a few minutes talking about it in advance. The events in Acts 15 are crucial in the life of James and the early church.

At first, my obsession with Acts 15 was something of a joke, but with time the situation has become more serious, as in, "OK, Melissa, you *really* need to move on now or we are never going to meet our book deadline." Suffice it to say, this is one of the most fascinating chapters in the New Testament. I know people say that about any and every passage if it's the one they're currently addressing, but I really do mean it, y'all.

This new thing God did meant Gentiles no longer needed to convert to Judaism to be included among God's people. In Peter's words, God has *purified* or *cleansed* (notice the ritual imagery) the Gentiles' hearts by faith (see Acts 15:9).

Hundreds of years before the Jerusalem Council the prophet Jeremiah spoke of a time when Gentiles would learn well "the ways" of Israel to be established among God's people (Jer. 12:16). Suddenly the time Jeremiah forecast has arrived. Unexpectedly, the promised gift of the Holy Spirit is poured out on Gentiles as well as Jews.

Suddenly the early church was experiencing something unprecedented in salvation history. They had no example to follow. While Old Testament Scriptures legitimized their experience, no instruction manual existed. Instead, they had to walk in the Spirit and improvise as they encountered new problems and conflicts. This was improvisation in the power of the Spirit, with the assistance of the Old Testament, of course, but, it was improvisation none the less.

A friend of mine is currently involved in the hard work of starting a seminary in a female prison. What does this look like, exactly? While we have no black-and-white answers in the Bible about a female seminary in a prison, what if God has called you to establish one? You would have to walk in the Spirit and ask God to guide you with the wisdom and knowledge in Scripture. Yes, you might even have to make some decisions of your own without a verse to back you up. Life is complicated, but God gave us the Holy Spirit to empower us for messy situations just like this one.

Back to the early church. These folks had to figure out how to transform the prophetic message into something practical and reasonable in the daily lives of both Jews and Gentiles. And it wasn't easy. While Jeremiah's message sounded great in theory, what did the particulars look like? After all, Jews and Gentiles could hardly even eat together. From a devoutly Jewish perspective, the Gentiles' entire way of life made them not just dirty but infectious. So, here, at the Jerusalem Council, the early church must discern how Gentiles could exist as the people of God without sacrificing the freedom to be Gentiles.

Our protagonist, James, has the loudest voice in this important discussion. In our next segment we'll pick up on some of the tedious but significant details of James' speech at the Jerusalem Council. Believe me, I will tell you more than you will want to know about the speech after you've spent day 5 with Mom.

Day Five

LISTEN TO ME!

FLASH FORWARD

"After they stopped speaking, James responded: 'Brothers, listen to me!' " Acts 15:13

I promised we'd pick up today on the determining point of conflict over Gentile believers and Jewish laws. Flip to Acts 15, the record of an account many scholars believe corresponds to the Galatians segment we studied yesterday. If you listen with even one ear, you'll hear the echo. We're going to work hard today, so I'll prime the pump with a sweet story that might ease the depth of research you're about to do.

My son-in-law Curtis made a public profession of faith in Christ and was baptized when he was 9 years old. In his denomination, such actions soberly qualified him for membership. He was serious about his faith even then and said he could hardly wait to attend a business meeting to act on his freshly acquired voting rights.

Perhaps it's a boy thing because I grew up in the same denomination and the thought never occurred to me to run like the wind to the next church council meeting. My thought was, hand over the Lord's Supper before some one gets hurt, and you can have your meetings. Not Curtis. He'd earned a vote he intended to cast.

If Curtis were the rebellious type, I'd say his parents had made him endure meetings, and his yea or nay was sweet revenge. His motive, alas, appeared pure. He described attending those business meetings with the adult "pillars" of the church, raising his short, skinny arm and seconding motions with a voice years from changing. Imagine how much they smiled. My heart spills over picturing how many of those same men later bent their knees and laid hands on Curtis at his ordination. You never know what God will make out of a 9-year-old.

You and I endure our share of meetings too, church or otherwise. Every now and then, one changes life as we know it. That's what happened in Acts. Read Acts 15:1-11; the segment appropriately splits the book down the middle. A heated debate led to what is historically called the Jerusalem Council.

What was this meeting? (See vv. 1-6.)

Take a good look at verse 5. Who insisted that the Gentiles be circumcised and keep the Mosaic law?

Don't just tilt the Pharisees' identity toward a negative light. Revel in the fact that numbers of them indeed accepted Jesus Christ as Messiah, notorious as others were for opposing Him. The claims Peter made in verses 7-9 were almost scandalous to some and of titanic importance to all.

In the margin list several of Peter's claims. Complete Peter's challenge in verse 10. "Why are you testing God by ...

Notice that Peter reframed the yoke, not as a test of men but as a test of God Himself, aiming the offense infinitely higher.

Write your own paraphrase of Acts 15:11.

Oh, that we would not try to make others earn what we freely received. Read the next segment, Acts 15:12-21, and reflect on verse 12.

Why do you think the whole assembly needed to listen to Barnabas and Paul as they told about these "miraculous signs and wonders" (NIV)?

Lock your gaze on verse 13. This is the point in the narrative when our James took the platform. Many scholars believe he was presiding over this ground-breaking (maybe earth-quaking) gathering. What hints do you see that James was in charge? Let's shine the spotlight on a few places that help us picture James in his bulging circle of influence. His presiding side doesn't smother his warm pulse. Look back at verse 14.

What name did he call Peter?

James intentionally called Peter by the Hebrew or Aramaic form of his common personal name, Simon, or more literally, Simeon. Don't doze off here. This is where I need to tell you up front to let go of all attempts of excising the Jewishness from James. To do so would be to miss him almost entirely.

When Peter went on the road, James took the lead position among the Jerusalem-centered followers of Christ who were (memorize this!) *Jewish*. Just as Paul had a natural affinity for the Gentiles he primarily served, James kept an affinity toward Jewish believers whom he not only served but whose unremitting Jewishness he shared. We will see evidences of this throughout his writings and will do well to remind ourselves often that he enjoyed the same inspiration of the Holy Spirit as Paul. Read the words of F. F. Bruce carefully.

> James had a statesmanlike breadth of vision, as appears from his policy at the Council of Jerusalem (15:13-21). But he was careful to retain the confidence of the ordinary church members in Jerusalem, many of whom were "zealots for the law" (21:20). In addition, he continued to the end to command the respect of the Jerusalem populace, largely because of his ascetic way of life and his regular participation in the temple services of prayer, where he interceded for the people and their city. Whatever Peter and other members of the Twelve may have done, James was free of any suspicion of fraternizing with Gentiles.[11]

In the margin, list the inferred characteristics of James that this excerpt helps shape in your perceptions.

Only with this backstory can we fully appreciate the stunning words out of James' mouth in Acts 15:14.

Simeon has reported how God first intervened to take from the Gentiles a people for His name.
ACTS 15:14

What exactly did God do, according to this verse?

One more time: "taking from the" who?

You are staring in the face of one of the most dramatic and critical moments in salvation history. Why so important?

What does Deuteronomy 14:2 say about God's people?

I was spinning on my stationary bike, reading a commentary on this chapter of Acts, when I realized the force of James' words and watched my heart rate spike on the monitor. I hope your pulse gets a little aerobic here, too. In Acts 15:14, James "does not speak of God's taking a people *in contrast* to the Gentiles, but of his taking a people *consisting of* Gentiles."[12] James deliberately inverted the Old Testament passage like the hand of God pulling a glove inside out.

Why do you think James was wise to quote an Old Testament prophet such as Amos in this council meeting?

How does 1 Peter 2:10 say something similar?

Back to Acts 15:16. James, then, quoted the prophet Amos, who predicted that Gentiles would also bear God's name. "The words of the prophets are in agreement with this" (v. 15, NIV).

Did you note the two words "in agreement"? You'll love the original term. It is the Greek compound word "symphonousin."[13]

What English word does that resemble?

We will one day worship in the presence of the One who orchestrated the perfect symphony.

Both words come from a combination of the terms "together" and "sound/ voice." After all our discord, clash, and clamor, we will one day worship in the presence of the One who orchestrated the perfect symphony of two different testaments and, more impressively, of a host of clay instruments. He will settle the score, all notes in place, and the exquisite beauty will be otherworldly.

Now, look back at Acts 15:20. What particular areas of abstinence did James suggest?

If you're like me, you might wish to come up with a different list. Abstinence from sexual immorality (interestingly, in Greek *porneia)* is no surprise even if keeping the commandment in this overexposed society is.[14] The food-related areas in verse 20 are more mystifying to us because we feel galaxies removed from their culture. When was the last time you went to a restaurant and saw "food sacrificed to idols" on the menu?

The explosion of the early church beyond the borders of Judaism threw shrapnel past their front doors and onto their dinner tables. If I may be so bold, the fallout couldn't have been any more shocking had it hit their bedrooms with mixed marriages. This fresh work of the Spirit could mean that Jews and Gentiles might actually find themselves eating together. The very idea left jaws agape and mouths empty. After all, who could eat?

The problem wasn't just the food, although a pig was plenty to choke on. The larger issue was the statement of covenant communion suggested by a shared table. What you find in Acts 15:20 is James' wise attempt to ensure that the Gentile diet at the common table did not throw food all over the faces of their Jewish brothers and sisters in Christ. Let's conclude our lesson with Acts 15:22-35.

How did they get the word out concerning the decision of the Jerusalem Council?

How did they distance themselves from those who tried to impose on the Gentiles circumcision and the Law of Moses? (See vv. 1,24.)

Note the phrase "troubling your minds" (NIV). The Greek term translated "troubling" is a military metaphor for "plundering a city."[15] How might the plundering metaphor fit into this context?

The NASB translates verse 25, "It seemed good to us, having become of one mind, to select men to send to you." Few things testify to the presence and power of Christ more vividly than two garlic-strong mind-sets melding into one. Ephesians 2:14-18 plays the piercing melody beneath the harmony of the letter to the Gentile believers.

Read these verses. What was the means of their peace?

How have you personally experienced this peace?

Our segment concludes with the bearers of good news "sent off by the brothers with the blessing of peace" (Acts 15:33, NIV). How perfect that the Gentile believers sent their Jewish "brothers" back to Jerusalem with the ancient, very Jewish blessing, *shalom*.[16] Surely, He Himself "is our peace" (Eph. 2:14).

The **NEXT LEVEL** with Melissa

JERUSALEM COUNCIL, PART TWO

The verdict James proposed at the Jerusalem Council was something of a compromise. While he affirmed the testimonies of Paul and Peter by rejecting the demand that Gentiles must keep the Law of Moses (see Acts 15:19), he qualified the judgment by concluding that Gentiles should abstain from: (1) food polluted by idols; (2) sexual immorality; (3) meat of strangled animals; and (4) blood. These four prohibitions are known as the apostolic decree.

Now hang in here with me. I know not all of this stuff seems culturally relevant to us, but it can be rewarding to know if we take time to explore it. I'd walk 500 miles to ask James where he got the four prohibitions in the apostolic decree. From where did they come? Why these four? What is their significance?

I'd walk 500 miles to ask James where he got **the four prohibitions** in the apostolic decree.

Although knowing for sure the source of the apostolic decree eludes us, Richard Bauckham makes a fantastic case that these prohibitions come from the rules for resident aliens in the land of Israel. Based on very technical arguments, he proposes that James' prohibitions grow from typical Jewish exegesis of Leviticus 17:8–18:18.

Keep in mind that the early church was trying to discern the appropriate relationship between Gentiles and the Mosaic law.

As Bauckham says:

> **All the evidence suggests that the apostolic decree was generally accepted by Jewish Christians as authoritatively defining the relation of Gentile believers to the Law of Moses. They did not think this meant abolishing the Law, as some supposed was Paul's position. They understood it to be upholding the validity of the Law, which itself distinguished between Jews, who were to keep the whole Law, and Gentile members of the eschatological people of God, on whom it laid only the four obligations specified in the decree.[1]**

Some have called into question the historicity of Luke's depiction of the Jerusalem Council, doubting that Paul would have ever supported James' more moderate judgment.

But, here are several points to ruminate over as you contemplate the text on your own.

1. James proposed that Gentiles keep a mere 4 of over 613 laws in the Jewish Scriptures and not as a means of salvation but to acknowledge the historical and ongoing significance of the Mosaic law in salvation history (see Acts 15:21).

2. Paul taught that strong Christians should lovingly and selflessly constrain their freedom for the sake of "weak" Christians (1 Cor. 8:9-13).

3. Paul did not believe the law was salvific (salvation generating), but in Romans 3:31 he says that faith upholds the law rather than nullifies it.

4. Paul did not explicitly mention the apostolic decree in his letters, but he, Timothy, and Silas delivered "the decisions reached by the apostles and elders in Jerusalem" as they went from town to town "for the people to obey" (Acts 16:4, NIV). Therefore, the Book of Acts presents Paul as supporting and spreading James' deliberation.

5. Acts 16:1-3 relays the surprising news that Paul himself circumcised Timothy because he wanted to take him along on the journey. But, wasn't the whole point of Acts 15 to prove that circumcision is unnecessary? Paul must have known that the Jews in that area would be particularly sensitive about these issues, perhaps especially since Timothy's mom was a Jewish Christian and his dad was a Gentile. Regardless of what motivated Paul to do this, it demonstrates to us that these matters were far from simple and that sometimes exceptions were made because the issues were simply too complex. Moreover, Paul seemed to take his own advice to the Corinthians: "Take care that this liberty of yours does not somehow become a stumbling block to the weak" (1 Cor. 8:9, NASB).

From a modern Christian perspective the revolutionary idea is that Gentiles would be required by the Jerusalem church to keep a couple of the Mosaic laws. The far more revolutionary idea for first-century Jews was that Gentiles could be the people of God, worship Yahweh, and not be circumcised.

The far more revolutionary idea was that Gentiles could be the people of God and not be circumcised.

When we think to ourselves, *How in the world did we get from Torah-keeping Judaism to "law-free" Christianity?* To some extent the answer lies in the Jerusalem Council. In Acts 15 we catch a quick but clear glimpse of the earliest Christians in action.

viewer guide | session two

James 1:1

We spent all of week 1 getting to know the man, James. Today we open our Bibles to the message of James where our attentions will be fastened for the next five weeks. Read James 1:1.

1. What James 1:1 __________ _______ about the writer is as telling as what it ________. Servant (Greek *doulos*)—"a ________ of God and of the Lord Jesus Christ"

2. The letter of James is addressed to the "twelve __________ __________ among the nations" (NIV). Points of particular significance:
   - The Greek word translated "scattered" is literally "in the ___________."
     (See Acts 8:1,4.)
   - __________ is the Old Testament name __________.[1]
   - Greek transliteration of James: __________.
   - Hebrew transliteration of James: __________.
   - James wrote this letter not as " 'a ___________ ______________' ... but a ______________ _______. ... He was writing with full hope that the Jews as a whole would turn to Christ."[2]

"The Epistle was penned in the days when Christianity and synagogue were not yet ____________, when Jerusalem was still as __________ ________ it and was, further, still the center of Christianity as a religion and as an organization."[3]

3. James might have been the ________ ________ of the New Testament ___________.

"The Epistle of James can take its natural place, alongside other literature in the process of formation in the second decade of the Christian mission, as the first surviving document of the church."[4]

4. James was one of the _______ New Testament books to be _________ into the canon.[5]

"Canon"—________ or _____________

5. James draws straight from the well of Jesus' _____________ more than any other New Testament author.[6]

6. The message of James can be captured in two words: _________ ____.

7. Our lesson's conclusion is James' salutation: (Greek *chairein*)

________ to ________!

Let Beth know at *lproof@lproof.org* if you memorize the Book of James.

1. Ralph P. Martin, *Word Biblical Commentary: James* (Nashville, TN: Thomas Nelson Publishers, 1988), 5.
2. James B. Adamson, *The Epistle of James* (Grand Rapids, MI: Wm. B. Eerdmans Publishing Co., 1976), 51.
3. James B. Adamson, *James: The Man and His Message* (Grand Rapids, MI: Wm. B. Eerdmans Publishing Co., 1989), 49.
4. John A. T. Robinson, *Redating the New Testament* (Eugene, OR: Wipf & Stock Publishers, 1976), 139.
5. Adamson, *James*, 6.
6. Douglas J. Moo, *The Letter of James* (Grand Rapids, MI: Wm. B. Eerdmans Publishing Co., 2000), 7.

WEEK TWO

A BOOK CALLED JAMES

Day One
JOY WHENEVER

FLASH FORWARD

"Consider it a great joy, my brothers, whenever you experience various trials, knowing that the testing of your faith produces endurance."
James 1:2-3

We spent week 1 getting to know James the man, so we won't mind if he doesn't mince words. If I were James, I'd tend to want to chat a while before counting it all joy when life pitches you into the food processor or breaks one foot and sprains the other. If I were going to say it at all, I'd probably save it till the end. Not James. He wrote like a man scared of running out of ink.

Please read James 1:1-4. We considered the first verse in session 2 and handwrote it on page 214. Please take the time to handwrite verses 2-4 on the same page.

The half brother of Jesus wrote as thoughtfully as he did succinctly. In the Greek, the opening chapter of James rolls off his pen in catchwords, forming links of a chain. He introduced a word then looped it around the neck of the following concept, piggybacking terms. For example, James' jump from "Greetings" to "Consider it pure joy" (NIV) seems abrupt to us, but the ancient listener could hear the play on words. In Greek, the term for "greetings" *(chairein)* and the term for "joy" *(charan)* are link words, as you can tell by glancing at them.[1]

I'd use a similar device if I wrote you an e-mail that began with "What's up? Consider that life's looking up if you're feeling down." You'd roll your eyes at me, but you wouldn't miss the wordplay.

Before we see what they mean, here's another word chain linked together by the fine art of alliteration. See the words "face trials of many kinds" (NIV) in verse 2? In the Greek you'd see *"peirasmois peripesēte poikilois."*[2] Try saying that phrase five times as fast as you can.

Devices like alliteration remind us that these epistles were mostly read aloud to their original audiences, so the inspired writers often gave thought not only to the words they said but how they sounded.

Easy for James to say, but I can't think of anything harder than counting hardships a joy. And it's the first thing he scratched on the scroll. Does anybody feel as if you're already making an "F" in this course and we're only at verse 2? Take heart. We're going to love this book if we can stand it.

Let's take apart verse 2. Swap *consider* for *feel*. In the margin describe how the meaning would change if the exhortation said "*Feel* pure joy" rather than "consider it" (NIV).

The word *consider* calls us to a mental exercise. Not an emotion. James isn't telling us to have a knee-slapper over all we're going through. He's telling us to think, to reflect, and to esteem the unalloyed joys available to us "whenever [we] experience various trials." Recall the word "experience" in your *Flash Forward*. The Greek word is *peripēsete,* which literally means to "fall into" as several other translations suggest.[3] I think you'll strike gold in another place the Greek verb is used, tucked into the parable of the good Samaritan.

Read Luke 10:30. Fill in the blanks: "A man was going down from Jerusalem to Jericho and ____________________ ____________________ the hands of robbers."

Now, set the two occasions of the Greek term side by side. Neither text is talking about looking for trouble or telling us we can jump deliberately and gleefully into a mud hole and count it all joy. Goodness knows I've tried. We fall into the kind of hardship James is talking about. Sometimes we don't even see the ditch coming.

In the margin tell about a recent time you fell into hardship.

Just so you know yours qualifies, the kind of thing James is talking about can take any form. From people-related problems to problem-related people, anything goes. From home to work to school to church to bed, everything's game. The primary meaning of the Greek wording for trials "of many kinds" (NIV) means "many-colored" or "variegated."[4] Go ahead and use a little imagination.

What two colors would you paint your current hardship? Why?

Viewing the wording of James 1:2 in the bloody and bruised traveler of Luke 10 paints a graphic picture of what trials can do to us. They can strip us, beat us up, abandon us, and leave us half dead. Sometimes you may feel so exhausted and demoralized by a dark difficulty that you can't imagine even finishing this study. You were simply on your journey, trying to get from here to there, doing your job, and minding your own business then it happened.

Luke 10:30 says he "fell into the hands of ________________."

You see, left alone, that's just what trials are: robbers. Takers. Let me show you one more vivid name for them. The Greek word for "trials" *(peirasmois)* is linked to the term *"peirates."*[5] Cross the first "e" out, and what do you have? They steal your security, dignity, dreams, and sometimes your spouse or friends. They board your ship and "pirate" the gold meant to be yours on the shore.

Unless you're in Christ. That's what James is saying. Trials don't get to steal from followers of Christ unless we hand over the goods. In fact, they're commanded to give goods *to us* if we're willing to receive them. Robbers or reapers, it's up to us. "What dividend could be worth the difficulty?" Take a look at James 1:3-4 and let's see what James considered worth the trouble.

Robbers or reapers, it's up to us.

What does the "testing of your faith" give you?

It's OK if right now you're thinking perseverance is overrated and you could really use your electric bill paid. Some of us are pretty beaten up. But we're going to see the high price on the head of perseverance and realize that, in effect, the perfect work at stake is us. The Greek word translated *perseverance* or *endurance* pushes beyond the passivity we tend to associate with patience.

Two definitions spoke loudest to me. First, perseverance means "nerving oneself" like a person determined to stay on his feet, holding tight to Jesus, while storm winds try to toss him like a yellow rubber duck on a swelling sea.[6] What this definition says to you and me today is that it's time we nerved up.

Second, perseverance means "heroic endurance."[7] I know a few people who could stand to see some heroic endurance in feeble flesh and blood. How about you? Who have you seen it in and how? Unless it's Jesus, that person is no more superhuman than you or me. He or she may have had more faith but not more potential. Focus now on verse 4 and respond in the margin.

What must perseverance or endurance do, and exactly why?

The NKJV says it like this: "Let patience have its perfect work, that you may be perfect and complete, lacking nothing." I don't know about you, but I feel a hundred country miles from perfect. Although without morality we can't be mature believers, sin-free is not what the word implies in this context. The Greek word for "perfect" *(teleios)* describes "that which has achieved or reached its goal, objective, purpose" and, therefore, "full-grown" and "fully developed."[8] The last few words of verse 4 capture it best: "lacking nothing."

The *teleios* idea is that we grow up fully in Jesus during our tenure here on planet Earth, bearing much fruit, giving God glory, and not missing a single thing Christ died on the cross to give us. He has a goal for each of us, and His desire is to completely fulfill it.

All of our discussion brings us to one big question: *So, what are you going to do with all you're going through?*

We don't *have to* consider it a great joy when we fall into all sorts of trials, but do we have a better plan? Let's do what the first word in our *Flash Forward* says: let's "consider" our options. What are my other plans, and how do they pan out? Sometimes our root issue is that we don't want to be forced into anything. We need to know we really do have options. Let's think through three. Identify your most pressing personal trial right now. Please do this next exercise with me because it could shed tremendous light on our path.

In the margin name three *different* things you could do with what you're going through. Consider making one obeying James 1:2.

Now, consider the fruit of each of the three. What do you believe the five-year ramifications would be for each of those courses of action? Write the result under each one. Get as specific as possible.

Food for thought, isn't it? While counting our trials joys because of the treasures they can bring may be the hard choice in the beginning, most of us would have to admit that the other options don't pan out as well. We'll see more on all this in session 3.

In case today's lesson has been heavy for you, let's wrap up with something lighter. Perhaps you caught the gender terminology in James 1:2—"Consider it a great joy, *my brothers.*" When the masculine plural "brothers" is used in a general sense regarding believers, we women can know we're included in it.

In Wendell Berry's fiction classic, *Hannah Coulter,* the main character speaks fondly of a woman who showed her kindness during a difficult time and, in doing so, quotes a man who may have understood women best of all.

> Miss Ora knew what it was to be out of place and ignorant and lonely. If she thought I was sad, shut up in my room, she would come and peck twice with one knuckle on my door. "Oh, Hannah," she would say, "don't you want to come out and sit a while on the porch? It's a lovely evening." Or, "Hannah, come back to the kitchen and let's have a cup of coffee. Or tea, if you'd rather."
>
> "All women is brothers," Burley Coulter used to say, and then look at you with a dead sober look as if he didn't know why you thought that was funny. But, as usual, he was telling the truth. Or part of it.[9]

After 30 years of women's ministry and so many shared joys and sorrows, I'd say he's onto something there. *All women is brothers.*

LEVEL 4

The **NEXT LEVEL** with Melissa

THE EPISTLE OF JACOB

I will never forget the first time I read the Greek text of James 1:1. My eyes scurried back and forth searching for the name of our author in Greek and found no resolution. I saw the Greek name Ἰάκωβος (the English transliteration would be something like *Jakobus)* and thought, "Surely this cannot be the word behind our English name *James?"*

After some searching through a lexicon, I learned that *indeed* it is the Greek behind our English rendering, *James*. For the nerds out there who care about this kind of tedium, I found out that Ἰάκωβος is the Hellenized form of the Greek transliteration Ἰακωβ which is in turn from the Hebrew name יַעֲקֹב *(Ya'aqov)*, or in English: *Jacob*.

I started to imagine all sorts of corrupt scenarios, like maybe James I, King of England, who was involved in the translation process of the Authorized Version of 1611 egoistically demanded that "Jacob" be translated as "James."

After hours of some pretty boring research, I happened on a brief footnote that indicated the name *Ia'acov* became "James" in English as a result of the Norman conquest at the battle of Hastings in 1066.[1] The Norman conquest was a major player in shaping the English language. Who knew?

What makes this discussion extraordinarily confusing is that the English language has two variants that have been derived from the same name: Jacob and James.

We would typically think of Jacob and James as two completely different names, Jacob as the more distinctly Jewish name. As John Painter points out, however, "there are clues that remind us of the connection between the two names in English. For example, the supporters of the Stuart Jameses are referred to as *Jacobites* and the period is named *Jacobean*."[2]

In case I have lost you, the bottom line is that the man we know as "James" is named, like numerous other men in first-century Judaism, after the famous patriarch in the Old Testament, Jacob. This is actually the case for all the men named James in the New Testament.

The man we know as "James" is named after the famous patriarch in the Old Testament, Jacob.

Matthew 1:15-16 indicates that Jacob was also the name of Joseph's father, which makes our author the namesake of both the patriarch Jacob and his grandfather Jacob.

The point of this discussion is to demonstrate that the more accurate translation of our protagonist's name is "Jacob." Throughout this study we will call our author "James" for the sake of simplicity and continuity with our English translations. But we would all do well to note at this point that the family of our writer (and by extension the family of Jesus Himself) was proud of its firmly Jewish heritage.[3]

Any time that we spend reminding ourselves of the blatantly Jewish roots of the early Christian movement is time well spent. So, in James 1:1 we see our protagonist, named after the father of the twelve tribes of Israel, addressing the twelve tribes in the Diaspora. Is that not absolutely gorgeous?

Day Two
JUST ASK

FLASH FORWARD

"If any of you lacks wisdom, he should ask God, who gives to all generously and without criticizing, and it will be given to him."
James 1:5

Last night before I climbed into bed, I got down on my knees and whispered to God, "I need wisdom! Tell me what to do!" I think I even rubbed my head with both hands. My first words to Him this morning after a restless night were echoes of the same plea. I didn't need wisdom for next week. I had a pressing work problem that had to be addressed today. It didn't just entail situations and circumstances. It entailed people: warm-blooded individuals who can be wounded, misled, or caused to stumble. Being somebody's boss was more than I signed up for.

Over the next half hour, I received enough insight from the verses in my devotional guide to know how to take the first steps when I got to work this morning. Throughout the day, I've reflected on a sacred experience that can be taken for granted: planning to go one direction, seeking leadership from God, heading another, and realizing soon that the latter way was the only wise way. Divine intervention is never trivial or routine. Let's recover some amazement today. I find myself awed—almost stricken—this moment by this miraculous, often intangible thing we call the leadership of the Spirit.

The Book of James has been coming alive in my life. Oh, how I pray it will come alive in yours as well.

Please read James 1:5-8 and write these verses on page 214.

Do you recall the part of our previous lesson where I told you that James loops or piggybacks concepts in the opening portions of his letter? How does verse 4 loop around verse 5?

If I asked the question clearly enough, you noted the repetition of the concept of lacking. James moves from the idea of endurance working to provide what is lacking in us to what we should do if our lacking is wisdom. This subject could blurt a double negative right out of the mouth of an English teacher: Lord knows I never, ever don't need wisdom.

You either? Give some thought right now to four different areas in your life where you could use the kind of wisdom only God can give:

I need wisdom

I need wisdom

I need wisdom

I need wisdom

We need knowledge, too, but it differs somewhat from wisdom. What do you think the differences may be?

We are rich beyond measure to have a sacred text that stretches its arms northward to the lofty promises of Heaven and touches its toes southward where the rubber meets the road. It's tough down here, and God knows it. We need practical advice. We need the wisdom to know what to do with knowledge. We need authentic leadership of the Spirit in areas that aren't black and white.

We need authentic leadership of the Holy Spirit.

Some of us need to find decent help with child care or to know where to educate a child with learning disabilities. We wonder how to deal with stepchildren. Or stepparents. Or in-laws. Some of our marriages are in trouble, and we don't know what to try next. Our businesses are about to go belly up, or our neighborhoods are getting dangerous. Some of us have stumbled on some volatile information, and we don't know what to do with it. We need help. Not the kind of help man can give. We need the wisdom of God. Now.

This next portion is where we could lose the focus of seasoned believers who already know so much. Please stay attentive here and open yourself to fresh awe over this privilege.

What are we to do if we lack wisdom (v. 5)? Write it in all caps.

Cynics are welcome in Bible study, too, so let me pose a few questions on their behalf: God already knows what we need. Why can't He just give it?

Why do we always have to ask? Take a shot at the answer.

The King of the universe wants a real, live relationship with us. He's not interested in just being a mind reader. He's not even interested in just being a provider. He's both of those things, but the role He relishes most is Father. He wants us—frail mortal creatures—to connect with Him and communicate with Him as the dearest relationship in human existence. He rejoices to hear our voices. He delights to be our sole and holy source for all things in life.

Read Matthew 7:7-8 with a soul willing to be revived. What is the bottom line of these verses?

Now, look back at James 1:5. How can we expect God to respond to our plea for wisdom?

You're gazing in the face of a solid-gold assurance. God will never one time mock us for lacking wisdom or sit back and think, *Seriously? How stupid can you get?* I love the NIV translation "without finding fault" (v. 5). Can we count all the times we chide ourselves in our lack of wisdom with the sick reassurance that, after all, this is our own stupid fault? I'm relieved to know that, even if my lack of wisdom got me into a mess, when I ask God for what I need, He won't delight to remind me that I'll never be enough.

Revel in knowing that the verb "ask" in James 1:5 is present tense. We're invited to ask as often or for as much wisdom as we need.[10] The same verse claims that God "gives to all generously." That includes you. That includes me. He doesn't just top off the glass of our lacking. He lets it spill over the edge and into our laps like a pitcher in the hands of an overanxious waiter.

No, God's not our waiter but make no mistake. Christ is the living Water, and living waters splash over their bounds. The unshakable promise of generous wisdom is not without condition, however.

What is the condition according to James 1:6-8?

In an honest life a time comes when a person gets sick of duplicity. When she gets tired of looking at two faces in her rearview mirror. When she can no longer respect her own unwillingness to make up her mind. There comes a time to drive a stake in the ground and lay claim to one life, one focused goal, and one God. The NIV term "double-minded" ("indecisive," HCSB) is an intriguing word. The Greek *dipsychos* literally means *double souled.*[11] This verse is the earliest known use of the wording. James may have made it up himself.[12] The idea behind it is well documented in Old Testament Scripture, however.

They lie to one another; they speak with flattering lips and deceptive hearts.
PSALM 12:2

Glance at Psalm 12:2. How exactly do flattering lips speak?

"Deception" (NIV) or "deceptive hearts" (HCSB) in Hebrew is literally "with heart and heart" or what the King James Version calls "a double heart."[13] You might picture the malady like this: the two chambers of our hearts trying to split off from one another and beat like competing drums facing different directions. It leaves the whole system out of sync and inauthentic.

What do you think could be an example of "two-heartedness"?

First Chronicles 12:33 offers the perfect antonym with the NIV phrase "undivided loyalty." It literally means the reverse: "*not* with heart and heart."[14] It means that we bring all that we are to all that He is and all that we need to all He can give. It means we quit tossing this way and that, backstroking toward God one minute and dog-paddling for the world the next. It means taking on the apostle Paul's words in Romans 11:36 as our personal confession: "From Him and through Him and to Him are all things." Including us.

James is talking about this kind of faith in 1:6 when he says we must ask without doubting. Like the psalmist, we know where our help comes from (see Ps. 121). We place our lives, our loved ones, our needs, and our wants in the hands of God alone. We pray and can know beyond question that God hears.

In the context of James 1:6, not only *can* we go to God for wisdom with the confidence that we will receive; we *must* go to God for wisdom with the absolute confidence that we will receive. Since starting this journey, I've practiced coupling my plea for wisdom with my advance gratitude for receiving it.

Look back at verse 7. Isn't it interesting that the person who doubts, waffles, and wavers "should not expect to receive anything from the Lord"? *Anything?* Wow. That means that doubt not only robs us of the wisdom we requested but other priceless provisions as well.

Matthew 6:33 represents the reverse: "Seek ye first the kingdom of God, and his righteousness; and all these things shall be added unto you" (KJV). Do you see the concept of overflow coming from both directions? Faith receives more than it asks. Doubt loses more than it disbelieved. Matthew 13:11-12 conveys a similar idea. A lot is at stake here. Let's look at our options again.

Faith receives more than it asks. Doubt loses more than it disbelieved.

What happens if we chuck all this single-mindedness and wholeheartedness for the natural life of duplicity? We get the grand prize: a life of instability. A double-minded man "is unstable in all his ways" (Jas. 1:8, KJV). I don't know if the word "unstable" makes you squirm, but it does me. How many of us can truly say we don't sometimes feel about a quarter of an inch from instability? About an eighth of an inch from the edge? One tiny crisis from a breakdown? Even a surge of imaginary harm can weaken our knees and quicken our pulse. The NET Bible® translation of Isaiah 33:6a has been in my memory verse spiral for years: "He is your constant source of stability." Yes, He is. And when the Enemy threatens to send me reeling like a weak-footed drunk on a slick sidewalk, I remind him of the One who is my constant source of stability.

Our lesson keeps looping my thoughts around Elijah's exhortation in 1 Kings 18:21. Let's conclude by writing it in the margin and seeing if we sense any word from God. Maybe today is a day for making up our minds in a personal area where we battle duplicity. I'm honored to journey with you. Rest assured, I share every bit of the conviction this kind of lesson causes. Our God is for us even when He confronts us.

Day Three

A WILDFLOWER IN THE MEADOW

FLASH FORWARD

"The brother of humble circumstances should boast in his exaltation."

James 1:9

At first we, with an abundance of possessions, will want to recoil from today's segment of James and trade true conviction for self-condemnation. Let's refuse to. Let's receive the Word like medicine to souls sick with selfishness and begging to be put out of their misery.

Narcissism is the rampant virus of the West, and the Book of James pierces our soft skin like a sharp vaccination. Behold the wonderful side of studying a whole book of the Bible: we can't pick and choose topics that dodge our discomfort levels.

Please read James 1:9-11 and handwrite the segment on the appropriate page. Afterward, write three summations you could compile on a first-glance basis with little thought:

1.

2.

3.

If your first one is that God loves the poor, your second that God hates the rich, and your third that you're pretty sure God hates you, too, then you (like me) could use a fresh theology lesson. Take heart from the start. You would have been right about number one. God does indeed have a heart for the poor. So did His servant James and with good reason. Those of humble means were within arms reach of him virtually every day of his ministry in Jerusalem. Toward the end of week 1, day 4, I asked you to record the one thing the "three pillars" (James, Peter, and John) asked Paul and Barnabas to do as they took the gospel to the Gentiles.

Review Galatians 2:10 and write the one thing they asked here:

Now, read Romans 15:23-29. Why was Paul on his way to Jerusalem?

From the terminology in verse 26, can you tell whether these poor people were Christians? If so, how?

What fascinating case did Paul make for reciprocation between Jews and Gentiles (see v. 27)?

Paul referred to this same trip in Acts 24:17. What purpose does it record for his journey?

Something happened in the early days of Christianity that spread poverty like a plague among Jewish converts in Jerusalem. We know from Christ's own words in Mark 14:7 that the poor had always been among them just as they will always be among us. Conditions changed rapidly enough, however, to cause evangelists like Paul to spread word all over the growing Christian world that the believers in Jerusalem needed help. Their situation was dire enough for Paul to actively take up offerings for them in his travels and haul them all the way back to the holy city at significant personal risk.

Remember that James was the shepherd over this poverty-threatened flock, so who on earth would have been more passionate about their needs? His constant exposure to the poor makes perfect sense of multiple mentions in such a brief epistle. If you and I worked among the poverty-stricken every single day (and some of you do), we would be willing to speak at any volume and beat down any door in their defense. We who are not presently assigned to serve those of humbler means in our workplaces must constantly tune our ears to the voices of those who are. Look up the following Scriptures and record a few reasons why:

We who are not presently assigned to serve those of humbler means in our workplaces must constantly tune our ears to the voices of those who are.

Deuteronomy 15:11

Proverbs 17:5

Proverbs 19:17

Proverbs 31:8-9

Scripture refers to the poor or poverty-stricken hundreds of times from Exodus to Revelation. The concept is so constant that, from a Bible student's standpoint, it's virtually impossible to remember God and forget the poor. The point is not to stir up guilt. It's to stir up giving. Simply put, we who have are to open our hands in complete humility to those who don't.

Look for James to circle back to the topic several times, but the action line won't waver: guilt is useless. Giving is priceless. Before we start glorifying poverty and considering it the only sacred condition, wrestle with this: "If scarcity of goods inherently improves one's spirituality, no biblical text would ever command help for the poor!"[15] God would never tell us to relieve people of their blessed state.

So, back to Jerusalem in the first century A.D. and God's servant, James. What on earth happened to cause such dire straights? Were the poor more open to the gospel of Jesus Christ? Probably. Or, were many Jewish converts persecuted for their faith? See for yourself.

Read Hebrews 10:32-34 and pinpoint the part that suggests an outbreak of poverty among early converts to Christ.

Reflect once again on James 1:9-11. Perhaps the backdrop helps us better understand James' passion toward the poor. His exhortation for those in humble circumstances to take pride in their high position and the rich to take stock in their low position had a leveling effect. Think of it as a sociological form of Isaiah 40:4-5. "Every valley will be lifted up, and every mountain and hill will be leveled; the uneven ground will become smooth and the rough places, a plain. And the glory of the LORD will appear, and all humanity together will see it."

The one who is rich should boast in his humiliation because he will pass away like a flower of the field.
JAMES 1:10

In the brotherhood of believers, those up high are called to bow down, and those crouched down are called to stand tall—each because of what Jesus has done. Stare at James 1:10 again and reflect on what James could mean by the rich taking pride in their low position. I don't know for certain that this mind-set applies here, but I can tell you from a personal standpoint that the only time I feel a vivid fellowship with suffering believers in other parts of the world is when I am humbled by extreme difficulty of my own. Otherwise, I wonder how in Heaven's name I will stand next to them around the throne of God and have any crowns at all to cast. Without frequent humblings, I am a cushy, lightweight Christian who doesn't know the first thing about denying myself and carrying my cross.

James called both extremes to take stock of what they had coming. Interestingly, one is in the long-term and the other the short. He called the poor to look *beyond* this life toward their ultimate position in Christ. He called the rich to look *toward* the end of this life and the futility of earthly riches. In other words, their positions dictated their perspectives.

Set 1 Peter 1:24-25 next to James 1:10-11. Who is James comparing to withering flowers?

Now, who is Peter comparing to withering grass or flowers?

You see, all human flesh quickly fades and passes away. The transience of this earthly existence is both hope to the poor and humility to the rich. The picture in James 1:11 captures the hustle and bustle of the self-important who really do think that the one who dies with the most toys wins. James carries over the teaching of his half brother in Luke 12:15-21.

How do these verses echo the same principle?

As I studied for this lesson, the thought occurred to me how Satan might have preyed upon new Jewish converts in suddenly humble circumstances. Many Jews believed a multitude of possessions showed God's favor and fewer possessions indicated His displeasure. Don't get me wrong. The Old Testament contains complaints about the prosperity of the wicked and accounts of the righteous of those of humble means. The overarching understanding among most, however, was that God would prosper the faithful and withhold from those who weren't.

Check out Psalm 112:1-3, for example. Who is "blessed" (NIV) or "happy" (HCSB), and what things are in his house?

In the black of night Jewish converts who suffered the confiscation of their property could have asked themselves whether God's favor was lost to them. Indeed, they'd been conditioned for centuries to do so. I also wonder if this confusion is one beautiful reason why James capped this portion of Scripture with a new beatitude in verse 12.

Who is "blessed" according to James 1:12?

Why do you think God placed such emphasis on the poor throughout His Word?

The incarnation stood blessing on its head. Glory graced a wooden manger. Flesh veiled the fiercest beauty. Bandages wrapped crowns around the heads of the broken. Bad news gave way to good. "Blessed are the poor in spirit!" "Blessed are those who mourn!" (See Matt. 5:3-4.)

Blessed are all who need Jesus!

"You say, 'I'm rich; I have become wealthy and need nothing,' and you don't know that you are wretched, pitiful, poor, blind, and naked" (Rev. 3:17).

Oh, to know.

The **NEXT LEVEL** with Melissa

WAS JAMES MARRIED?

As we set out to learn as much as we can about the man James, a natural question that may occur to us is, *Was James married?* After all, most married folks I know regard this particular relationship as one of their most fundamental relationships. While we have no way to be certain that James was married, 1 Corinthians 9:5 presents it as a possibility. In that seemingly incidental text Paul asked the Corinthians: "Don't we have the right to take a believing wife along with us, as do the other apostles and the Lord's brothers and Cephas?" (NIV).

The issue for Paul in 1 Corinthians 9:5 was not primarily about having the right to marry, since we know from 1 Corinthians 7:7 that Paul's preference was celibacy. Rather, in the context, the verse concerns Paul's refusal to invoke his various *rights,* specifically his right to the Corinthians' financial support. So, admittedly, the question we ask is somewhat tangential to the context of 1 Corinthians 9:5. Nevertheless, it is striking that Paul mentioned "the Lord's brothers." I interpret the phrase "the Lord's brothers" literally as a reference to Jesus' physical, earthly brothers. If this interpretation is correct, then Paul included Jesus' brothers as among the early Christian leaders who were married. Since James was by far the most prominent of Jesus' brothers, it is at least a possibility that James was a husband.

Since we believe that, for the most part, James remained in Jerusalem to head the local church there, we should not envisage James as an itinerate preacher like Peter or Paul. But it is possible that he did travel from time to time. Whether single or married, James may have been financially supported by the church in Jerusalem. According to Paul, plenty of Christian leaders were supported by early Christian communities, apparently *excluding* him.

The moral of this little segment is that sometimes in the most unlikely verses we get a glimpse into something that could be significant, and, even if a matter is not verifiable, the possibilities are still worth exploring.

Day Four
BAITED BY OUR DESIRES

FLASH FORWARD

"No one undergoing a trial should say, 'I am being tempted by God.' For God is not tempted by evil, and He Himself doesn't tempt anyone."
James 1:13

Picture your closest social circle, the one in your real life, not online. The people in it don't have to know each other. Their common denominator only needs to be you. Now picture each of their faces.

- Who is most prone to tell you what you want to hear?
- Who will talk you into feeling better even when you shouldn't?
- Who is your friend, the dependable liar?

Now, turn in that circle of friends like an arrow on a game board. Stop at the one who seems to lack the social skills to beat around the bush. The one who blurts out what you need to hear even when your fingers are in both ears. Point at the one you avoid if you're not feeling up to the truth.

Put the face of James on him. (Minus the missing social skills perhaps.) He's not going to be just our friend for the next six weeks, he's going to be our big brother. He's going to tell us what we need to hear and, if we're smart, we'll listen. We stand to learn something today, for instance, that could help us pinpoint the exact spot where things keep going awry. Some of us keep trying to protect ourselves from the Devil, and we should, only to find ourselves back in the ditch. Something's not working, but who knows what?

No one in existence has more to gain from our selective hearing than the Devil. Don't think for a second he's incapable of being nice to you. If you want to stay in bondage to self-deception, he can be your best friend.

Let's take a courageous look inside today. Not only is holiness at stake, authentic happiness is at stake. In God's economy, those aren't exclusive terms.

Not only is holiness at stake, authentic happiness is at stake.

Please read James 1:12-15 and write it on the appropriate page.

The word "blessed" in verse 12 can also be translated *happy*. This blessedness or happiness anticipates a future event so thoroughly that it receives a deposit of gladness in advance.

Who did you say was "blessed" (1:12) yesterday?

Up to this point in James 1, the emphasis has been on the testing of our faith through harsh circumstances; but with the slightest variance in wording and context, it shifts in verse 13 from trials to temptation. Here are a handful of facts that, put together, could honestly save our lives:

1. *Each person is tempted.* Temptation is one of the great equalizers in our world. No one escapes temptation. We're all tempted, but we're not all tempted by the same things. Temptation is an "each person" kind of thing, and the bait fits the fish.

2. *God Himself doesn't tempt anyone.* Some of us are asking what I might have wondered years ago: *Who would think that He does?* Don't most of us believe that God is holy and righteous, incapable of wrongdoing and absent of darkness? Isn't that what Scriptures says? Ah yes, but the temptation to blame God for our temptations is as ripe as the fruit on the forbidden tree.

A man's own foolishness leads him astray, yet his heart rages against the LORD.
PROVERBS 19:3

What does Proverbs 19:3 say about temptation?

Like you perhaps, I've blamed God at times for "making me this way," but playing the nature card doesn't make us the perfect poster child for Proverbs 19:3. What cuts and pastes our faces onto this glossy poster is doing something extraordinarily stupid, making a big mess, then getting mad at God for letting us do it. The NLT says it like this: "People ruin their lives by their own foolishness and then are angry at the LORD." Ouch.

Some of us more often lean toward self-reproach, but I'd be lying to say I've never blamed God for not stopping something inane. Abnormality made the argument appealing. "Lord, that wasn't me. That wasn't even in my heart." Wrong. The actions may not have been in my plan or even in my conscious mind, but they undoubtedly sprang from something in my messed up heart. Sounds like bad news to face, but it's good news if it ends up setting us free.

3. *We are baited by our own desires.* Look carefully at James 1:14. The word "desires" translates from the Greek *epithymia*. By itself, the term simply conveys a strong desire or craving. The context determines whether it's positive or negative. Take a look at Luke 22:15 for a positive rendering.

How exactly did Christ feel about sharing the Passover meal with His disciples?

The wording "eagerly desired" (NIV) or "fervently desired" (HCSB) translates the same Greek word. I love knowing Christ feels strongly about His followers and possesses a holy craving toward us. I like thinking He can hardly wait until we're all there with Him. An emotionless relationship holds absolutely no draw for me. Apathy makes the dead out of the living. Created in God's image, He means for us to have passion for people, zeal for life, and a calling to righteous causes, but not to be eaten alive by them, we need healthy hearts.

I can't quit thinking about Dr. K.A. Richardson's definition for *epithymia*. In the negative context of James 1:14, he translates it *deformed desire.*[16] Does that wording drive a stake into your heart like it does mine? I can't think of a more vivid and disturbing way to label my condition for so many years. I so often willingly reached for exactly what would burn me. I was drawn to it like a moth to a flame. I loved it then hated myself for loving it. Then I'd hate it but hate myself more for choosing it. Lord, have mercy.

Somewhere along the way we have to own our own deformed desire. We have to take responsibility for setting out our own bait and biting it, too. While the Bible by no means absolves Satan in this process, in this one vital spot we're forced to reckon with our sinful selves alone. Once I realized the problem was in me and not just around me or done to me, I knew Jesus was my only hope. He alone can change us from the core. He alone can seep into the dark crevices of our souls where destructiveness drives us.

Jesus alone can change us from the core.

Tell me, have you ever been forced to recognize your own "deformed desire"? If so, what forced you into awareness?

Beloved, you might stop and thank God for that conviction. We could be doing a lot of things besides walking with God through Bible study right now.

"Desire conceives, it gives birth to sin, and when sin is fully grown, it gives birth to death" (Jas. 1:15, NET). Unsettling, isn't it? All of us who are honest have experienced the process in this verse. We feel the craving or desire and, this time, instead of fighting it, we give way to it. Thomas à Kempis put it this way: "At first it is a mere thought confronting the mind; then imagination paints it in stronger colours; only after that do we take pleasure in it, and the will makes a false move, and we give our assent."[17]

According to James, this "assent" is the point of conception and soon gives birth to unabashed sin. Then we all know what happens: it grows, and grows, and grows until standing before us is a fire-breathing dragon that resembles a twisted version of our old selves. It whips us with its tail, hurls us further than we dreamed we'd go, and buries us deeper than we meant to hide. And then, the death. There's always a death of some kind when it's done.

In the margin name a few deaths that can result from full-grown sin conceived out of deformed desires. This can be a topic for your group to discuss.

One commentator suggests that sin is full grown "when it becomes a fixed habit."[18] I can certainly nod to that from personal experience. The deaths that addiction can bring are innumerable. They can kill relationships, security, self-respect, and livelihoods, and that's just for starters. A friend of mine fell dreadfully sick a few nights ago and couldn't get up or reach her telephone.

Her husband was passed out cold from drinking too much ... again. She tried to scream to wake him and even resorted to throwing things at him to no avail.

I asked her afterward how she felt about him, and I could tell that her heart was fighting deadness. That's just one way full-grown sin kills. Where on earth would we be without a Savior who can raise the dead? If you happen to recognize your own pattern somewhere in this lesson, there really is another way. In fact, we studied it earlier this very week.

Look carefully back at James 1:3-4. What exact progression is described here?

Now, look at both segments side by side. James 1:14-15 is the antithesis of James 1:3-4. Can you see it? The common center point between the two is the testing of our faith. Make no mistake. A tidal wave of temptation is as surely a test of our faith as a time of suffering. Both boil down to whether or not we are going to believe God. Each also has an antithetical progression. If, when we are tested, we decide to be faithful and endure, endurance will bring about its perfect effect. Something we've been missing all our lives will be completed in us and we will mature. Verse 12 says that's not all.

Ultimately, God Himself will give us the "crown of ___________."

On the other hand, if we decide to distrust God and instead give way to our own deformed desires, they will conceive sin. Ironically, sin also has a maturing process.

Sin matures and brings forth ____________________ (see v. 15).

This is the James version of Deuteronomy 30:19: "I have set before you _______________ and _______________. ... Choose _______________."

OK, one last look at James 1:12. To whom exactly has God promised the crown of life?

Loving God with everything in us is the key to a healthy heart.

Beloved, you are gazing at the very antithesis of deformed desires. I could stand and shout with joy as one who has discovered long, lost treasure. My dear Sister, loving God with everything in us is the key to a healthy heart. A good friend of mine often says that those who don't love God will love anything. If you make only one solitary request for yourself or someone you care about, let it be this! To love the Lord your God with all your heart, soul, mind, and strength. A way leads to life. And a way leads to the *crown of life*.

Day Five
FATHER OF LIGHTS

FLASH FORWARD

"Every generous act and every perfect gift is from above, coming down from the Father of lights; with Him there is no variation or shadow cast by turning." James 1:17

I'm keeping a secret from my husband. It's a delicious feeling really. So far, the baiting is the best part. I keep telling him there's something I'm not telling him. Finally, after all these years of marriage, I think I've found the perfect gift.

Keith is almost impossible to buy for, a fact that brings considerable consternation to his wife and daughters on special occasions. Three challenges stack up against us. First, he's the consummate outdoorsman, making his three girls like fish flopping on the shore at his favorite stores. Second, if he can afford it, he probably already owns it. This frustrates me to no end. Third, his preferences toward fishing poles, shotguns, and surrounding accoutrements are so specific that we have about a 1/1000 chance of pegging them.

This year is different. This year I think I've got it. It's already wrapped in manly, deep purple paper with a slightly less manly white bow. All I'm waiting for is the right timing.

Our segment today is James 1:16-18. Please read these verses and handwrite them on the appropriate page.

Look carefully at James 1:13-15,17-18. Set them side-by-side in your thinking and note the variance in tone. The two segments seem to be poles apart, but verse 16 masterfully ties them together by creating a deliberate contrast.

What does verse 16 warn against?

Consider the whole portion falling between James 1:13 and James 1:18. Do you see any repeated concepts? (See vv. 15,18.)

Write a one-sentence synopsis of these six verses, drawing it all together.

Never be duped into believing that the flesh gives and heaven takes away.

Since dusk fell on the garden of Eden, man has fallen prey to the paranoia that God is trying to cheat him. James 1:13-15 draws a picture of what happens when we decide (perhaps subconsciously) that God is holding out on us and we're going to take what we want for ourselves.

All rebellion is essentially the attempt to take *now* what God won't give. The object of our deformed desire looks so alluring and promising that we can't imagine it birthing death, yet eventually it always does.

James gives loud caution to his readers never to be duped into believing that the flesh gives and Heaven takes away. Deep inside the marrow of our belief system, we are prone to think of God as the gigantic minus in a life full of pluses. Only by the integrated revelation of the Holy Spirit do we comprehend the great reversal: God gives and the flesh takes away. God bestows. The flesh bereaves.

Every good and perfect gift is from above, coming down from the Father of the heavenly lights, who does not change like shifting shadows.
JAMES 1:17, NIV

James 1:17 takes our perspective toward gain and tilts it upward like arms wide open. James sets before his readers the God of Heaven and earth who literally, actively, perpetually, and generously gives divine gifts to His children. I'm talking about presents like the ones under a Christmas tree, only infinitely better and marvelously less restricted by seasons. All of us have received a host of them. We just don't always recognize them.

Indeed, every good and perfect thing that has ever come into our lives has come as a gift to us from God Himself. It did not bubble up like crude oil from this earth. It flowed down like rain from the riverbank of Heaven. It was intentional. It was personal. Yet we see ourselves at the mercy of random events, abilities, and coincidences.

Reflect on the NIV terminology again: "Every good and perfect gift is from above." Maybe you can see some "good" but the whole idea of "perfect" is completely foreign to you in such a flawed world and, if you're like me, in such a flawed *life*. Keep in mind the expanded definition of the word *teleios* that translates *perfect* in the Book of James. The word describes that "which has achieved or reached its goal, objective, purpose."[19]

Out of God's astounding grace, a very imperfect person can still receive a delightfully perfect gift precisely because it's perfect for her. God's gifts are given with goals. They're perfect because they're perfecting. They don't just give today. They give toward every tomorrow.

One of the most impactful tasks we could accomplish today is to acknowledge various gifts from God. To do so, take your present age and divide it by four.

My present age ___________ / 4 = ___________

Reflect on the course of your life in quarters. As rough as it may have been in various seasons, let's try to recognize several good and (dare we say?) *perfect* gifts God poured into our lives. We'll record them in the exercises to follow.

Let's stop and pray for God to open our eyes to His goal-driven activity in our roller-coaster histories. I'll add a few of my own acknowledgments to help you get started.

First quarter (newborn to _______________):

The gift of a big family and sharing a bedroom with my grandmother.

Second quarter (______________ to ______________):

Taken to church. Money for braces! Got to go to college. Built some impactful relationships. Met my man. Had two little girls.

Third quarter (______________ to ______________):

Caught Bible study like a virus. Found freedom in Christ from several persistent strongholds and measurable redemption from the pain of my past.

Fourth quarter (___________ to ___________):
My wonderful co-workers. Sons-in-law. Grandchildren!

Beloved, listen carefully to what James is claiming under the inspiration of the Holy Spirit: *If it was good, then it was God. If it was perfect, then its goal was precise.* As we take a look back at discernible gifts of God in each quarter of our lives, we might feel tempted to glance at each other's lists and roll our eyes over a veritable dream life. If so, you'd be as woefully off base about my life as I'd be about yours.

Many hard things happened in those quarters. Some weren't just hard. They were horrible. Yet, I can see how God continued to pour down gifts on me from Heaven that would sustain me and lift me. Some would end up being the life of me. I'm a terribly imperfect person, but an insatiable love for books was a perfect gift for me. I am an inherently selfish person, but God has given me an odd affection for women I serve like I've known them for years and most I've never met. I'm a self-absorbed clot of frayed nerves on my own, but through Christ I've caught glimpses of corporate vision.

Are these examples stirring up thoughts toward a few more of your God-given good or perfect gifts? If so, boldly list them.

Deuteronomy 26:11 tells us to "rejoice in all the good things the LORD your God has given you and your household." If you haven't stopped lately to thank Him for innumerable gifts, do it now! Honor Him by rejoicing in the good things He's given you and your household. Don't try to ignore them in the name of humility. Pride takes credit. Glory gives credit. The point is to glorify God through those good gifts.

Parts of our lives were more nightmarish than good. What then?

I can look at my life in retrospect and see how several of those very things morphed into gifts. I am convinced that desperation became a gift to me because it saved me from a life of mediocrity. Gray wasn't an option for someone as self-destructive as I was. Looming disappointment in some key people in my life also turned into a gift. I couldn't get anybody to mend or tend to my tattered soul the way I craved.

A lifetime of snuggling up to folks with scissor-hands scars you, but those scars become a road map that leads straight to Jesus. There He becomes the uncontested love of your life and the unexpected fountainhead of cleaner affection for others. Every gap in your life makes room for the Lover of your soul. God uses time to unwrap presents that appear as curses.

Now, look back at James 1:17. How is God referenced in this verse? "The Father of ... ________________."

See the reference in tandem with James 1:18. What did He choose to do according to this verse?

Our Father in Heaven fathered the entire universe in its impeccable order and spectacular beauty. He who calls the stars by name calls us the very "children of God! And that is what we are!" (1 John 3:1, NIV).

He is perfectly acquainted with every circumstance in our lives and every cell in our bodies. He knows what we need. He knows what we crave. He knows a good gift for us when He sees one and has a goal for every perfect present He sends down to us from Heaven.

He birthed us through the word of truth. Nothing is more contrary to our new natures in Christ than to birth death through our deformed desires. A word of deception hides behind every temptation and the word of truth behind every timely gift. Temptation attempts to tear open the package before its due date and, in so doing, disfigures what's inside.

Temptation attempts to tear open the package before its due date and, in so doing, disfigures what's inside.

Wait on the Lord! So many presents are wrapped under your tree that it will take a lifetime to open them. That's God's way. He keeps telling us that there's something He's not telling us, like exactly *how* this whole thing is going to work out. This we can know: it's going to be perfect.

The **NEXT LEVEL** with Melissa

THE GENRE OF JAMES

One key to interpreting a biblical book, like any other written work, is its literary genre. Because it has been a while since seventh grade English class, *genre* simply means a kind, category, or type of literary work. As E.D. Hirsch notes, "All understanding of verbal meaning is necessarily genre-bound."[1] We know this intuitively. For example, we read a satire differently than we read a selection out of an encyclopedia.

We have **different expectations** of a text based on our knowledge or perception of the work's content, structure, and purpose.

We know that different literary genres convey meaning in different ways. The Bible contains numerous literary genres including but not limited to: poetry, narratives, prophetic oracles, law, wisdom, gospels (something like an ancient biographical sketch), letters, parables, apocalypses, and countless subgenres we can't address here for the sake of brevity.

As you probably anticipate by now, the Book of James does not fit neatly into any one category. No scholarly consensus exists about the genre of James, but we can discuss some of the most important and generally maintained observations.

1. **An Epistle:** First, James is an epistle but somewhat irregular even as a letter. Unlike most of Paul's letters, James did not write to a specific congregation or individual. His identification of the recipients as "the 12 tribes in the Dispersion" (Jas. 1:1) leads many to subclassify James as a "diaspora letter."

2. **A Diaspora Letter:** This was a circular letter sent by an acknowledged spiritual authority in Judea to Jews living outside the land. A diaspora letter aimed to unite scattered Jewish communities with the beliefs and customs of the motherland and to urge them to live faithfully as the covenant people of God in a land not their own. As evidence, note that some passages seem to refer to particular historical situations (see Jas. 2:2-7, 15-17; 4:1-4,13-17).

3. **A Paraenesis:** One influential James scholar argued that the book is paraenetic literature.[2] That big word means a specialized form of advice or exhortation that includes at least some of five major features.
   a. the use of precepts and imperatives (commands)
   b. the use of moral examples
   c. a close relationship between the author and the recipients
   d. the use of traditional materials
   e. general applicability[3]

James definitely contains these five characteristics, especially the use of commands. James has the highest frequency of imperatives in the entire New Testament.[4]

4. **Wisdom Literature:** Because of the overlap with the wisdom literature, recently scholars have suggested that paraenesis is actually a subcategory or subgenre of the broad category called wisdom literature.

Indeed, the Book of James has a lot in common with Jewish wisdom literature.

Several years ago when I first began to study James, I begged an insightful classmate to read James in one sitting and, without overthinking it, to relay his initial thoughts to me. He was kind enough to answer my plea and his first remark was, "James reads like the Proverbs of the New Testament." His suggestion has a lot of truth to it.

James does share common elements with Proverbs. For example, James references "wisdom" several times (Jas. 1:5; 3:13,15,17). He echoes themes from Proverbs like wealth, poverty, and the tongue. He posits some short and choppy but profound aphorisms (adages or maxims). He moves quickly from topic to topic, sometimes without showing a smooth flow of thought. James even alludes to Proverbs itself several times (see Jas. 4:6; 5:20). But, even though James has a lot in common with wisdom literature, many commentators are reluctant to classify it as such.

James is a difficult writer to pin down, for in spite of all the aforementioned similarities, James is not wholly concerned with wisdom as a theme. He also uses legal texts like Leviticus 19, and even more paradoxically, he speaks in the tenor of the prophet Amos (see the prophetic oracle in Jas. 5:1-6). So although James has many features of wisdom literature, we should not be quick to classify this eclectic text as pure wisdom literature like the Book of Proverbs.

Neatly classifying James is a daunting and perhaps impossible task. James' voice reverberates with prophet and sage. We would say he is altogether unique, but then again, he sounds a whole lot like Jesus Himself. We can confidently conclude that James uses many features of wisdom and paraenetic literature to creatively express traditional Jewish materials through the vision and teaching of Jesus.

The purpose of James' letter, as Cheung puts it, is to "reorient his readers to a new and different meaning system grounded on the faith of Jesus Christ the Lord of glory."[5]

The purpose of James' letter, as Cheung puts it, is to "reorient his readers to a new and different meaning system grounded on the faith of Jesus Christ the Lord of glory."

viewer guide | session three

John 16:20-24

On week 2, day 1 of our homework, we saw the exhortation of James to "consider it a great joy ... whenever [we] experience various trials" (Jas. 1:2). Today we will widen our scope on joy by studying a concept in Christ's own teaching in John 16:20-24.

Two terms from John 16:20-24 are going to preoccupy our attentions today:

________ (Greek *chara*) ⬅ ➡ __________________ (Greek *thlipsis*)

The word "anguish" is often used to convey the added element of

___________ ____________.

Consider two examples:

- __________ + ______________ = anguish
- ______________ + ___________ = anguish

The etymology of the word "anguish" (Latin *angere)* includes the meaning "to _________."

Consider the similarity in the Greek definition of "anguish" in John 16:21:

> Greek *thlipsis*—from *thlibō*—"to crush, press, ____________, ___________. *Thlipsis* conveys the picture of something being crushed, pressed, or squeezed from a great weight. It is used to denote grievous physical affliction, or mental and spiritual distress."[1]

1. __________ and joy can ________ (Jas. 1:2).

Also compare Romans 9:1-5 to 2 Corinthians 7:4-7.

2. __________ and joy can _______ _________.

"The Spirit of the Lord GOD is on Me, because the LORD has anointed Me ... to provide for those who mourn in Zion; to give them a crown of beauty _____________ of _________" (Isa. 61:1-3).

3. The source of anguish can ________ into _______ (John 16:20).

Compare Psalm 30:11. Hebrew *hapak*—"to turn, ... ____________, ____________. ... Frequently used in connection with the acts of God."[2]

4. Mental anguish can be like the ________ in ____________ (Ps. 55:1-5, see v. 4).

Hebrew *hiyl*—"to turn in a circle, twist, revolve; to writhe, travail (in childbirth), bear a child. ... The main idea is that of writhing in pain, which is particularly associated ________ ______________. Also denotes ... suffering torment, ... experiencing anguish or distress."[3]

5. Anguish is ________ to ______ to a _______ (John 16:20-22).

1. *Hebrew-Greek Key Word Study Bible* (Chattanooga, TN: AMG Publishers, 1996), 1632.
2. Ibid., 1512.
3. Ibid., 1515.

WEEK THREE

WORDS THAT FREE US

Day One
QUICK TO LISTEN

FLASH FORWARD

"My dearly loved brothers, understand this: Everyone must be quick to hear, slow to speak, and slow to anger." James 1:19

Has anybody besides me recently gotten caught not listening? I know it's painful, but go here with me for a moment. Does anyone else doodle your way through conference calls and then have no idea what to say when it's your turn to talk? Or, on the other hand, is it always your turn to talk? Is anyone besides me particularly proficient at butting in? God forbid we wouldn't be the one to get to talk next. Does anybody besides me keep your cell phone in your lap while having lunch with a new friend so you can give it a sly glance when she picks up her iced tea? It's pathetic.

Thanks to God alone, not even yours truly is that inconsiderate all the time—but often enough to squirm as we turn to our next segment. In fact, I've improved my listening skills just recently for the solitary reason that I knew this lesson was coming. That's the thing about knowing a book of the Bible fairly well before you ever start writing a study on it. You have a heads-up to straighten up before conviction hits like a sledgehammer. With the study of the Book of James, you can either change or quit. Let's not quit.

Instead, let's handwrite James 1:19-21 on the appropriate page.

Now let's literally "take note" of the three imperatives in verse 19. List them in the margin.

1.

2.

3.

Star the one (or ones) most challenging to your natural personality. If you starred all three, take heart. We are supposed to need God. With full assurance that we are dearly loved sisters, let's focus first of all on the pairing, "quick to hear, slow to speak."

You may share my stronger devotion to "slow to hear, quick to speak." In fact, much of the time I quit listening once the topic is established because I'm rehearsing what I want to say. Then, if I'm in a cordial humor, I bite my tongue while the seconds drag by at a snail's pace until it's my turn to talk. It's a terrible habit that smacks of narcissism and one I mean to break during the course of this study.

The only way we're apt to develop the art of listening is to become rabidly intentional.

Electronic means of communication are here to stay, but forget looking at them to help you sharpen your social skills. Most of us agree that connecting electronically has its upsides, but *USA Today* suggested a serious downside: "Often, we're effectively disconnecting from those in the same room."[1] Face-to-face repartee is slipping through our fingers lightening-fast, so the only way we're apt to develop the art of listening is to become rabidly intentional. Our first big assignment this week is to lock down our lips and listen. Here's a little extra motivation.

Write out Proverbs 17:27-28 here:

You've got to love Proverbs 17:28. We don't even have to be wise to seem wise. All we have to do is hold our tongues. Here's where the issue grabs my attention: even more than I like to talk, I genuinely like to learn. You, too? Well, when we're talking, we're usually not learning. That active realization is enough to shut me up. Keep in mind that God gave us mouths on purpose so the point is not to cease talking. Our most effective speech can be measured with a yardstick though, not a 50-foot industrial tape measure.

Now, let's shift to the next imperative while we still have a toe left: "quick to hear, slow to speak, and ________________________."

In the privacy of your own intimate relationship with God, on a scale of *1-10, 1* being a *nonissue* and *10* being *substantial,* how much of an issue do you have with anger?

1 ____ 10

Regardless of your answer, reflect on the last seven days. What kinds of things sparked feelings of anger? Get as specific as possible, down to the driver at that stoplight.

Keeping in mind how loved you are by God and how He is on your side, answer these prodding questions: How often is your anger expressed in words (of any kind)? What, if anything, have you said in recent weeks or months out of anger that you wish you could take back?

Keep in mind that your anger may have been masked or suppressed when you said what you regret, but you may know in all honesty that it helped shape your words.

Let's intentionally complicate the matter. When was the last time you felt your anger was justified?

In fact, could your anger have been considered "righteous indignation"? If so, in the margin briefly explain how.

Now, look back at James 1:20 and record the harm of anger:

Few internal motivators rival anger. It's not just a pointer. It's a screamer. It doesn't just suggest a direction for you to go. It shoves you there with a whiplash. Notice that James does not refute anger as a plausible emotion. He refutes a quick temper as a holy conspirator toward a righteous life.

Rabbis of past eras might have been more likely to forbid it all together. "While man may imitate certain divine qualities, according to the Jews, certain ones, notably anger, are forbidden: 'Thrice was Moses angry, and thrice he failed to produce the mind of God.' "[2] I found this perspective toward anger most intriguing among those prevalent in ancient Judaism: "It was believed that the 'angry' man had not mastered his *yetser* [essentially, his *impulse]*. To lose one's temper was to lose the Shechinah (Jas. 2:1)."[3] That last word refers to a resting or settling of the glory of God. The commentator associates it with James 2:1 for a glorious reason. Keep it in the back of your mind until we reach the second chapter.

For now, how might Ephesians 4:30-31 imply that anger could affect the manifestation of the Spirit in us?

Now, read James 1:20 again. It may have particular relevance to us when we believe we possess righteous indignation. David P. Nystrom says James may be "instructing us to be slow to assume the mantle of righteous indignation, because in so doing we implicitly claim to speak for God."[4] The prospect is chilling, isn't it? If the implications were frightening in James' day when letters were written longhand and delivered foot-slow, imagine the impact in a culture where we can instantly voice our heated opinions in a public forum without the benefit of an editor or a permanent eraser.

Man's anger does not accomplish God's righteousness.
JAMES 1:20

When natural disaster strikes, the natural man rises up in us wearing a religious robe and claiming to be God's mouthpiece. Make no mistake. God can and does speak, but, according to this segment of James, He rarely speaks through the rash-hearted and, according to a later segment of James, He passes over the proud like they have a spiritual plague. This is the point where verse 21 chimes in. *Day 1 continues on page 76.*

The **NEXT LEVEL** with Melissa

HEARERS, NOT JUST READERS

Last week Mom and I headed out to grab some lunch when I noticed a tattered piece of laminated paper containing the words of James chapter 5 on her car floorboard. Mom told me several months ago that she was memorizing the whole book; but you know, we all hope to do that sort of thing, so I figured I would believe her *after* the fact. After all, I've been known to get a wee bit overambitious myself. I once composed a list of life goals and memorizing the entire Bible might have been mentioned. Let's be honest, I haven't gotten past Genesis 1.

Since she had clearly made it to the final chapter and we had a few more minutes alone together in the car, I asked her to recite the book from memory. As she recounted this familiar text, she inflected and accented particular words and phrases in a way that the words fell on me in a fresh way. The content of James' message was still the same, but the words took a new shape as she orally declared them.

The content of James' message was still the same, but the **words took a new shape** as she orally declared them.

Listening to Mom narrate the book from memory all in one sitting was so incredible to me that I asked her to do the same for our Living Proof staff during our weekly prayer and devotional time. The responses from the staff were remarkable.

One staff member was so emotionally moved by the experience she nearly burst into tears in the first chapter. She said somehow the message resonated more deeply in her than simply reading portions of the book.

Another colleague said she never realized how prominent a certain theme was in the Book of James until she heard it spoken aloud. Most of us agreed that it was easier to follow James' flow of thought from chapter to chapter when we heard the words spoken than when we simply read them.

It was easier to **follow James' flow of thought** from chapter to chapter when we heard the words spoken than when we simply read them.

While I am unspeakably grateful I can curl up alone on my couch with my own personal copy of the Scriptures, for several reasons hearing Scripture recited in a group setting was a rewarding experience. First, to hear the entire epistle all in one sitting was beneficial. The entire book takes about 15 minutes from beginning to end.

Since verse and chapter divisions in modern translations are, at times, unhelpful, it was quite the payoff to hear the message uninterruptedly without an artificial break. We also too often camp out on one or two verses without recognizing the immediate context of the verses.

Although verse-by-verse, in-depth meditation has some profound benefits, something is also to be said for the compelling cohesiveness of reading or, in this case, listening to an entire epistle or Gospel in one sitting.

Second, since our society relies so heavily on written and visual forms of communication, it was refreshing to absorb and process information entirely by hearing. Silently listening to the Scripture read or recited uses a different learning muscle, one that does not get a whole lot of exercise in our culture.

Finally, the vast majority of the earliest Christians would have heard James' words read out loud. Coincidentally, in 1:22 James himself indirectly mentions the ancient practice of hearing texts read aloud when he commands his readers to be doers of the word and not just hearers (as opposed to readers).

The vast majority of the earliest Christians would have heard James' words read out loud.

We tend to imagine the first-century Christians with leather-bound Bibles in hand, but this was not the case. Not only were books rare and expensive in the ancient world, but only a tiny percentage of the population could even read (and the bulk of that tiny percentage was male).

If you like numbers, scholarly estimates for literacy rates in first-century Roman Palestine range from about 3 to 10 percent.[1] For the sake of perspective, literacy rates in America today are around 99 percent; even my 5-year-old nephew is learning to read.

The mass literacy we know and experience in America is completely foreign to the ancient world where publishing a book literally meant providing one or more copies of a work, each copy made separately and by hand.[2] Even "reading" was a thoroughly oral phenomenon since books were written primarily to be read out loud.[3] Although it sounds counterintuitive to us, for the most part, an ancient person "read" a book by listening to someone else read it out loud.

Immediately after Mom finished reciting the book to our staff, one of my co-workers exclaimed, "I felt like I was a member of the early church!" She was exactly right since the first Christians lived in an oral culture that favored the spoken rather than written form of language. Listening to James' epistle read out loud makes for a special kind of continuity between the modern reader and the early Christian audience.

... a special kind of continuity between the modern reader and the early Christian audience.

Creating this continuity with the early Christians is by no means a necessity, but it does make for a special encounter.

You can easily access audio files that contain readings of James, even for free on *www.biblegateway.com* or of course you can listen to my Mom in the bonus material with this study on DVD or audio CD.

In view of James 1:19-21, what are we to do (v. 21)?

The command to "get rid of" means to "strip off" something as you would a constricting jacket. One commentator suggested that James may have meant to remind his readers of Zechariah 3:1-7.[5]

Read these vivid verses and describe what happened.

Under the New Covenant, believers in Christ become members of the holy priesthood (see 1 Pet. 2:5; Rev. 1:6). Does anything about Joshua the priest in Zechariah 3 remind you of your own experience?

If so, what? Respond in the margin.

The NET Bible® specifies a dimension of "evil" in James 1:21 that might help us grasp what we're supposed to strip from ourselves. It reads, "Put away all filth and evil excess and humbly welcome the message implanted within you, which is able to save your souls."

Circle the word following "evil" in the previous sentence. So, how do "moral filth" (HCSB) and "evil excess" (NET) supplant the words of God extended to us? I think perhaps they each pretend to fill a hole or void in our lives that was intended by God to give the Word room to grow. Though virtually all of us with the education to read this book and the money to buy it have more than we technically need, a wide gap can exist between having extra and having evil excess.

If you agree, in the margin explain the difference.

Since I began research on this convicting book of the Bible, I started attacking some places of evil excess in my life. Places where my possessions were purely nauseating. As a rule, I don't give away gifts my husband has given me, but some other extras went up for grabs. Every area of my life still bloats with surplus, but God is helping me strip off a little sickening excess.

We'll have more of these discussions further down the road, but don't develop a case of dread. If God insists on making more room in our lives, it's so He can bless us with things that really satisfy. Remember! Every good and perfect gift comes from above! Now, let's spend our last few moments fastened to the end of verse 21.

What does James tell us to humbly do?

Today's segment of Scripture comes full circle here. Above all, God desires for us to be quick to listen *to Him. To His Word. And to His words.* He says to us in effect, "Those words I planted in you have the power to save your very soul. Welcome them!"

God reminds us that He didn't plant His word in us just so we could divert it toward someone else's conviction or deliverance. That's true even when we have righteous indignation. We need humility to receive a word from God down into the soil of our humanity. We tend to take God's message to us and hang it around someone else's neck, but its first target was our own souls.

We who trusted Christ as Savior were instantly saved from eternity apart from God, but we have continual need of deliverance until He brings us "safely into His heavenly kingdom" (2 Tim. 4:18). The Greek lexical term translated *save* in most of the New Testament and here in James 1:21 is *sozo* meaning "to save, deliver, make whole, preserve from danger, loss, or destruction."[6] Another way of saying " 'save your souls' is 'rescue your lives.' "[7]

Those words could bring me to tears today. Christ has used His implanted word to rescue my life so many times. Yours, too? He is so faithful, Sister. Let's move our hand away from the rich soil of our hearts and welcome seed that sows salvation "to the uttermost" (Heb. 7:25, KJV).

Day Two
THE PERFECT LAW

FLASH FORWARD

"The one who looks intently into the perfect law of freedom and perseveres in it, and is not a forgetful hearer but one who does good works—this person will be blessed in what he does." James 1:25

Squeeze in the palm of your hand the verses we're studying today, Sister, because they are the keys to flourishing life, bone-deep transformation, and divine blessing. What James will teach us is the difference between *talking about* living in victory over things like self-centeredness, addiction, seduction, and temptation and actually *doing it.* If we had the space, this whole lesson would be in a size-72 font, bold and italicized. So, promise me you'll see it big and hear it loud.

James can teach us is the difference between talking about living in victory and actually doing it.

Please read James 1:22-25 and handwrite it in the back of your book.

At the end of our lesson, I'll ask you to make up a five-word acronym, starting with the letters *W-O-R-D-S,* that reflects a dimension of these four verses. Keep that assignment rolling around in your head while you study today.

A darling woman approached me and said, "Beth, I did *Breaking Free* three times and I still have the same stronghold." She wasn't the first person who'd told me something like that. Her question was genuine and I was endeared to her instantly, but my mentor instincts started arm wrestling with my maternal instincts. Her freedom had to take priority over her feelings.

"But did you actually do what the Scriptures said?"

She couldn't say for sure. It seemed like she did because she'd been so devoted to the homework. We can work a study until the desert turns to ice and still be stuck in the same bondage. The doing causes the changing. Not the hearing. We're intelligent women, so why don't we recognize that sooner?

James offers the bottom line: *because we deceive ourselves.* And I mean both of us. Glance over all of James 1 for a moment. How many times does he mention self-deception? __________ Listen carefully, Sweet Thing, because I know this one by heart: There is no lie so sly as the one we tell ourselves.

Look back at verses 23-24. In the margin draw the visual James poses to make his point.

Never mind wondering if a man would look in the mirror the same way a woman would. A man it is. The Greek doesn't suggest that he gave too quick a glance at himself to remember what he looked like. The strength of the original wording is obvious in the ESV: "He is like a man who looks intently at his natural face in a mirror." Circle the word that describes the way the man looked in the mirror. And he still forgot.

One commentator "highlights the absurdity of this picture of a person who 'examines intently his very own face in the mirror, but within seconds he cannot even pick himself out of a police lineup.'"[8] Imagine if that were us.

Self-deception slithers in when we mistake appreciation for application or being touched with being changed.

We can underline our Bibles till our pens run dry without a drop of ink splattering our lives. The self-deception slithers in when we mistake appreciation for application or being touched with being changed. The tricky part is that hearing all by itself really does lend a certain satisfaction. Think about the last time you closed your eyes and listened to an instrument that nearly brought you to tears. Something similar can happen when we listen to Scripture being read or a message being taught. The hearing itself can be satisfying. "Deep calls to deep" (Ps. 42:7), and we nod our heads with genuine resonance.

The Word of God, however, is meant to do more than penetrate. It's meant to activate. It can bore holes through obstacles. It can tumble defenses. It can plant wandering feet of clay in places of divine purpose. It can sanctify the sin sick and steady the aimless and confused. It can light a blazing torch in a black hole. Simply put, the Word was meant to work. And, through it, we were meant to bear fruit. Romans 10:17 tells us that faith comes by hearing, but James will soon teach us that faith with no fruit is dead on the vine.

James' older half brother taught a similar activity of faith all over the Gospels. We can well imagine that Christ's claim in Luke 8:21 echoed like a broken record in James' memory: "My mother and My brothers are those who hear and do the word of God."

Lock in on this section of James 1:23: "like a man looking at his own face in a mirror." Circle the phrase "his own face." The KJV uses "his natural face," giving perhaps a stronger deference to the original wording. Actually, the Greek is *genesis*. While the adjectives "own" or "natural" unquestionably translate the word, some scholars think the "genesis" face could layer the meaning.[9] James does, after all, refer to aspects of creation several times in his letter (see 1:18; 3:9). If genesis carries the deeper meaning, the reflection in the mirror would not only reveal grime or sore. It would also remind the gazer of his true identity, bringing conviction with an upward spin: *I want to be who I was created to be: a bearer of the very image of God.* Sadly, however, he goes out and forgets who he really is.

We were created to be satisfied with nothing less than the fulfillment of our original purpose. James 1:25 depicts a gaze toward a different source.

What does this person do?

What is the promise at the end of the verse?
"This person will be ______________________________."

Let's repeat that concept for the sake of clarity: "This person will be blessed in what he __________."

Do you see the concept? It's not until the hearing turns into doing that believing leads to blessing. Our "doing" may not always show up in physical activity. The initial act of obedience might be waiting upon the Lord or setting our minds zealously upon His faithfulness.

For Abraham in Romans 4:20 the "doing" was giving glory to God and refusing to waver in unbelief. Please note that James 1:25 records the second blessing in the Book of James. The first one appeared in James 1:12 for the one who endures trials. We'll see the significance of the inclusion of blessing later in today's lesson. Now, what kind of "law" is mentioned in James 1:25?

What on earth is this "perfect law that gives freedom" (NIV)? Is James referring to the Old Testament or to the Jewish Torah? Or is he referring to the gospel message of Christ? We assume he couldn't have been consciously referring to the entirety of the New Testament because so little of it, if any, had yet been written. To further muddy the waters, we also can't hastily throw out the Old Testament law because of Christ's claim in Matthew 5:17.

What did Christ say about the law?

If we really want to do justice to James' voice in the context of his world, we need to leave room for the possibility that he may well have been referring to the Mosaic law. But, with his entire letter in view, he would have been doing so in such a way to prioritize the moral code over the ritual code and, thereby, echo the teachings of Jesus. Keep in mind that, to many first-century Jews and those long before them, the law was precious. Further, the early church had yet to receive the full revelation of the New Testament canon.

Dr. Peter H. Davids offers another perspective on the "perfect law that gives freedom."

> It is within this Jewish world that one can understand the phrase. For the Jewish Christian the law is still the will of God, but Messiah has come and perfected it and given his new law. … Thus one finds the Sermon on the Mount (especially Mt. 5:17) and other similar passages in the early Christian tradition that present Christ as the giver of a new or renewed law. James' contact with the tradition behind the Sermon on the Mount is certain, and one must agree … that James sees Jesus' reinterpretation of the law as a new law.[10]

Stick closely to this next part because it has the capacity to connect some of the most important dots between Jesus and His half brother James: What did Dr. Davids say "is certain"?

I saw scholars make a connection between the two teachings over and over in my research. In your mind's eye, picture one rope dangling from the Sermon on the Mount and another rope dangling from the Book of James. See them? Now, tie them squarely together. If you'll hang onto that one big knot for dear life while the topics in James swing here, there, and seemingly everywhere, you'll land somewhere in the heart of his teaching when we're done. Let's turn that knot two quick angles in our hands.

1. What word do James 1:12 and 1:25 have in common with Matthew 5:3-10? (You only have to glance to see it.)

Relationships are the goal of regulations.

2. What connection do you see between Matthew 7:26 and James 1:22?

That both texts contain beatitudes and exhortations to put the Word into practice is beyond coincidence. We will see James tag along behind his half brother in taking the letter of the law and sticking it in the land of the living where relationships are the goal of regulations. One scho lar explains,

"James defines law in such a way that it grants freedom from self-interest and immorality, allowing the Christian to grow into what God intends. It is not unlikely that James is here reflecting the words of Jesus relative to the law."[11]

One classic interpretation of the Sermon on the Mount is to see it as a sort of reenactment of Moses coming down from the mountain with the tablets of stone and proclaiming the law to God's people. In the Gospel of Matthew, it is not Moses, the servant of God on the side of that hill. It is Jesus, the Son of God, and this time, He's proclaiming the law of the Kingdom. A kingdom that lives within us (see Luke 17:21). True to His claims in the Sermon on the Mount, He does not abolish the law but lifts up the heavy layer of stone to expose the fleshy heart. He is not interested in behavior alone. He is interested in motive. "He pierced to the heart of its intention, and in so doing elevated the law."[12] If the law was to truly liberate, it had to be turned inside out. Jeremiah 31:31-34 records the prophetic process.

What did God promise He would do?

Compare Ezekiel 36:26-27. How would recipients of this new heart be moved to follow God?

When have you known in your heart that your act of obedience could have only been a move of the Spirit?

When Jesus pierced the heart beneath the broken law, our realization of guilt and failure would only have increased without a Savior on His way to the cross and the promise of the Holy Spirit to infiltrate our lives. By His patient, meticulous plan, God etched this perfect law of freedom on human hearts through Christ and, thereby, Torah "reached its ultimate redemptive purpose."[13]

Stay with me for a final thought. What, after all, is God's "ultimate redemptive purpose" for each of us? Romans 8:29! "To be conformed to the image of His Son." Hebrews 10:5-7 attributes the prophetic words in Psalm 40:7-8 to Jesus Christ. Hear the messianic melody from the psalmist's pen: "Behold, I come; In the scroll of the book it is written of me. I delight to do Your will, O my God, And Your law is within my heart" (Ps. 40:7-8, NKJV).

Even before Moses descended Mount Sinai with the tablets of stone that were broken to pieces, the heart of the law pulsated with unbroken life within the Son of God. When God sends the Spirit of His Son into our hearts (see Gal. 4:6), the law on His heart beats within our own, etching our declaration of liberty ever deeper. Therein lies the transformation. *I delight to do Your will, O my God. Your law is within my heart.* And Imago Dei appears in my mirror.

W
O
R
D
S

Now, in the margin write an acronym drawn from the lesson.

The **NEXT LEVEL** with Melissa

THE IMPLANTED WORD

The more I study James, the more convinced I become that the phrase "implanted word" in 1:21 carries huge significance to the meaning of the book.

Just a few verses earlier James referred to himself and his readers as "firstfruits" because they are the beginning of God's new creation (v. 18). Thus, the "implanted word" that James referred in verse 21 is not something embedded in every human being but rather it takes up residence in a believer when God sovereignly grants the gift of new birth.

The phrase "implanted word" is unprecedented in the Bible but, as Mom mentioned today in your homework, it echoes a theme promised by the prophets Jeremiah and Ezekiel. In those texts the authors speak about a time when God's word/law will be planted in the hearts of the covenant community.

We find support for this proposal in the *Epistle of Barnabas,* one of the earliest Christian works outside the New Testament. There we also find James' rare Greek word ἔμφυτος "implanted."[1] Barnabas said, "He who placed within us the implanted [ἔμφυτος] gift of his covenant understands. No one has ever learned from me a more reliable word, but I know that you are worthy of it."[2] This close parallel adds weight to the argument that James used "implanted word" to refer to the New Covenant of Jewish prophecy.

I find it striking that a foreshadowing of the inwardness of the covenant appears not only in the Prophets but also in the Torah, specifically in Deuteronomy. Moses commands the people, "Circumcise your hearts and don't be stiff-necked any longer" (Deut. 10:16). Then 30:6 displays a remarkable shift in tone. The rather prophetic chapter anticipates a time when Israel, the covenant community, is dispersed among the nations but returns to God with all its heart. Moses promises that no matter how far away Israel is, God will restore and bring the Israelites to the land of their fathers. Moses promises, "The Lord your God will circumcise your heart and the hearts of your descendants, and you will love Him with all your heart and all your soul so that you will live" (Deut. 30:6).

Moses anticipated unfaithful Israel receiving the covenant cursings but one day being restored. Upon genuine repentance she would receive divine heart surgery. All in one book, Moses shifted radically from commanding the Israelites to "circumcise" their own hearts (10:16) to declaring that, sometime in the future, God Himself would circumcise their wayward but repentant hearts for them (see 30:6).

God's word through Moses was near to and within the reach of God's people from the beginning (see Deut. 30:11-14), but the anticipated New Covenant promised something unique, different, and internal. As something embedded or planted in the human heart, "the word is permanently established in the individual and like inborn assets functions in an exceptional manner."[3] Although the language is not identical in Jeremiah, Ezekiel, or Deuteronomy, it is likely that James viewed the birth of the Jesus/messianic movement as fulfillment of the prophecies of the New Covenant. If this argument stands, it provides a stunning example of the continuity between the Old and New Testaments.

Day Three
PURE RELIGION

FLASH FORWARD

"Pure and undefiled religion before our God and Father is this: to look after orphans and widows in their distress and to keep oneself unstained by the world." James 1:27

"Man is the Religious Animal. He is the only Religious Animal. ... He is the only animal that loves his neighbor as himself, and cuts his throat if his theology isn't straight. He has made a graveyard of the globe in trying his honest best to smooth his brother's path to happiness and heaven."[14] Mark Twain makes you think twice about whether or not you want to be called religious, doesn't he? In fact, if you're like me, you never know if someone is using the word toward you as a compliment or an indictment.

Before I give you a definition, how would you define *religious*?

From crusaders on horseback to terrorists on airplanes, history has earned humanity its dubious relationship with the term *religious*. In a room by itself, however, the word carries no inherent negativity. Once we drag folding chairs into it and invite people to sit down and make themselves comfortable in our indoctrination, all bets are off. The English word *religious* means "manifesting faithful devotion to an acknowledged ultimate reality or deity."[15] The biblical concept of piety is similar, but the "deity" is solely the Lord. To most, the issue is not that people manifest faithful devotion to deity. It's *how* they manifest it. James weighed in on the subject before the ink on his hello could dry.

Please read James 1:26-27 and write these two verses on the appropriate page.

Verse 26 stirs up a question I wish we could discuss in person: do we consider ourselves religious? Wait a second before you shake your head or nod. Evangelicals have been trained to insist that we have a relationship instead of a religion, and in matters of salvation that is a biblical fact. We are Christians because we know Jesus Christ as Savior. At the same time, out of that relationship can come practices that manifest our devotion to Him. In fact, we're engaging in one of them this very moment.

Because we know Jesus Christ as Savior, our practices manifest our devotion to Him.

In the margin name ways you manifest devotion to Christ through the course of a month. Don't be shy. It's important.

If you mentioned things such as prayer, corporate worship, blessings over meals, taking communion, witnessing baptism, or many others, we're probably in the same boat. So, rowing up next to Merriam-Webster's definition, we'd have to say we seem religious. I know, I know. I'm resistant to it, too, but let's face it. You and I may be considered by some of our neighbors, co-workers, or friends to be one of the most religious people they've ever met. Scary, isn't it?

Let's try one more definitive question: if being religious became illegal tomorrow and you or I were arrested, would there be enough evidence to convict us? Throw us an orange jumpsuit and show us the cell. Like it or not, technically we're religious. And this, dear Sister, is where James lights up the subject like a stick of dynamite. It starts in verse 26.

If anyone thinks he is religious ...

then his religion is ...

Complete the sentences in the margin.

Not the tongue again. It won't be the last time either, but at least he builds something new onto the concept with each additional mention. On this occasion, we play the part of the rider, and our tongues play the part of the horse. This analogy is more obvious in the NKJV and ESV in the use of the phrase, "bridle his tongue." The command shouting over the verbal stampede is, "Rider, control your horse!"[16]

What if we don't? To quote various translations of James 1:26, our religion is *useless, in vain, empty, worthless, futile*. Eugene Peterson floats it this way in The Message: "This kind of religion is hot air and only hot air."

Is there nothing in between? What about warm air for those of us working extra hard at devotion? Good grief! Doesn't reciting Scripture from memory count for anything?

Useless, in vain, empty, worthless, futile. James doesn't budge one religious inch. See, we keep falling in the trap of thinking that if the good outweighs the bad, it's all good. James suggests if we show all sorts of devotion to God but don't bridle our maverick tongues, it's all worthless. Glance at the last phrase of 1:26 where James again pegs self-deception.

Stirring it up with our definition of *religious*, what do you think can be self-deceiving about manifestations of devotion?

After James tells us what true religion is *not*, he sketches two quick images of what true religion *is*. Read James 1:27 and describe his idea of "pure and undefiled" religion.

We're not meant to limit all manifestations of faithful devotion to these two practices. We're meant to see them as living, breathing exhibitions of real religion. Think of them as the reality TV of true piety.

Let's camp on the first exhibit: "to look after orphans and widows in their distress." James sketched the two classes of people in his culture with the least rights, the least hope, and the greatest vulnerability. Helpless on their own, they were subject to shameless oppression, exploitation, and neglect. Notice that he also described them as people in marked distress in case well-wishers were hoping they were handling it well. Images on the screens of our TVs, laptops, and cell phones have helped paint faces of the world's helpless.

What images come to mind as you picture the exploited and neglected in our day?

The KJV "to visit" them doesn't complete the picture though. Let's not kid ourselves. A warm hand can reach a mighty long way. Actually caring for them and easing their distress exhibits pure religion. As God would time it, while studying for this series I've heard a number of voices point out the strong trend toward social concerns among younger believers. Many of our Christ-professing college students and young adults resonate deeply with hands-on initiatives toward the poverty-stricken and oppressed. To them it's not political. It's spiritual.

Describe how these Old Testament prophets would agree.

Isaiah 58:5-7

Deuteronomy 14:28-29

Read Deuteronomy 24:17-22 carefully. What were the Israelites to remember as they left behind part of their harvest?

You see, the young believers we talked about earlier aren't so much experiencing an awakening as a revival of a prominent command in Scripture. They may not be as tied to traditions, but watch them quick-draw their wallets for those ravaged by sex trafficking. We could argue for balance all day long and each generation still suffer lack; but, since God has us in the Book of James, let's turn up the volume on his voice. Dr. Peter Rhea Jones writes:

> There will be a recurring temptation to tame the powerful social message of this flaming letter, to domesticate it and calm its biting, all too relevant message into palatable terms. If the message of James is allowed to go out unmuffled, it will rattle the stained glass windows.[17]

Fewer of our churches have stained glass, but James could still crack some serious panes. Crouched with our Bibles at the foot of the cross, trying to find God's will in its wake, we can't afford to muffle this message. True religion is at stake. Social consciousness beckons each of us across the board, but the ways we could respond are as varied as our holy passions. We are called to tend to the poor, but adjust your lens and see what specific opportunities make your heart jump … or maybe sink. Casting your bread upon an ocean doesn't seem to do much good, but find a clear pond and suddenly you see the fish. Ministries that particularly resonate with me are often geared to the abused or to those demoralized by addiction.

What about you? Where does God stir up your passion?

True religion is all hands on deck and all heads out of the sand.

God is practical. He doesn't ask us to do what doesn't matter. What seems a drop in the bucket to you is a sip from the wellspring of life to someone about to thirst to death. Let's muster the courage to ask Him to show us who to help and how. True religion is all hands on deck and all heads out of the sand. The mystery is that, there, we often find our own healing and fulfilling.

OK, one last element. Look back at James 1:27 for the final image in James' sketch of pure and undefiled religion. The NIV wording is especially powerful: "to keep oneself from being *polluted* by the world" (emphasis added). Think on the concept for a moment: *world pollution*. It pervades the terrestrial air we breathe. It hangs a heavy veil of smog between us and God's horizon, distorting our vision and weakening our resolve. But the hands-on message of James isn't written to those who have sequestered themselves from the world.

James wrote for people serving actively, openly, and humbly right in its thick, pungent pollution. So, how on earth do we serve in it without smelling like it? With serious discipline and determination, that's how. With courage and deep conviction. With a large daily dose of the Holy Ghost, as my girlfriend says. You don't live this kind of life accidentally. You make up your mind who you want to be and daily die to the rest. You surrender yourself to living in the tension where you'll always be stretched and often be broken. Religion pure and undefiled is grit without the grime. You accept that far easier ways to live exist, but you were born for nothing less.

And when we sniff ourselves and smell the world, we run to the One who can wash us.

Day Four
THE FOLLY OF FAVORITISM

FLASH FORWARD

"My brothers, do not show favoritism as you hold on to the faith in our glorious Lord Jesus Christ." James 2:1

Brace yourself. We are actually going to study seven verses today. You might need a head start, so I'll wait here while you go ahead and write James 2:1-7 on page 216. Yes, do it. I promise you're going to be so glad you wrote out the entire epistle when we say good-bye.

At first glance, James seems caught in a loop of repetition. The larger picture shows the first chapter introducing a host of topics that he spends the rest of the book illuminating. Themes like perseverance, faith, speech, and wisdom appear in the opening number and will each take the spotlight again before the final bow.

Case in point: yesterday we devoted the smallest amount of space to the second picture of pure and undefiled religion: "to keep oneself unstained by the world." If we stop abruptly at the end of chapter 1, a 50-gallon topic seems to get a drop of ink. Resist equating the end of a chapter of Scripture with the end-all of that inspired thought. Remember, Bibles weren't originally formatted into chapters and verses. In 2:1-7 James talked right on about keeping ourselves unstained by the world with an example as spot-on today as it was in the first century: our vast propensity to treat people differently.

Left to ourselves, we're mud pies baking in the elements of preference and prejudice. We favor one, dismiss another. Entertain one, endure the other. A glance can garner respect or recoil. We stereotype. We assume. We speak of individuals as "they" and "those kind." Our prejudices are buried so deep in our pores that we don't recognize them wrapped in our skin. If we show basic cordiality to the person we've devalued, we call it even. But that's not what James calls it. Feeling sorry for one group doesn't balance the scales of our favoritism to the other. Let's let this segment of Scripture speak its brutal truth to us because, if this shoe fits, we need to burn it.

Left to ourselves, we're mud pies baking in the elements of preference and prejudice.

Anne Lamott once said, "You can safely assume you've created God in your own image when it turns out that God hates all the same people you do."[18] Think that one through. Then see if Scripture might raise its brow with something similar.

Please look up each of the following verses and note both the main idea and the context.

Leviticus 19:15

Deuteronomy 10:17

Acts 10:34-35

Galatians 2:6

Romans 2:11 (Write this summation in all caps.)

We want so badly to think that we who spend time in God's Word and pursue life in the Spirit are long past the ignorance of prejudice, but we dare not make those assumptions. Prejudice in its most obvious form, racism, is an abomination to God and blasphemes His Name. Prejudice of any form is never harmless, never funny, and never to be taken lightly. To sit back and say nothing is to cast a vote of approval. Some things call for zero tolerance. Maybe after the atrocities of the last century, we are scared enough of human nature not to let ourselves get away with racial prejudice.

Our greater bait to discriminate, however, may not be racial. It dangles right here in front of us in James 2:1-7. Maybe it's more about some who seem like winners and others who seem like losers. The thought is, "haves" must be smarter or, at the very least, wiser and bless the hearts of those poor "have nots." Our prejudices are as different as our personal values. At the end of the day, what impresses us dictates us. We each naturally prefer those who possess what we esteem—whether money, social status, power, talent, spirituality, intelligence, celebrity, style, or beauty—and we devalue those who don't. Do we ever catch ourselves giving preferential treatment? Paying overt attention to one and covert attention to another? Ever caught a strong whiff of social snobbery and realized it was you? Yep. Me too.

Faith and favoritism are oil and water. ... We kid ourselves when we think we're a blend of both.

James would say the source of that stench is world pollution. The worldlier we are, the less we can smell it. Take another look at today's *Flash Forward*. See how James pits faith against favoritism? The bottom line is that, try as we might, we cannot make a cocktail of them. Faith and favoritism are oil and water. Vinegar and nectar. Baby powder and gunpowder. We're kidding ourselves when we think we're a blend of both.

Next, James casts each of us in a role-play where we're among those who belong in a given environment and in walk two kinds of visitors. Think of it like a "What would you do?" reality show. Scholars are divided on whether James 2:2 describes a church-service setting for worship or a church-court setting for judicial cases among believers. A church-court is less common today, but it was very familiar to first-century Christians. With either interpretation, the point sticks.

Look carefully at verse 2 and fill in the following one-word blank: "For example, a man comes into your ______________."

The Greek is *synagoge*, which we recognize as *synagogue*.[19] The term may whisper a loud secret regarding the dating of the Epistle of James. These new believers in the Messiah Jesus were still glued to the local Jewish synagogue. Picture it as the original setting of the role-play.

Or picture it as your local church, small-group Bible study, Christian event, or maybe even a counseling session. You belong. Two contrasting people walk in who don't. What happens then? Which one do we seat well, so to speak? Note how pitifully little has changed in what determines our prejudgment. Isn't much of it still about attire?

Describe the first person listed in verse 2.

The Greek that translates "wearing a gold ring" is what scholars call a *hapax*. That means it's the only time the exact term is employed in Scripture. Furthermore, James' pen was the first to scratch it on parchment, causing some scholars to believe he coined it. The Greek "colorfully describes a person as having, literally, 'gold fingers.' "[20] For you lovers of ancient movies, it predates James Bond. Those of you who were raised on home-sewn clothes like my sisters and I won't struggle to wrap your minds around this fact: "Ancient mercantilism suggests that all but the wealthy wore homemade clothing. ... One of the clearest markers of status in the Roman world was attire."[21]

Wow. What a surprise. The poor person is described in filthy clothes, suggesting he also reeked of need. Add smelly to shabby and what then? Picture a greeter so thoroughly embracing the one poorly dressed that no one else can smell a thing besides Christ. Love covers.

Reread James 2:4. If we discriminate, what do we become?

Now, how does James begin verse 5?
"______________________, my dear brothers."

This is the only time in the letter he uses this exact attention-getter. God has placed a wise woman in my life about 10 years my senior to be a primary voice of counsel to me. On occasion she leans forward on her elbows, interlocks her fingers, fixes her gaze, and says, "Listen to me." And I do. I'd be an idiot not to. James is doing the same thing here and, much like my friend, he targets his counsel to someone he loves.

That word "dear" in verse 5 means *beloved*. Check verse 5 again. Did you see what God chose the poor in the eyes of the world to be or do?

Listen, my dear brothers: Didn't God choose the poor in this world to be rich in faith and heirs of the kingdom that He has promised to those who love Him?
JAMES 2:5

Amazing, isn't it? Everything is right-side-up from a God's-eye-view but, from where we sit, it seems upside down. Make sure you don't hear that verse say that all poor people are rich in faith and all rich people, poor. The biggest qualifier of the blessed-poor is at the very end of verse 5.

To whom did God make the promise?

Blessed are those who need God enough to know Him enough to love Him enough to know He's enough.

While Christianity's canvas is speckled with exceptions, the tendency is that believers with less trust God with more. Believers with more trust God with less. In some ways, it's simple math. Have much/need little. Have little/need much. Blessed are those who need God. Blessed are those who need Him enough to know Him enough to love Him enough to know He's enough.

Describe the explanation in 1 Corinthians 1:26-29 why God tends to choose the weak over the strong.

What feelings surface when you somehow feel dishonored? How might those feelings translate to those dishonored over their poverty? Respond in the margin.

Did you see it? How is it that our nature is so often inclined to prefer those who would not even prefer us? How often do we drool over celebrities who mock the very One to whom we belong?

One commentator said this about those showing prejudice in James 2: "The Christians do not simply discriminate against the poor, but they do so in favor of the rich. This means that they are siding with the very class which both historically and at present persecutes the impoverished believer. They have made the church into a tool of persecution; they have, in effect, sided with the devil against God."[22]

Lord, have mercy on us. Help us see any hint of our faces in this mirror. Thank you for persevering through this lesson. What it lacked in pleasantness, maybe it made up for in relevance. Linger a moment here at the end on the diamond in the coal: God chose the poor in the eyes of this world to be "heirs of the kingdom."

I've clung to James 2:5 every time I've returned to relative riches after awkwardly trying to serve the poor with a drop in a bucket. A foaming sea of slums doesn't leave you the luxury of feeling proud of yourself for going or giving. We have the forgotten poor right in our own cities, but right now my mind runs waving the banner of James 2:5 to the ones crammed into squalor in spots bereft of human rights. *Make it up to them in Heaven, Lord. Give them our shares, however small they seem. Exceed every fairy tale and dress this temporal world's poor in Your finest apparel and parade them as the honored princes and princesses of Your kingdom. And we will cheer.*

Day Five
THE ROYAL LAW

FLASH FORWARD

"If you keep the royal law prescribed in the Scripture, 'Love your neighbor as yourself,' you are doing well." James 2:8

I'm glad you came back today. I've thought a lot about you since we closed yesterday's lesson and wondered if, right about now, you could stand to hear somebody say "Well done!" A soul needs that kind of encouragement from time to time and it means twice as much coming from a person who doesn't throw around sticky-sweet words like gum on a sidewalk.

We're about to hear James tell a certain kind of person that he is "doing well," and in that commendation, we get to squint through a keyhole at the entire law. Please take a few minutes to handwrite James 2:8-13 on the appropriate page. The Scripture referenced in James 2:8 is Leviticus 19:18.

Read this Old Testament verse and fill in its closing declaration: "I am ________________."

What does it mean to you when God follows up a statement with that kind of declaration?

On occasions with this particular emphasis, God reminds the reader that the weight of a saying is not so much in the words. The weight is in the one saying those words. As the people of God, we don't answer to dried-up ink. We answer to a living Orator who still oxygenates His Word with warm breath and, as in the days of Jeremiah, still watches to see that His Word is fulfilled (see Jer. 1:12). All this week's talk about "law"—old or new—has a way of stirring up the cloud on Exodus 24:9-12 again. Picture this scene with fresh vision:

We answer to a living Orator who still oxygenates His Word with warm breath and ... watches to see that His Word is fulfilled.

> Moses went up with Aaron, Nadab, and Abihu, and 70 of Israel's elders, and they saw the God of Israel. Beneath His feet was something like a pavement made of sapphire stone, as clear as the sky itself. God did not harm the Israelite nobles; they saw Him, and they ate and drank. The LORD said to Moses, "Come up to Me on the mountain and stay there so that I may give you the stone tablets with the law and commandments I have written for their instruction."

The words on that stone came from a throne, "inscribed by the finger of God" (Ex. 31:18). The law cannot, like a dead limb, be amputated from the Lawgiver. It had to be animated by an outstretched arm with a racing pulse and upheld by royal edict. Glance back at our text in James 2:8.

What does our protagonist call the command originating in Leviticus 19:18? "If you keep the ____________________ prescribed in the Scripture."

And, for emphasis, what is this "royal law"? "Love ...

One commentator translates the intention of the Greek in James 2:8 as "the law of the Great King."[23] It reverberates from the heart of the Old Testament no less than seven times in the New. Matthew 22:32-40 records the bubbling wellspring from which all the others flow. There in that glorious Gospel you get a glimpse of the Great King to come and the law as He summed it.

Record what Jesus said in Matthew 22:40.

Look up two other segments that include the command to "love your neighbor as yourself." Record all summations and anything else you find noteworthy in the contexts.

Romans 13:8-10

Galatians 5:13-14

God could have said, "You shall love your neighbor." Period. Or, He could have said, "You shall love your neighbor as you love your parents." Or, better yet, "You shall love your neighbor as you love your children." But He didn't. He adamantly said, "You shall love your neighbor as yourself."

Loving God and loving others does not equal hating ourselves after all.

Well, what do you know? Loving God and loving others does not equal hating ourselves after all. We were hardwired to love and care for ourselves or we wouldn't hasten to draw our foot inside the car before someone slams the door. Imagine how mangled our bodies would be if we took care of them the same way we tend to our hearts. But, before we curl up like a pill bug in obsessive self-analysis, let's run like the wind to this excerpt: "James's use of 'yourself' ... does *not* promote modern psychologies ... that intentionally enjoin 'self-love' before we can love others. Rather, the love commands throughout Scripture *assume* that people have a healthy, balanced view of self, rather than taking pathologies into account."[24]

That's what we need, Lord. A healthy, balanced view of ourselves because, frankly, all of our pathologies are exhausting. We're rolled up in a ball here on planet Earth. Unfold us, Lord.

In this unfolding, we run aground onto something definitive about James' regard for the law in the whole of his letter. Our devotion to God and true religion is illustrated most poignantly on the pages of other lives. That's where much of our story is told. We think we want this massive biography written by God with our name as the title, but His way is a much better read. And the character development? Sublime.

James used the royal law as a summation of true obedience. Loving our neighbor as ourselves is the Arc de Triomphe of "the perfect law of freedom" he referenced in 1:25. In other words, this is how it reigns. How all sides win.

Look carefully at James 2:12. How are we to "speak and act"?

Think about this carefully: how could loving others as we love ourselves turn out to be liberating to us? Think practically as well as theologically and write your thoughts in the margin.

Watch for the concept for the remainder of James' letter and note how many of his principles fall under the category of loving others as we love ourselves. In our present context, it not only cures our favoritism. It cures the selfishness that propels it. Boiling a lot of things down to one sentence is a relief. If you're like me, the deeper you get into this epistle, the more you feel you need to do.

We're meant to take pause at this point in the letter and hear these words: if, out of your love for God, you are loving to others, "you are doing well" (v. 8). Sometimes I just need a clear goal. You, too?

Alas, ending the lesson here would be a wonderful thing, but we're not finished yet. About the time we give a sigh of relief, James said, "Whoever keeps the entire law, yet fails in one point, is guilty of breaking it all" (v. 9).

James no doubt got that holy notion from Jesus in Matthew 5:19-20. The primary kind of righteousness Jesus associated with "the scribes and Pharisees" in this segment was ritual rule keeping. Remember, Jesus called His followers to something beyond righteous rules. He called them to right relationships.

In the very next segment in Matthew, Christ interjects anger toward a brother into the conversation about murder. Then while heads are spinning, He says: "If you are offering your gift on the altar, and there you remember that your brother has something against you, leave your gift there in front of the altar. First go and be reconciled with your brother, and then come and offer your gift" (Matt. 5:23-24). Jesus didn't let His listeners get away with feeling smug about their good standing with God while they were in poor standing with others.

Whoever breaks one of the least of these commands and teaches people to do so will be called least in the kingdom of heaven. But whoever practices and teaches these commands will be called great in the kingdom of heaven. For I tell you, unless your righteousness surpasses that of the scribes and Pharisees, you will never enter the kingdom of heaven.
MATTHEW 5:19-20

Today we're His listeners. Yes, we live this side of the finished work of the cross, but so did James. No, we're not bound to ritual laws but we are indeed bound to love. Jesus Himself said, "I give you a new command: Love one another. Just as I have loved you, you must also love one another" (John 13:34). And Paul, behind Jesus said: "Love, therefore, is the fulfillment of the law" (Rom. 13:10).

What is love if it shoves away reconciliation? Let's resist conviction that could lead to freedom by rushing past this precept quickly. Perchance are you hoping you and God are so busy in your relationship that your need for reconciliation with someone has gone unnoticed? I've been there, hoping God was distracted, but, all the while, He wasn't.

Several years ago a dear friend told me something she felt God was asking her as she resisted reconciliation. "Do you just want to be right? Or do you want to have relationship?" I think, to James, she just expressed the royal law.

Are these thoughts resonating with you in any way? If so, how?

God knows the tendency of the pious to use preoccupation with Him as an excuse to ignore people. The "I'm too busy looking up to look out" kind of mentality doesn't hold water with Jesus. He'd just as soon pour that water from a pitcher and wash somebody's feet. From His teaching and then from James' we can come to no other conclusion than this: Because we look up, we're compelled to look out. This is a fount from which blessing flows: "Blessed are the merciful, for they will be shown mercy" (Matt. 5:7, NIV).

Because we look up, we're compelled to look out.

We want this looking up, looking out kind of life but the fact is, we falter and fail. Should this royal law be the only one we vowed to keep, sooner than later we'd succumb to selfishness and stand judged as violators. And, God help us, as we're judged in the same way we've judged others and have measured to us what we've measured to others (see Matt. 7:1-2).

We need something bigger than justice. We need mercy—the kind of mercy that arches triumphantly over the seat of judgment like wings of golden cherubim over the mercy seat. We need eyes pried wide-open to mercy so great and so rescuing that it cannot help but make us merciful. We need the mercy of a holy, righteous God who is good enough for us.

Should we ever forget, we need a wild-eyed reminder of the rock from which we've been hewn and the pit from which we've been pulled so that, if we err toward our brother, we err on the side of mercy.

Lord, shake us out of the slumber of our self-helplessness and awaken us to a mercy so wide that we rise to the light of the east while our transgressions set in the west. This is the mercy that breeds mercy. This is the love that loves others as itself. This is the law of the Great King.

The **NEXT LEVEL** with Melissa

PERFECT LAW OF LIBERTY

"The perfect law of liberty" sounds like an oxymoron, doesn't it? The truth is that we are unaccustomed to the law bearing such positive connotations. This is fairly understandable since the majority of us are Gentile Christians and the apostle Paul fought vehemently for us not to have to abide by the Old Testament law. But the function of the law for Jews who believed in Messiah Jesus was a different issue than it was for Gentiles. We must bear this distinction in mind to understand the dynamics of the earliest Christian movement. Here are three general points to remember when we discuss the law:

1. According to our own Bible, God Himself is the author and initiator of the law handed to Moses.

2. That many Jews believed the law to be both perfect and liberating is consistent with statements in Deuteronomy (see 31:11-19), the Psalms (see 19:7), and the Mishnah (Abot. 6:2b). As Mariam Kamell points out, "The Torah was a law of liberty both because it was given at the time of [Israel's] liberation from Egypt, and because failure to obey it led to repeated enslavements to nations."[1]

3. First-century Judaism was extremely diverse (not unlike modern Christianity). We cannot assume that all Jews *literally* kept all 613-plus laws in the first five books of the Old Testament. Folks differed on precisely how to interpret and obey the commandments.

This explains why Jesus asks a religious expert, "How do you read it?" (Luke 10:26). Although Mom alluded to this already, James interprets the law (the Torah) through the lens of Jesus' teaching, emphasizing both love for God and love for neighbor.

James interprets the law through the lens of Jesus' teaching.

Ironically, even though we honestly struggle theologically with the phrase "perfect law of liberty," I think we understand its meaning experientially. For example, the other day someone asked my mom how obedience to God has changed her life.

Mom spoke movingly of how the practice of persistent Scripture reading and memorization repaired and restored her broken mind. She told stories of how bathing her mind in the knowledge and wisdom of God changed her behavior and her life.

The way Mom kept linking her personal freedom and liberation to God's Word is the heart of the phrase "perfect law of liberty." Most of us are Gentile Christians. We do not keep the 613-plus Mosaic laws, but as canonical Christians we do consider the Mosaic law to be God's Word. We certainly believe that the Mosaic law as reinterpreted by Jesus, particularly in the Sermon on the Mount, is still fully authoritative for us today.

Jesus promised that those who hear and act upon His words will be like a wise man who builds his house upon a rock (see Matt. 7:24). In other words, Jesus preached that His own words are life-changing and life-giving for the one who performs them.

Maybe we know more about this phrase than we actually think. Take heart if you struggle to grasp James' understanding of law because you stand in a long line of Christians who have gone before you. From ancient Christianity, issues related to the Mosaic law have been among the most daunting.

viewer guide | session four

A wonderful part of taking a book of the Bible at this pace is the luxury of mining treasures out of single words or phrases. We are going to return to segments from this week's homework and draw out two phrases that could offer riches beyond what we'd recognize on the page.

Part One: Revisit James 1:25—"______ ________________"

Greek *parakupto*—"The verb has the basic meaning of '______________ ___________' but comes to be applied especially to the action of '_______________ by ______________ ________.'"[1]

Consider two other places this word is translated in the New Testament:

- John 20:11
- 1 Peter 1:12

Note particular wording in the following translation: "The one who peers into the perfect law of liberty and fixes his attention there, and ________ ________ _____________ a forgetful listener but one who lives it out—he will be blessed in what he does" (Jas. 1:25, NET).

Part Two: Read James 2:1-9. Focus on verse 1—"_____ ____________ _______ ________ ________"

- James 2:1—*The New International Commentary of the New Testament* translation of the phrase: "the Lord Jesus Christ, ________ ___________."[2]

Consider the following excerpts:

"The Lord Jesus Christ is the __________ ________. ... Jesus is the very ________________ of the divine glory made present in the world. ________ the ______________ to the people of God in the Old Testament and the Immanuel who is Jesus, the very glory of God is embodied in the person of Christ. An interchangeability between Christ and ________ is observable here."[3]

Dr. C.H. Dodd writes of the "well-known maxim of *Pirqe Aboth:* 'When two sit and there are between them words of ________, the ______________ ________ between them.' "[4]

- James 2:1—*The New International Commentary of the New Testament* translation of the entire verse: "Do not try to combine faith in the Lord Jesus Christ, ________ ________, with the ____________ of men's __________ __________."[5]

Reread James 2:3. Reflect on a literal translation of the Greek: "while you say to the poor man: 'Stand there,' or 'Sit here ________ my ______________.' "[6]

Concluding thought: Faith and ____________ don't ______.

1. Douglas J. Moo, *The Letter of James* (Grand Rapids, MI: Wm. B. Eerdmans Publishing Co., 2000), 93.
2. James B. Adamson, *The New International Commentary on the New Testament: The Epistle of James* (Grand Rapids, MI: Wm. B. Eerdmans Publishing Co., 1976), 101.
3. Kurt A. Richardson, *The New American Commentary,* vol. 36, *James* (Nashville, TN: Broadman & Holman Publishers, 1997), 109
4. C. H. Dodd, *New Testament Studies* (Manchester: Manchester University Press, 1953), 60.
5. Adamson, *New International Commentary,* 101.
6. Ibid.

WEEK FOUR

LIVING THE FAITH

Day One
DEAD BY ITSELF

Day Two
FAITH PERFECTED

Day Three
CALLING ALL TEACHERS

Day Four
FIRE & WATER

Day Five
WISDOM BELOW, WISDOM ABOVE

Day One
DEAD BY ITSELF

FLASH FORWARD

"In the same way faith, if it doesn't have works, is dead by itself."

James 2:17

A few days ago two of my beloved co-workers were driving full speed ahead on a Houston freeway when three cars collided and spun in circles right in front of them. Sabrina stiffened both hands on the wheel and shoved both feet on the brakes while tires squealed and Diane summoned, "Jeeeeeesus!" They came to a screeching halt about 10 feet from the wreckage.

Our series is flashing by. We've sped through three weeks of homework and four sessions. Today we are going to slam on the brakes and park in a segment of Scripture that has caused no few theological wrecks. Please read and handwrite James 2:14-19 in the back of your book.

What do you think makes this segment so controversial?

In today's lesson and tomorrow's, we'll wrestle with the very verses that caused such a ruckus in the heart of Martin Luther toward the Epistle of James. To him, the teaching in this segment and Paul's (profuse!) teachings on justification by faith simply could not coexist. In Luther's estimation, one of them had to be wrong and James was outnumbered.

My pastor of 25 years never claimed to be a Bible scholar, but he always said something that seemed brilliant to me: "When two texts appear to contradict one another, which is right? Both of them. We just don't always have the understanding to see how. But God certainly does."

Overriding all else in the tension between Scriptures on justification is the unshakable truth that we are saved by the power and grace of God alone. He accomplished our salvation through the offering of Christ who "was delivered up for our trespasses and raised for our justification" (Rom. 4:25). Let's go carefully to the text and draw out three major themes that might veer us clear of some wreckage. The first two float to the top with repetitive terms.

Read James 2:14-16 in the margin and circle the identical phrases that serve as bookends for the segment.

What good is it, my brothers, if someone says he has faith but does not have works? Can his faith save him? If a brother or sister is without clothes and lacks daily food and one of you says to them, "Go in peace, keep warm, and eat well," but you don't give them what the body needs, what good is it?
JAMES 2:14-16

For extra emphasis, write the phrase here.

James meets us on the page with perhaps the single most convicting question any believer in Christ could be asked: *What good is your faith?* Let's have the courage to ponder it. How are our individual worlds any better off because we believe in Jesus? Do those we encounter in passing, in working, or in playing receive any direct benefit because we are Christians? James might argue that bringing benefit to our worlds from our faith is the chief reason we're still here after we are born again into eternal life with Christ. This line of thought brings us to our first major point from today's text: *Faith is meant to do some good.*

Someone will say, "You have faith, and I have works." Show me your faith without works, and I will show you faith from my works.
JAMES 2:18

Take a look at James 2:18 toward our second point and circle every set of repeated terms. (Look beyond common words like "you", "have," and "will.")

If my directions were clear, you caught the repetitions of the words *faith, show,* and *works*. These repetitive words line up for our second point: *Faith shows works*. Remember, we're trying to get through today's lesson without wrecks so before anybody starts spinning, let's be clear: we are not saved by works.

According to the apostle Paul in Ephesians 2:8-10, what is the relationship between faith and works?

James 2:14-18 throws suspicion on whether or not a person is saved if her faith is a complete no-show.

Read each of the following translations of James' question in 2:14b and circle what seems to be the qualifying word or words for "faith."
NIV: "Can such faith save him?"
NET: "Can this kind of faith save him?"
ESV and NASB: "Can that faith save him?"

One believes with the heart, resulting in righteousness, and one confesses with the mouth, resulting in salvation.
ROMANS 10:10

The bottom line for James is that real faith is demonstrative. The Spirit surfaces sooner or later. In Romans 10:10, Paul says that we believe in Jesus with our hearts. Like the heart pumps blood to every limb and any limb without it is dead, our faith is pumped into our actions and extremities without it are dead.

Before we cry foul over our freedom in Christ, James probably got this part of his theology from his big brother in the Gospels. You will know a tree by its fruit, for instance (see Matt. 12:33). You and I are free from the law. But if we are "free" to live continually and completely absent of all signs of Christ's Spirit in us, something is dead wrong.

According to *Word Biblical Commentary*, the Greek verb forms in this section could be stated like this: "if a person *keeps on saying* he or she has faith but *keeps on having* no works" (emphasis added).[1] Then the person may not be saved. That is what's at stake here if I decide to tidy up these Scriptures.

Somebody who is lost but thinks she's saved could just go on living in deception to the shocking end. Sound application here could be the difference between life and death. The Holy Spirit does His job. He convicts and compels. If we can *keep on living* without any intervention, interference, or empowerment from Him, He may not be present within us.

I say these next words absent of all triteness or routine. If you think this may be you, praise God that the very conviction you're feeling is a crystal clear work of His Holy Spirit. Ask Jesus to come into your heart this very moment, to save you to the uttermost, and to bring forth much fruit through the course of your life. He loves you so and wants you to be wholly secure in Him.

I'd sit right here with you for a long time if I could. I care so much. Please let someone know if you've come to this realization today and asked Jesus to save you and show Himself through you. If you asked, He accomplished it. That's a guarantee.

After soaking in James 2:19, how does that revelation hit you personally?

As we've embarked on this study of the life and Letter of James, one of the freshest and most profound elements for me has been awakening to the deep river of Judaism coursing through his veins. He wrote every word of this epistle as a Christian Jew, riveted by the life-saving sight of the resurrected Messiah. The Jewishness of James is never more blatant than right here in verse 19. Every truly Jewish reader would have recognized the words lifted right out of Deuteronomy 6:4, a verse with unsurpassed vitality to them.

Read its context in Deuteronomy 6:4-9, then write verse 4.

The segment you just read was combined with Deuteronomy 11:13-21 and Numbers 15:37-41 to comprise what is called the *Shema*. The word in English translates "Hear!" You can see its prominence in the verse you wrote in the preceding space. Circle the English word for emphasis. The Shema (pronounced "sh-MAH") bore such significance to the Jews that it became their formal creed, a liturgy reflecting their very essence and recited twice a day by loyal Jewish men. It was dear to them as John 3:16 is to us.

With this brief background, read James 1:19 again. With no compromise of inspiration, James almost certainly assigned the statement shock value. In my research, I learned that "the pious Jew even attached merit to the way the *Shema* was said."[2] One rabbinic writing suggested that "Whosoever prolongs the utterance of the word One shall have his days and years prolonged unto him."[3] Then comes James: "You believe that God is one; you do well. The demons also believe—and they shudder."

Whew. Faith shown by works was not a foreign concept to the old order of his day but, if they dozed off during the reading of the last few paragraphs, they awakened here with a jolt like a man dreaming he was falling, all limbs flailing. By now you and I know James well enough not to think he was casting disparagement on the spoken creed of Deuteronomy 6:4. No telling how many times he'd said it in the previous month. He was simply making sure they knew it wasn't enough.

James was simply making sure they knew a spoken creed was not enough.

That brings us to our third and last point today: *Faith does more than nod with devils*. Realizing that we share a certain amount of our belief system with demons from hell is humbling and frightening. Make no mistake. They are monotheists. They have seen the glory of the Lord God Himself. They know there is no one like Jehovah. They also know that Jesus is His Son.

- Mark 3:11 reads, "Whenever the unclean spirits saw Him, those possessed fell down before Him and cried out, 'You are the Son of God!' "
- In Mark 5:7, a demon-possessed man cried out, "What do You have to do with me, Jesus, Son of the Most High God? I beg You before God, don't torment me!"

Oh, they believe, Sweet Thing. They believe. Every satanic temptation to discount God's supremacy comes from a demon who knows better. Many people lead us into deception because they themselves are deceived. The father of lies is not one of them. He knows the truth and means to lie.

Go ahead and say he's ruthless but never credit him as fearless. Fear and anger (see Rev. 12:12) have a long history of traveling in tandem. Satan wears them on his back like bristled hair down a mad dog's spine. Yes, we believe that God is one, but we place our faith steadfastly in something more.

- We believe that God "gave His One and Only Son, so that everyone who believes in Him will not perish but have eternal life" (John 3:16).
- We believe that He bore all of our sins so that we could become His righteousness.
- We believe that we are who He says we are and not the numbing sum of Satan's accusations.
- We believe that to find ourselves, we lose ourselves in all that is glory and grace.
- We believe that we are loved and not despised, held and not forsaken, cherished and not rejected, enjoyed and not just endured.
- We believe that "at the name of Jesus every knee will bow—of those who are in heaven and on earth and under the earth—and every tongue should confess that Jesus Christ is Lord" (Phil. 2:10-11).

Let the demons tremble.

Day Two
FAITH PERFECTED

FLASH FORWARD

"You see that faith was active together with his works, and by works, faith was perfected." James 2:22

Where I come from, you mind your manners. If you have something ugly to say, you say it nicely. And, if you don't like how a person does something, you tell someone else. Using endearments as insults can be an art form.

While these stylized southern manners can be charming or ridiculous, they might help illustrate how often we can miss a point by objecting to the tone. Having the privilege to communicate with people from various regions has caused me to see that we're often saying the same things, just in very different ways. Sometimes I need a person to flower it up and she needs me to spit it out. And somewhere in the middle is a spitty flower.

James came from a world of diatribe. It was a speaking style that was well understood in his circles and shared widely among teachers and students. All of this is to prepare you for James' rather straightforward approach in our opening Scripture today. After all, Mom said name-calling was naughty. Under the inspiration, however, James was just stating the facts to those for whom the church bells toll. Please read James 2:20-26. We have substantial writing to do today in the back of our books but, if you take the time to do it, you will reap so much more. I love the HCSB version of the lead-out verse: "Foolish man! Are you willing to learn that faith without works is useless?" Look carefully at the first five words of James' question in this translation.

Complete the question from the verse above. "Are you ...

In this context, anyone unwilling to learn is an empty-headed fool. Our human tendency is to figure out quickly what we believe then, from that point forward, stick to materials that affirm our early-determined belief system. We end up barely making it into our spiritual adolescence before binding our own systematic theology books in our heads.

You hold a great big Bible in your hands with 66 books strung together like pearls on a crimson thread. The only way to pick and choose, keep or lose, is to cut the thread and send pearls flying. Let's stay *willing to learn,* Beloved! Don't be afraid Scripture is going to fall apart at the seams if one bit doesn't seem to fit. God holds His own Word together.

Fill in the rest of verse 20: "Are you willing to learn that ...

This commentary excerpt gives us a glimpse beneath the surface: "James even makes his point with a bit of wry humor in the form of a wordplay: Faith without works *(ergon)* does not work *(arge= a + ergos)*."[4] Don't you love the mere possibility that James might have had a sense of humor here?

So, let's consider his question: Are you and I *willing to learn* that faith without works doesn't work? Yes? Then let's look at the evidence our protagonist pitches on the table.

A.

In the margin list the two Old Testament figures James offers as exhibits A and B.

B.

I purposely left space below A and B so I could ask you to go back and record any biographical information offered about each in James 2:21-25 *alone*. Please do so now.

In Abraham, James cited the single most pivotal figure in ancient Jewish history. Their birth as a people of God came through his specific divine calling, explaining why "father" (HCSB) or "ancestor" (NIV) is probably at the top of your biographical information under his name.

One of the biggest controversies of scholars through the centuries has been over the different ways James and Paul applied Genesis 15:6: "Abraham believed the LORD, and He credited it to him as righteousness." In Romans 4, the apostle Paul views it in its original Genesis 15 context. God promised that Abraham would have an heir from his own body and, from him, descendents beyond number. There, the justifying faith occurred when Abraham believed Him. In Paul's words:

> He believed, hoping against hope. ... He considered his own body to be already dead (since he was about 100 years old) and also considered the deadness of Sarah's womb, without weakening in the faith. He did not waver in unbelief at God's promise but was strengthened in his faith and gave glory to God, because he was fully convinced that what He had promised He was also able to perform. Therefore, it was credited to him for righteousness (Rom. 4:18-22).

James applies the same Scripture to a scene 30 years later when Abraham offered his beloved son Isaac on the altar. In this stunning act of obedience that preached the gospel of Christ beforehand, God interrupted the slaying of Abraham's beloved son and substituted a ram caught by its horns in the thicket (see Gen. 22). The glorious irony is that, in the actual fulfillment thousands of years later, the substitutionary offering would be the one and only beloved Son of the Father. We are depicted by Isaac, escaping death, and Jesus is the perfect Lamb of God, slain for the sins of the world.

So, how can James take the statement in Genesis 15:6 and apply it to Genesis 22? He makes his case in 2:24.

List everything works accomplish according to James 2:24.

We've already learned that, to James, faith without a shred of works is nonexistent. He doesn't prefer works to faith or faith to works. He sees them as conjoined co-workers. The part of James 2:22 that I especially want you to see is where James says that Abraham's faith "was perfected" by works. That's a key concept in this epistle. It forms the basis on which James is able to use Genesis 15:6 in reference to an act in Genesis 22 that occurred many years later. Think of it as Abraham's life verse. The faith that Abraham exercised when he believed God in Genesis 15 was brought to its ultimate goal and maturity in Genesis 22 when he offered Isaac on the altar, foreshadowing the gospel.

Dear friends, if God loved us in this way, we also must love one another. ... If we love one another, ... His love is perfected in us.
I JOHN 4:11-12

In the margin, carefully observe the portions of 1 John 4:11-12. How is a similar concept in play?

We aren't likely to unravel the thick theological knots tied through the centuries around Paul and James, but they had two different objectives. "James was combating a superficial faith that had no wholesome effect in the life of the professed believer. Paul, on the other hand, was combating legalism—the belief that one may earn saving merit before God by his good deeds."[5]

In your own life, do you struggle more with superficial faith or with legalism? Why?

For some of us that satisfies our minds enough to move to James' second example of faith at work. Others might consider delving much further into justification outside of our series. You will find no few materials. One of my favorite things about any study is what it makes me want to study next.

Now, let's take a look at Rahab. That I keep wanting to spell her name "Rehab" should tell you something about my family history. The fact that she appears among the faithful in Scripture and someone like me appears among the students of Scripture is a testament of God's inexhaustible grace written on both sides of one page.

Rahab's appearance in James 2 could send us to our faces. James only mentions two models of faith evidenced through works. One is a man. The other is a woman. One of them is the *Pater* of Israel and the other is a prostitute of Canaan. *Day 2 continues on page 108.*

The **NEXT LEVEL** with Melissa

THE UNITY & DIVERSITY DANCE

James most attracts me because of his unique voice. To me, his theological uniqueness makes him relevant and interesting. But, as I've studied and interacted with people about the epistle, I've come to wonder if his uniqueness poses a threat for some people.

The great reformer Martin Luther definitely considered James a problem. After determining that James did not fit comfortably with his strict law/gospel antithesis (see pp. 118–19), Luther subjected James to inferior canonical status by detaching it from its regular order and placing it (along with Hebrews, Jude, and Revelation) at the end of his edition of the German New Testament.[1]

Luther opined that James does not sufficiently preach Christ since James fails to mention Christ's death and resurrection.[2] But, if we really believe the Bible is divinely inspired and thus, our ultimate authority, then who gave us the right to establish parameters for how a biblical author should do theology? As Frank Thielman puts it:

> Believers have a good reason for carefully bracketing presuppositions that do not call into question the basic insight that the New Testament is the Word of God; they are motivated by a desire to listen, not to an echo of their own prejudices when they read the New Testament, but to the voice of the text itself. Only by doing this will they hear the Word of God. … The believer who is a student of New Testament theology must honor the theological diversity within it.[3]

While Christians have long maintained the unity of the Bible, we should be careful that we don't simplify it. The Bible is more than just one big book. It is a massive library comprised of numerous literary genres and authors. While I often enough refer to God's written Word as "the Bible," I also like to call it "the Scriptures" because it is, after all, a collection of writings.

The Bible is more than just one big book. It is **a massive library** comprised of numerous literary genres and authors.

We would expect a library of writings with numerous human authors to have a significant amount of diversity. I suspect we fear some will wrongly interpret diversity as contradiction, but even this fear should not cause us to force our own synthesis on God's Word. Again Thielman is of help.

> If we try to minimize [an apparent divergence] either by trimming the canon down to a size that fits us theologically or by advancing implausible harmonizations, we impoverish our understanding of God. The theological diversity of the New Testament shows us that at the same time God is near us he is also beyond our comprehension.[4]

We may not appreciate the tension that diversity causes, but what if God does? It should tell us something about God's creativity that

He gave us four Gospel writers and not just one. Though all four wrote about the meaning and significance of the life and death of Jesus, they each have their own style and distinctive themes.

Significantly, even in the second century, believers tried to synthesize the Gospel material. The early church resisted this pressure to harmonize the material since they believed all four writers were united in message and the manifold witness to the one apostolic message had merit.

The early church resisted this pressure to harmonize the material since they believed **all four writers were united in message** and the manifold witness to the one apostolic message had merit.

Some argue that various branches of the church and/or academic world overemphasize diversity in the New Testament at the expense of unity. I believe that is a very fair assessment, but it is also fair to say that others of us overemphasize the unity of the New Testament at the expense of diversity. The difficult interpretive task for the Bible student is to be both tenacious about the unity of the biblical text but also honest about and open to its divinely-intentioned theological diversity.

For example when we arrive at a thorny text like James 2:14-26, a text that has long been thought to stand in direct contradiction to the apostle Paul, let's think differently. Rather than defensively comparing James with or pitting him against Paul, let's first hear James out. We must let the man speak before we develop hostility toward him. What is he actually saying?

Our duty as Christians demands that we seek to understand how James conceives of faith and works before we start clearing up how he means exactly the same thing as Paul in Galatians. Maybe James does mean the same as Paul or maybe he means something slightly different—complementary, not contradictory.

Whatever the case, we must first let James have his own word. We could talk about these issues all day long, but we do not have time or space.

By way of conclusion, I would like to again quote Thielman because he is just so helpful on these matters. He warns:

> Students of the New Testament should therefore resist the temptation to flatten the theological diversity of the New Testament into a series of logical statements so tight that the mystery of God's greatness is missing from them.[5]

I don't know about you, but I want my hermeneutic—my method of interpreting the Scriptures—to factor in that perhaps God knows some stuff that I just don't fully understand.

When He who was, who is, and who is to come sees each one of us, He sees who we were, who we are, and who will become.

Maybe Abraham and Rahab are not Exhibits A and B after all. Maybe they are Exhibits A and Z. Maybe, between the two of them, anybody can qualify. Yesterday's failure can become tomorrow's hero of the faith.

The actual Greek word translated "prostitute" in 2:25 is *porne*. She could have been the porn star of Jericho, and God still called her to faith. When He who was, who is, and who is to come sees each one of us, He sees who we were, who we are, and who we will become. I love Him so much for that. James' specific focus on what Rahab had done moves me deeply. Do you realize how much of her adult life had been characterized by what she had done?

This may be too basic for some of our tastes but I can't resist saying it: God can change what people do. He can change behavioral patterns that have been in play for decades. He can change what we do to cope, to find comfort, to survive conflict, to count. Like me, Rahab had done a same old thing for years ... and then she did something new. She believed God and acted on it. That definitive action won her a spot in the Hebrews 11 Hall of Faith. More importantly, God won her a place of honor in Matthew 1:5.

According to Matthew 1:1, what do verses 2-16 of that same chapter comprise?

Four women appear in that genealogy of our Lord Jesus Christ, and each of them could have been associated with shame if humankind alone got its say. Instead, drops of their blood ran through Immanuel's veins.

Write Matthew 1:5 in the margin.

If you know anything about the story of Boaz, maybe his compassion for Ruth and his willingness to see her as more than a foreigner makes perfect sense. After all, he was his mother's son. Rahab's boy grew up and became Ruth's kinsman redeemer, taking her as his bride. Mesmerizing.

Today as we will draw our most pointed discussions about faith and works to a close, we're hard-pressed for the perfect summation. One commentator pointed out the truly gorgeous irony that "no one has captured the basic message of [James] 2:14-26 more forcefully than [Martin] Luther" in his preface to the Book of Romans.[6] So, with all due and sincere respect, we will let him voice our benediction:

> O it is a living, busy active mighty thing, this faith. It is impossible for it not to be doing good things incessantly. It does not ask whether good works are to be done, but before the question is asked, it has already done this, and is constantly doing them. Whoever does not do such works, however, is an unbeliever. He gropes and looks around for faith and good works, but knows neither what faith is nor what good works are.[7]

Day Three
CALLING ALL TEACHERS

FLASH FORWARD

"Not many should become teachers, my brothers, knowing that we will receive a stricter judgment." James 3:1

At 30, I had barely reached toddlerhood as a teacher. Only a few years had passed since my maiden voyage as the worst Sunday School teacher in the safe harbor of my church. I didn't say the class wasn't fun. I said it wasn't good. Bereft of a single ounce of training, I spent the week thinking up what I wanted to talk about and then spent Saturday night in a Bible-flipping frenzy trying to find a Scripture that applied.

God alone knows how much better the class would have been had I simply used the teacher's Sunday School quarterly but, to be candid, I hated the name *quarterly*. That should give you some idea of the maturity level involved. The class and I survived by the skin of our teeth and both counted the weeks till my one-year commitment was complete. Desperate, I signed up for a Sunday-evening Bible doctrine class and fell in love.

As I sit at this computer screen and glance over to my right at an open Bible, by the grace and patience of God, I am still in love. Jesus swept me off my feet by the gusty, warm breezes of sacred pages turning. A mind broken by hypocrisy, abuse, sin, and crushing guilt was gradually saved by getting madly lost in a world of prophets, priests, and kings.

At 30, I was very early into the process and still leading a spirited aerobics class in my church gym on Mondays. The second it was over, I'd toss the leg warmers, throw on a skirt, and sprint across town to the best-kept, Bible-class secret in Houston, Texas. It met in a small room packed with a hundred women who eyed anyone new. Upon asking "How come nobody knows this is here?" I realized that this wonderful band of women were fighting to stay small against the high tide of their immensely popular Bible teacher.

On one of those Mondays, our masterful teacher, Jeannette Clift George, lifted her eyes from opening prayer and said, "Good afternoon, friends. Go ahead and turn to James 3:1 with me." And we did. I'd like to request the same thing of you right now. Would you read James 3:1-5 and write all five verses on page 219 please?

Why would a new teacher feel shaken by the first sight of James 3:1?

Our teacher that day was the epitome of grace. She wasn't my problem. James was. In my maroon Bible with the gently-gnarled, gold-rimmed pages, here's what I saw in store for teachers: "We shall receive the greater condemnation" (KJV). I was looking for extra condemnation about like I was looking for a wad of rattlesnakes. I clicked my spiked heels out to the car after class as fast as I could and told the Lord out loud that I was never teaching again.

Moments when you believe you have heard from God are difficult to describe, but on that day two thoughts hit me with hurricane force. First, I would teach. Second, I would never again teach without getting down on my knees in front of the group for prayer. Though I heard no audible sound, the instructions were clear enough to sink my feet in cement for 24 years and counting.

With your patience, today I'll weave the splintered twine of my personal experience among the Scriptures we'll seek. Aside from Rabbi Jesus, no teacher masters teaching, least of all this one. As Bible teachers, we deal with a text that will neither submit to us nor shrink to our view. In the spirit of Acts 3:6, I don't have an overabundance of insight, "but what I have, I give you." Some of you *are* teachers and some of you *will be* teachers, but, for those of us who operate within the biblical structure of the church, all of us *have* teachers. The following are a handful of land mines that go with the territory.

The temptation to teach more than we know. First Timothy 1:7 pegs this one: "They want to be teachers … but they do not know what they are talking about or what they so confidently affirm" (NIV). I look back on some of the things I've taught and think, *Girl, you did not know what you were talking about!* Resist the temptation to teach more than you know, particularly in the face of natural disaster or human suffering.

The capacity to mislead. Any leader is a potential misleader. Take that one to the spiritual bank.

What will surely happen among us according to 2 Peter 2:1-2?

Carefully read 1 Timothy 6:3-5. Write a descriptive profile of a person who does not agree to sound instruction.

The capacity to be misled. Teachers are not the only ones who can mislead.

According to 2 Timothy 4:3-4, how can an audience lead a weak teacher astray?

Complete 2 Timothy 4:5: "*But …*

The temptation to use the platform for personal agendas or opinions. Oh, that the line were always clear. Sometimes we can assume we've walked with God so long that every "religious" thought we have is from Him. Untrue.

The best advice is to feverishly seek the filling of the Holy Spirit so that, when we cross the line, we feel conviction. At that point, we redirect ourselves or apologize to the group. Several years ago I memorized these words of Christ and find them immensely centering: "My teaching isn't Mine but is from the One who sent Me. The one who speaks for himself seeks his own glory. But He who seeks the glory of the One who sent Him is true, and there is no unrighteousness in Him" (John 7:16,18). Jeremiah 45:5 is also taped on the inside cover of my Bible: "As for you, do you seek great things for yourself?" We want our answer to be an unwavering *No!* Ultimately all comes full circle in God's economy, and His glory turns out to be the greatest possible thing for us.

While we're at it, let me save you an immense amount of pain: whatever you do, refrain from using the public platform as a disguised means of calling out someone in your group. We don't call out his or her name, of course, but we know who we're really talking to. Such a ploy is playing God and not just arrogance. It is cowardice. If the person really needs confronting, Scripture teaches the proper means.

My worst infraction replays often in my thoughts and led to the severest season of discipline and humbling of my life. I could tremble thinking about it. Keep check on your motives, stick to the Scriptures, and ask God to give you the supernatural capacity to love those listeners more than you love your own skin.

You take a turn before I proceed. Use the margin to list a few other enormous temptations for teachers, either from experience, observation, or human nature.

The demand for self-discipline. A decent teacher has to study. Hard. One of the signs of a teaching gift is an unexplainable thirst to study followed by the difficulty of keeping to yourself what you learned. A teacher who doesn't like to study is a talker. Don't mix up the two. The greater self-discipline is fighting ferociously to hang on to your intimate relationship with Jesus. God will never call you to sacrifice your intimacy with Him on the altar of ministry. We have to zealously maintain our prayer lives and our love lives and teach out of the overflow of what Christ is teaching us. Otherwise we trudge blindly through the graveyard where teachers turn to dust.

God will never call you to sacrifice your intimacy with Him on the altar of ministry.

The pride and humiliation. Teaching can be a status thing today just as it was in the first century. The credit, another word for glory, to the teacher bleeds irony since we can't earn a distribution of the Holy Spirit to save our lives. The gifts of the Spirit are unmerited graces.

What gets less press is the humiliation that can go with teaching. Sometimes I'll be in the middle of a lesson and have no idea where God has gone or what on earth I'm talking about. Or my eyes will spring open in the middle of the night with, "You said what??"

Write Proverbs 10:19a in this space.

Moral of the story: Want to teach? Prepare to apologize a lot.

God often likes to teach the bigger lesson to the teacher. Yep, many lessons will be taught to you before they're profitably taught through you. Exodus 4:12 doesn't say, "I will tell you what to say." It says, "I will *teach* you what to say" (emphasis added).

The human judgment. I'm not sure which is more toxic: the criticism of people or their adulation. The former tastes like poison but a steady drip of the latter can make you twice as sick. Let's quit trying to take people's pulse to see how much they love us. "Am I now trying to win the favor of people, or God? Or am I striving to please people? If I were still trying to please people, I would not be a slave of Christ" (Gal. 1:10). If you can get people pleased, you cannot keep them pleased. Bind your wrist to the One who isn't fickle.

Stricter divine judgment. Why? Because "much will be required of everyone who has been given much. And even more will be expected of the one who has been entrusted with more" (Luke 12:48b). The judgment referenced in James 3:1 is toward the quality of our works and the loss or gain of reward, not the eternal destination of our souls (see 1 Cor. 3:12-15).

When a teacher stumbles, she is apt to be charged a group rate.

Others stumble with us. As James 3:2 says, we all stumble in many ways, but when a teacher stumbles, she is apt to be charged a group rate. No gift should be received with greater sobriety than influence.

But, wait a second. What if you're called to teach? If God calls a person to teach, in the words of Romans 12:7, "Let him teach." To shrink back is disobedience. Muse on a key word used in the NIV: "Not many of you should *presume* to be teachers" (Jas. 3:1, emphasis added). To do so is to presume enormous scrutiny upon our lives. But, Beloved, if Jesus has summoned you, you must go!

Amid every challenge I've mentioned, plus failing sight from a thousand footnotes, digestive problems from anxiety, and a dozen other teaching-related maladies yet unshared, I would not trade one moment of this wild ride for anything in the world. I've had to type at times with one hand so that I could put my other hand in the air in praise. I discovered true worship with Moses. I found my freedom with Paul. I danced before God's throne with David. And I've found Jesus through them all.

Teach, teacher! But fall to your face before it knocks you there.

Day Four
FIRE & WATER

FLASH FORWARD

"Praising and cursing come out of the same mouth.
My brothers, these things should not be this way." James 3:10

Between yesterday's lesson and today's, we slid down a shiny slide into the second half of our journey. You've already beat the odds and, from what I've observed, will probably stick it out to the finish. A bonding takes place through these lessons, doesn't it? For months now I've thought of you every day and hoped and prayed that you're encountering words from God that "are spirit and are life" (John 6:63).

You are not taken for granted here. If not for you, I'd just be listening to myself talk and, at this point, I'd rather hug a cactus. Do you have a good pen handy? Grab it and write James 3:6-12 in the back of your book.

Finished? Now, look back carefully at James 3:1-3,9 and circle (in your Bibles or in your handwritten version) every appearance of the word "we."

How many times does "we" appear in these four verses of James?

Prior to this section of the epistle, James has used the word "we" only once (see Jas. 1:18). All other references so far have been to "you," to "my brothers," and to "my dear brothers." Suddenly in chapter 3, from the ball of his pen bounces we, we, we, we, we, we. Why? And why in the world is James back on the subject of the tongue again and, this time, with all the delicacy of a firing squad?

I don't know about you but the subjects that stir up the most passion in me tend to be those most personal to me. Could it be that, of all the reprimands or corrections in the entire letter, this one hit the closest to home?

Watch James throw himself into 3:2 alongside us: "We all stumble in many ways." Then, under God's leadership, is it possible that James proceeded with an exposé of the specific area where he felt most prone to stumble?

Look at the segment again. Without detracting an iota from divine inspiration but basking in the wonder of it, do you hear any hint of frustration in the voice of James over the tongue? This I know, Sweet Thing. Nobody on the planet frustrates me like I frustrate myself. Usually when I'm most passionate about a subject in my teaching, it is either because I struggle with it myself or because I've been personally injured by it. Note again how clearly James lumps himself into the sum of teachers in 3:1. "Not many should become teachers, my brothers, knowing that we will receive a stricter judgment."

Circle "we" again.

As a teacher, maybe James was challenged at times to bridle his tongue just like most people who use many words. Imagine how often he'd also been injured by the maverick tongues of others.

Let's look at two of the metaphors James used in this section: (1) the tongue as a fire, and (2) the tongue as a fountain. First, the tongue as a fire.

Look carefully at verse 6 and complete this sentence:
"It pollutes the whole body ...

In the words of the New Living Translation, the tongue "can set your whole life on fire." We'd have to live under a rock not to know it. No human relationship or dimension of earthly life is fireproofed from flaming tongues.

When was the last time you were aware of the tongue's capacity to blister and scar?

The NET Bible® offers a translation that keeps drawing my attention: "[The tongue] sets fire to the course of human existence." Imagine how many wars have been waged over words, how much prejudice has been passed down through generations, how much hate has been seeded into family lines, and how much slander has been planted by the old into the young.

Eugene Peterson puts James 3:6 like this: "By our speech we can ruin the world, turn harmony to chaos, throw mud on a reputation, send the whole world up in smoke and go up in smoke with it, smoke right from the pit of hell" (Message).

Glance at James 3:6 again in your own Bible. What is the source of the tongue's fire?

- ☐ hell
- ☐ in-laws
- ☐ the pit
- ☐ human depravity

Before you're tempted to jerk your tongue from your throat, turn to Acts 2 and read verses 1-4. Ironically, these tongues were lit by fire, too.

What was the source of this Acts 2 fire?

Remember, James and the other half brothers of Jesus had already begun uniting with the disciples in Acts 1:14. James was almost certainly among those on whom these "tongues, like flames of fire" (2:3) came to rest. Suddenly they began to speak in the languages of those who'd come to Jerusalem from many nations, and "each one heard them speaking in his own language" (vv. 5-6).

You see, the human tongue can be lit by either source: Heaven or hell. God can draw people to the gospel by enabling us to speak in ways they understand or our tongues can cause people to hightail it like their heels are on fire. It can bring comfort and courage, or it can bring destruction and deafness. We do have a choice which fire lights our tongues. Just keep in mind that the natural default setting leans south.

The tongue can bring comfort and courage, or it can bring destruction and deafness. We have a choice ...

Ready to move to the next metaphor? Second, the Bible portrays the tongue as a fountain. Reread James 3:9-12.

In one sentence, write your own version of James' point in these four verses.

James' wording in verse 11 is fascinating. What two kinds of water does he mention?

Several major versions use the adjectives *fresh* and *salt* to describe the water. According to scholarly definitions of the Greek words, the HCSB nails the translation with: "Does a spring pour out sweet and bitter water from the same opening?" Circle both adjectives. The Greek transliteration of the word *fresh* or *sweet* is *glykos.*[8] Do you recognize the similarity to our word *glucose?*

The Greek word *salt* or *bitter* is *pikros.* Bitter most closely captures the word. Why all the haggling over sweet and bitter? Because James, a proven devotee to Judaism and raised to love the books of Moses, may well have been thinking of Exodus 15:22-25. Relish it from the NKJV.

> Moses brought Israel from the Red Sea; then they went out into the Wilderness of Shur. And they went three days in the wilderness and found no water. Now when they came to Marah, they could not drink the waters of Marah, for they were bitter. Therefore the name of it was called Marah. And the people complained against Moses, saying, "What shall we drink?" So he cried out to the LORD, and the LORD showed him a tree. When he cast it into the waters, the waters were made sweet.

Go back and circle the words *bitter* and *sweet.*

Marah means *bitter* in Hebrew, so every mention of the name reemphasizes the unfitness of the water. You may as well go ahead and circle it, too.

What did the Lord do when Moses cried out to Him?

God wasn't just showing Moses something. He was teaching and instructing him.

Don't you love the fact that the Lord showed it to him? If so, you'll really love this commentary excerpt: "The verb 'showed' is from the root that in the causative conjugation means 'to teach' or 'instruct' and is the same root from which we derive the word 'Torah' ('instruction,' 'law')."[9] So, God wasn't just showing Moses something. He was teaching and instructing him. Hang on because this is the part of the excerpt I particularly want you to see.

> Ferdinand de Lessups, builder of the Suez Canal, was told by Arab chiefs that they put a thorn bush into some types of water to make it palatable. Others have suggested that certain aromatic plants were used to disguise the bad taste of the water, but the text is clear that God gave Moses special instructions in response to the despair of the people. The tree may have had little more to do with the actual temporary healing of the waters than did the salt in Elisha's healing of the Jericho spring in 2 Kings 2:19-22. In both cases it may only be the power of God and a test of obedience that are present.[10]

First Peter 2:24 keeps swirling in my mind: "He Himself bore our sins in His body on the tree, so that, having died to sins, we might live for righteousness." I'm not remotely suggesting that James had this in mind or claiming here that the waters sweetened by the wood in Exodus 15 foreshadowed the tree that held our Savior. I will also stop short of making something big out of the thorn bushes used by Arab chiefs to make the water drinkable.

I won't stop short of telling you that I have been one bitter woman in the course of my life and I'm not anymore. That is the sweetness of redemption and a miracle of God if I've ever experienced one. Does anybody else need to testify to some bitter waters that have been sweetened by the deep, plunging work of Christ?

Go right ahead. Share your example and plan to be ready to share with your group if you will.

The very section of Exodus 15 we've considered today pours like a torrent into one of the most profound introductions God makes of Himself: "I am Yahweh who heals you" (Ex. 15:26). Beloved, anything God has ever been, He still is. He is everlasting, He is immutable, and He is Healer.

You can be rescued by God from your Egypt and still be filled to the brim with bitterness. I certainly was. Research suggests plausible reasons like mineral content to explain why that body of water in Exodus 15 was brackish and undrinkable. Likewise, plausible reasons suggest why people like us get bitter. All of us have been hurt and offended, misled and misused. Who in the world could blame us? We can find plenty of people who'll give us permission to keep that whirlpool of bitterness churned up within us, but we can only find One who can plunge beneath those waters and make them sweet. He alone can fill us through and through with the new wine of His Spirit and purify all the murkiness until it's as clear as a crystal sea.

If you're like me, sometimes you don't even realize you still have some of that old bitterness inside of you until something foul springs like a fountain from your mouth. Jesus pinpointed the source in Matthew 12:34: "The mouth speaks from the overflow of the heart."

Maybe it's time for a fresh work of Jesus right there in the wellspring of our hearts. Right there where the offense hit. Right there where the loss hit. Right there where the betrayal hit. Right there where the abuse hit. Right there, Child. He is the Lord your Healer.

The **NEXT LEVEL** with Melissa

LUTHER, LAW & GOSPEL

This excursus explores the theme of law and gospel in the theology of the great reformer Martin Luther. In the final couple of paragraphs, I will offer up a couple of my own thoughts, but my *primary* intention here is to explore Luther's doctrine, not assert my own theological views.

Luther's distinction between law and gospel lay at the heart of his theology. Borrowing the phraseology of Carter Lindberg, Luther saw the Bible as made up of two fundamentally different "kinds of speech"—law and gospel.[1]

Luther saw the Bible as made up of two fundamentally different "kinds of speech"— law and gospel.

For Luther, law communicates demands and conditions in the language of covenant.[2] It comprises the statements in Scripture that expose our sin and condemn us. Conversely, the speech of gospel communicates *promise* in the language of testament.[3] Gospel appears in Scriptures that speak of God's unconditional promise, grace, and redemption.

In essence, for Luther, the difference between law and gospel is between demands made by God and gifts given to us by God. In the category of law, the human being *actively* imitates God while in the category of gospel, the human being *passively* receives from God.

Luther saw the twofold law and gospel as working together, even if antithetically, "to produce in sinful man the dynamic dualistic struggle of self-righteousness against God's righteousness."[4] The spiritual and emotional trajectory of this experience, for Luther, mirrored his own personal story and theological history. He saw law leading to ultimate despair in one's tragically sinful state while gospel then triumphantly leads to total belief and ultimate reliance on Jesus for all things, chiefly to those pertaining to salvation. So, although law and gospel are directly opposed in Luther's theology, the law does have ongoing significance insofar as it exposes humanity's sinful nature.[5]

The Old Testament may naturally contain more law and the New Testament more gospel, but, for Luther, one can't assume the Old is law and the New is gospel. Rather the two Testaments each contain both "kinds of speech." Luther could point to passages in the Old Testament that preach gospel and passages in the New Testament that preach law. For Luther, theological sophistication means developing the ability to carefully distinguish between these two opposite kinds of speech in God's Word.

While not *every* verse in the Bible can be neatly categorized into law or gospel, in Luther's thought these two categories must be *distinguished* and not be *intermingled.*

We see Luther struggling through this in his commentary on Galatians when he said,

> It seems a small matter to mingle the Law and Gospel, faith and works, but it creates more mischief than man's

> brain can conceive. To mix Law and Gospel not only clouds the knowledge of grace, it cuts out Christ altogether.[6]

I hope this rather tedious discussion makes the reasons for Luther's personality clash with James more clear. Luther's law-gospel antithesis was not very compatible with James' theological emphases.

I also wonder if you are seeing where some of our own theological tendencies are rooted and why we too can be a bit uncomfortable with James. Whether we know it or not, as Protestants, our theological impulse to keep law and gospel as two binary opposing categories is an attribute we inherited from the 16th century German Reformation.

As Protestants, we inherited our theological impulse to keep law and gospel as opposites from the 16th century German Reformation.

James boggles our minds when he equates the law with freedom or unites faith and works because he mixes categories that we, as heirs in the theological line of Martin Luther, prefer to keep separate.

As we conclude, I need to express a couple of final thoughts to frame the conversation. First, context is king. We have to place Luther in his own historical context before we can grapple with some of his writings.

Martin Luther experienced a papacy so corrupt that, to fund the construction of Saint Peter's in Rome, it sold the promise that dead loved ones would experience relief from punishment in purgatory. Folks were literally buying their eternal destiny. After witnessing such contemptible pastoral abuse, no wonder Martin Luther was dead set on the passive role of human beings in salvation, even if, regrettably, it meant denigrating James in the process.

Though we greatly owe Martin Luther for a host of reasons, in the spirit of the Reformation's own slogan, *Sola Scriptura,* we must be certain the biblical texts themselves judge the law-gospel study method we have inherited and not the other way around. In other words, if we really believe Scripture alone is authoritative, then even the law-gospel hermeneutic lacks authority to judge James' theological worth; rather, James himself, in conversation with all the other voices of Scripture, must shape our understanding of law and gospel.

Day Five

WISDOM BELOW, WISDOM ABOVE

FLASH FORWARD

"The wisdom from above is first pure, then peace-loving, gentle, compliant, full of mercy and good fruits, without favoritism and hypocrisy." James 3:17

I grew up in a household popping at the seams with two parents, five children, and one grandparent. My mom's mom moved in with my parents immediately after they returned from their unforeseen honeymoon. The keener observer might have wondered if her formidable presence was their punishment for eloping. If revenge was my grandmother's motivation, she took her time doling it out since she didn't move on until she went home to Jesus at 87.

My nanny was both a delight and a handful and not one more than the other. One of her quirks was to consolidate anything of the remotest like kind. For instance, if three boxes of cereal were ⅔ eaten, she'd pour them all into one box. A poster could have been made of my older brother staring dazed and confused down his spoon into a sea of corn puffs, shredded wheat, and Cap'n Crunch®. A person trying to discover his true self got precious little help from Minnie Ola Rountree.

Now is a time I so wish I could sit with you in a group and hear about your family. What happy or annoying quirks would you tell me about your family when you were growing up? Your group might decide to share these together if you like.

We have a bowl full today, Sister, with too many concepts to wolf down in one sitting. Lest you look wild-eyed down your spoon, we will spend our final day of week 4 on our next verses in James then pick them back up again in session 5. I come from a long line of messy consolidators, so cornflakes are liable to fly; but when we're finished with the process, we'll know we've had a meal. Please read James 3:13-18, then write the segment in the back of your book.

This portion of Scripture is like an article begging for a column, so let's give it one. James masterfully contrasts "wisdom from above" with "wisdom" from below. Go meticulously through all six verses and find every description of each kind of "wisdom."

List them under the proper heading. Start at verse 13.

"Wisdom from above": "Wisdom" from below:

We'll hit a few high points now and save others for session 5. Are you game for taking the hard part first? Then lock in on verse 14.

Where do bitter envy (or jealousy) and selfish ambition reside?
□ the mouth □ the life □ the heart □ our dreams

Remember, James wrote his letter to believers. Unsaved people might have fewer qualms with openly demonstrating jealousy or selfish ambition, but seasoned Christians are notorious for disguising them. Sometimes we dress up jealousy and call it *discernment,* and sometimes we stick a mask on selfish ambition and label it *calling.*

James has a weak stomach for pretense. He cautions us to tend to our hearts where thorns of the flesh embed themselves deeper and deeper until they infect our character. With his penchant for the Hebrew meaning of peace, James switches the light on in our closets and says, "Let's stop playing games and get well." I can't move on in the lesson without blurting out how much I loathe the feeling of jealousy. I never find myself less tolerable than when jealousy rears its head. Anybody else?

If so, try to articulate why it's so miserable.

Jealousy takes root in the soil of insecurity. Without hesitation, let's ask God to pluck every splinter of jealousy from our hearts while we hold still in His hands; but those holes aren't meant to stay hollow. Let's ask Him to plant within us a thriving, healthy sense of our security in Him. Never forget that God is a giver (see Jas. 1:17). Every time we ask Him to take something from us, let's be bold enough to request divine riches in its place. Isaiah 33:6 says He's "a rich store" and a "treasure."

Back to James 3:14. What did he tell us *not* to do if we have bitter envy and selfish ambition in our hearts?

James' blunt approach can take some getting used to, but we're better off not trying to soften a point that's meant to hit hard and leave a long impression. Here's one summation of verse 14 using a James-like method: "Braggers are liars," period. The people most prone to boast or brag are those permeated by jealousy and selfish ambition. Whew. The Scripture gets up in our business, doesn't it? But how many people in our mile-wide, inch-deep social networks are willing to confront those kinds of flaws in us? I'd rather hard truths come from a gracious God who truly loves me. Consider the wording again: "Don't brag and deny the truth" (v. 14).

Don't brag and deny the truth.
JAMES 3:14

List one way bragging denies the truth:

The beautiful thing about new beginnings in Christ is that we're one confession away from being able to say, "That's the old me." Today could be the day for somebody new. Let's glance now at that second column for "wisdom from above" (v. 17). Look first at the intentional pairing of words in James 3:13.

Fill in the blanks:
"Who is __________ and has ____________________ among you?"

These two words claim a prominent place in the Law of Moses, specifically in Deuteronomy 1:13. Moses described the God-ordained delegation of authority with these qualifications: "Appoint for yourselves wise, understanding, and respected men from each of your tribes, and I will make them your leaders." Underline the two key words in common with James 3:13. I can't stand for you to miss Deuteronomy 4:5-8 where these two qualifications get a broad sweep from the leadership corner to the entire nation. It's well worth the trip, so turn there now and read all four verses.

The specific impact of wisdom and understanding is profound and immensely powerful. What is it?

Wisdom often knows what to do, what is right, or what is awry. Understanding often knows why.

What is the difference between wisdom and understanding anyway? At the risk of oversimplifying, first try thinking of it this way: wisdom is the *what.* Understanding is the *why.* Wisdom often knows what to do, what is right, or what is awry. Understanding often knows why. For instance, wisdom knows that pride is serious sin and should be shunned. Understanding knows that pride is the fastest way to a painful, ugly fall.

In any area of your walk of faith where you've accurately learned a "why" (even if the process was ugly), you've gained what the Bible calls understanding. Wisdom and understanding in the believer are as practical as they are beautiful. I used the example of pride.

Now, offer your own example of a "what" (wisdom) and a corresponding "why" (understanding).

What

Why

I love the HCSB version of the second half of James 3:13. "He [the one who is wise and has understanding] should show his works by good conduct with wisdom's gentleness." Aren't those last two words rich? Wisdom's gentleness.

List the names of two people you know personally who you'd characterize as wise and understanding. Why?

Now, let me ask you a question. Are either of them harsh?

Why do you think that is so?

True wisdom has a gentleness about it, doesn't it? Harsh people are never wise people. They may be smart. They may even be right. But they are not what the Bible calls wise. Most of your list in the second column under "wisdom from above" probably comes from James 3:17. Read it again: "The wisdom from above is first pure, then peace-loving, gentle, compliant, full of mercy and good fruits, without favoritism and hypocrisy."

Draw a circle around the first three descriptions and a square around each of the remaining descriptions.

James artfully and brilliantly etched these words on the page so that, when they were read aloud, their glorious assonance would ring in their emphasis like a golden bell. The words you circled all begin with an "e" in Greek. The words you squared all begin with an "a." If we could hear them all fall from a well-spoken tongue, one after another in their original form, we might just wish to accuse Bishop James of some pure, unadulterated rhythm.

I think you've worked plenty hard today. I'm going to let you out of class a little early and pick up with you in session 5 where we left off. In closing, I want you to know how much I appreciate you. I often glance back on the last 20 years of my journey with Christ Jesus and imagine how different my study life would have been without fellow sojourners to coax me, encourage me, and stretch me along the way.

The **NEXT LEVEL** with Melissa

GENTLENESS & WISDOM

James 3:13-18 is one of my favorite passages in the epistle, perhaps because the entire section is so insanely contrary to my nature and personality. I just can't help but be challenged. A couple of points profoundly speak to me: the first is James' surprising link between wisdom and gentleness and the second is his connection between peacemaking and righteousness.

In your lesson today, Mom alluded to the link between wisdom and gentleness in James 3:13. The Greek word rendered "humility" (NIV) or "gentleness" (HCSB) is πραΰτης, and it refers to "the quality of not being overly impressed by a sense of one's self-importance."[1] Douglas Moo notes that the quality this word (πραΰτης) refers to "was not usually prized by the Greeks" because "they thought it signaled a servility unworthy of a strong and confident person."[2]

Things are not so different in our society, are they? Even within our church communities, the wise people are usually the outspoken, the ones winning the theological debates. You know, the apologetics types who can devastate all their theological opponents? The gentle ones may be respected as good, down-to-earth folks with servant hearts, but we rarely deem them wise.

What is it about not being overly impressed by a sense of one's self-importance that makes one wise? If I were really courageous enough to admit I am not as significant as I think I am, then I wouldn't always need to have the last word.

In my woundedness and in my flesh, I delude myself into thinking that harshness and severity are worth it if another person is fortunate enough to gain my superior perspective.

Wrong.

The gentleness that is linked to wisdom in this context means living out of the knowledge that I am not the priority here. When I combine this disquieting yet liberating truth about me with the awareness that each

I desperately wanted to know Him through the depths of His Word, but I fear that, left alone in the pursuit, the tyranny of daily life and the harassment of the Enemy would have eventually caused me to lose heart and go lite. With you along the road, I'm accountable. I can't just twist my ankle and sit in the ditch and whine for the next month. I have to shake it off and get back up and walk. It's a beautiful, beautiful thing, isn't it? And it's God's way. He did not mean for us to do this alone. He meant for us to sit next to one another, even hundreds of miles apart, point at His Word, and say, "Did you see that?"

"If we walk in the light as He Himself is in the light, we have fellowship with one another, and the blood of Jesus His Son cleanses us from all sin" (1 John 1:7).

person I meet is worth far more than I could ever imagine, perhaps I will be on my way to exuding this wisdom from above.

The passage ends in verse 18 with the assertion, "Peacemakers who sow in peace raise a harvest of righteousness" (NIV). So, now we aren't just talking about wisdom here, we're also talking about a link between righteousness and peacemaking.

You just gotta love James, right? He simply will not allow us a pass to talk about peace without doing it.

We do love to talk about peace, don't we? We talk about peace a whole lot. But are we *really* peacemakers? Do we *actually* sow in peace? Do we promote peace and remove divisiveness in our communities, or do we secretly like to stir it up? More often than not, we rant about peace as a distant concept, like peace for the Middle East, but then, at home, we cannot even resolve conflict with specific people in our lives such as spouses, parents, and neighbors.

Our tendency so often is to champion some kind of abstract notion of peace for the masses, all the while failing to bring peace to specific people we encounter in our daily lives. Moreover, causing "disharmony in the community" for one's own selfish gain is earthly, not heavenly, wisdom.[3]

So often gentleness and peacemaking are virtues and attributes for "other" people, such as a Christian counselor or a young and tender housewife. But, here James preaches that these attributes are basic for all Christians, male or female, who seek to embody "wisdom from above" (v. 17) or "raise a harvest of righteousness" (v. 18, NIV). The powerful combination of these two unlikely connections results in a refreshing and inspiring paradigm shift, especially for the cantankerous person (I'm pointing to myself!), who brushes off gentleness and peacemaking as idealistic attributes that simply are not part of her God-given personality.

viewer guide | session five

James 3:13-18

For those of us who were willing, the opening pages of week 4 sketched James' signature verses across our hearts. Long after our journey is over, you and I will know its mission was accomplished if we're still willing to ask ourselves the prying question: When it comes to my faith, ________ ________ _____ _____? (2:14,16).

The key word pops up again in James 3:13, offering us a prime opportunity in today's session to pose a philosophical question:

What is the ________ ________?

1. One that _________ us from _________________ (v. 14).

   In preparation for the next point, consider James 3:17 in the New King James Version: "The wisdom that is from above is first pure, then peaceable, gentle, ____________ _____ ________, full of mercy and good fruits, without partiality and without hypocrisy."

2. One with a _________ record of ________________ (v. 17).

   Compare the wording of Matthew 27:50 (NASB, ESV)—"Jesus cried out again with a loud voice, and __________ ______ His Spirit." The Greek word *aphiemi* means "______ ________ ________."

   Keep in mind a vital difference in motivation: we yield out of wisdom from ________, not out of ________ ____________.

3. One that is __________ of ____________ (v. 17).

Mercy morphs into ____________________ when we take God's ____________________ instead of our possibility.

Glance back at James 2:16. Consider the wording of the New Living Translation: "Good-bye and have a ________ ________."

Consider the following quote:

"It is not the form of the statement that is reprehensible, but its functioning as a _____________ ________ for the ___________ to ________."[1]

4. One that is ____________ of ____________ fruit (v. 17).

Reflect on a rich statement written by Dr. James B. Adamson: "Fruit is both ______ ________ and ____ ______________, the crown of one process and the ________ of the ________ being present in the ________."[2]

1. Luke Timothy Johnson, *The Anchor Bible,* vol. 37, *The Letter of James* (New Haven, CT: Yale University Press/Doubleday, 1995), 239.
2. James B. Adamson, *The New International Commentary on the New Testament: The Epistle of James* (Grand Rapids, MI: Wm. B. Eerdmans Publishing Co., 1976), 157.

WEEK FIVE

DRAWING NEAR

Day One
CONSIDER THE SOURCE

FLASH FORWARD

"What is the source of wars and fights among you?" James 4:1

Today is one of those times I wish we could hash out our study face-to-face. Actually, I'm not leaning so much toward a conversation today as an interview. Somehow the segment we're about to discuss makes me imagine myself sitting across from you with a pen and paper asking a series of questions and challenging you to answer on the spot. Then, to be fair, we'd switch places but, to be unfair, I'd already have a hunch where you were headed.

Perhaps it would help to know that I've been on that side of the table a number of times. Some of them I lived to regret but, for the most part, if I knew the interviewer was sincerely interested and genuinely seeking understanding, even the meddling didn't bother me as long as I had the freedom to decline an answer. The best interviews of all have caused me to pause, scratch my head, and say, "Wow, I haven't really thought about that before."

So, what do you say? Would you agree to a short interview today to break up some ground so our lesson can sow deeper seed? What if you knew I was sincerely interested and genuinely seeking understanding and that you could decline a written response? Or what if you could answer in code so you knew what you meant but someone flipping through this workbook couldn't figure it out? Here's the best part: what if the questions caused you some needed introspection but gave your interviewer no ammunition to exploit you? That's the ultimate interview! So, why don't we try it?

I'm going to give you nine questions. I'm asking you to complete them with the provisions above, and then we'll proceed.

1. What is the biggest battle you have going on inside of you right now?

2. How long has it been going on?

3. The whole idea of *battle* implies that several different sides of the situation (for example, options, feelings, or conflicts) are clamoring against one another inside of you. If you are the uneasy home to an internal wrestling match right now, try to describe the sides at war.

4. We each have internal, unspoken conflicts with any number of people but most of us have a few people in our life with whom we actually engage in external conflict or quarreling. Who are those people for you?

5. Now, switch tracks with me for a moment. What is something you've wanted for a long while that you do not have?

6. Do you know someone who has this thing, situation, or relationship that you've longed for? If so, who? Keep in mind that naming the person doesn't automatically mean you envy them. What we're establishing right now is whether or not your deep longing is a sustainable reality on planet Earth. That said, who possesses what you really long for?

7. Have you consistently and earnestly asked God for this thing, situation, or relationship? If so, name a couple of reasons why you think you haven't yet received it.

8. Can you identify any link between the person or people with whom you are most prone to quarrel and something you want but you do not have? If so, what?

9. Has anything good or beneficial come to you or to others as a result of your lack? If so, list every bit of fruit you can identify or even remotely discern.

Are we still friends? I'm not going to give you space to answer that one right now in case the interview wasn't a pleasant experience for you. Anyway, the subject matter wasn't my idea. It was James'. See for yourself. Read James 4:1-3, then write the segment on page 221.

I know the agony of a battle raging within. In fact, the soil of my soul is a fairway of divots over one right now. As to whether or not mine is tied to something I want but don't have, picture me with whiplash from nodding.

Let's get this out on the table as fast as we can: all of us, no matter how much we have, desire something we don't. Something that doesn't seem unreasonable. Something that others in eyeshot appear to have. I don't know masses of people with this thing I long for but I know just enough to keep me thinking it's attainable. This I know after five decades of living: nobody has everything they've ever longed for.

All of us, no matter how much we have, desire something we don't.

Part of that comes from our insatiable flesh nature and sinful discontent. Another part sprung from the dust in God's busy hands when He molded us in His image and "set eternity in the hearts of men" (Eccl. 3:11, NIV). Our eternal souls were purposely fashioned for more than this world can spare. We long for "a better place—a heavenly one" (Heb. 11:16). In fact, the whole concept of faith assumes something we're hoping for and have yet not seen (see Heb. 11:1). In those ways, unrequited desire will be stuffed in the backpack of every sojourner marching to Zion. Not that I'm letting us off the hook. I confessed my abject sinfulness to God this very morning over a dust devil of resentment stirred up by an unmet longing in my heart.

Let me tell you something, Sister. This whole notion of human desire has huge implications. We touched on the subject matter in week two and talked about deformed desires. Let's add another term to it. In James 4:1, the word translated "desires" (NIV) and "cravings" (HCSB) is *hedone* from which we get our English word *hedonism*. "This term implies the very physical feelings associated with the bodily appetites. The sense is not of the inherent evil of desire but rather the conflict of desires that cannot all be satisfied simultaneously or without one canceling out the other."[1]

What part of this explanation of the word *hedone* most resonates with you and why?

"One canceling out the other" is crawling all over me like red ants. One of the things I've most longed for through the years isn't sinful. When I'm in a good frame of mind, I know that my lack has been far more profitable in my calling than a gain could have been. When I'm in a poor frame of mind, I don't care. I just want the thing. That's when it shifts from healthy desire to sinful desire even if the only action I take is bitterness.

Glance back at today's verses. "What is the source of wars and fights among you?" Our goal is to answer that question. "Don't they come from the cravings that are at war within you?" For me? *Yes, absolutely.* Verse 2 "You desire and do not have." *Correct.* "You murder and covet and cannot obtain." *Uh, negative on the murder part. Unless* James is using the term like Jesus in the Sermon on the Mount or the apostle John in his first letter.

Matthew 5:21–22

Look up the Scriptures in the margin and describe how they color the concept of murder.

1 John 3:15

James may indeed mean to use the term metaphorically in his letter. If you've put in much time here on earth, you've probably felt the kinds of things that qualify as murderous hate or anger. I certainly have. Those feelings can be lethal. If they aren't taken before God quickly for treatment, they strangle relationships to death. And, oh, it can be a slow, ugly death.

So, that's one way we can apply James 4:2. We better leave room for a literal rendering of the word "murder" (HCSB) or "kill" (NIV) in James as well. If we knew exactly when he penned it, we'd have a better idea which one he meant. If James wrote his letter very early in his tenure, murder was probably used metaphorically for anger, oppression, or overall carelessness. For instance, if people of means did not care about the poor, they were, in some respects, responsible for individuals perishing in their poverty. On the other hand, if James wrote his letter later in his ministry, he may well have intended the term "murder" literally. Uprisings of all sorts took place in Jerusalem before the city fell and the Temple was destroyed in 70 A.D. Lives were taken and kills often celebrated. Don't get the idea that the Jews *or* the new Jewish converts to Christ were always victims and never those retaliating.

The Jewish terrorists of James' day, "who pursued a campaign of violence against the Romans in order to restore the purity of Israel as a theocracy," were called *zealots*.[2] One commentator proposed that "the letter of James was most likely written in a period when murder was accepted as a 'religious' way to solve disagreements."[3]

James clearly begged to differ. Murder was dead wrong whether it rose from the heart or from the hand.

Let's shift to the next segment of verse 2: "You do not have because you do not ask." What a waste to let a voluntary deficit become the solitary reason for our unmet desires. For crying out loud, let's ask Him for what we need. If we don't feel like we can, let's ask ourselves why.

One way I can know from the get-go that my longing isn't godly is a reluctance to forthrightly ask Him for it. If I can't ask God for it, He's not in it. Remember James 1:17 and how we learned that, if it's a good gift, it's a God-gift? The reverse is also true. If it can't come from God, it can't be good.

Mind you, a wide gulf exists between feeling uncomfortable asking from God and feeling uncomfortable talking to God. We might not feel we can ask Him for something, but we can tell Him anything. Look at it this way: He already knows. We might as well talk to Him about it. When you're struggling with an unmet desire, Psalm 38:9 is your best friend.

Write the verse below.

You are nothing so inanimate as an open book before God. You are an open heart, warm and beating. All your longings, lackings, disappointments, and delays are ever before Him. He sees. He knows. He is never deaf to your sighs.

We still have one Scripture to go. According to James 4:3, what is another reason we might harbor an unmet desire?

In case you're trying to figure out whether you qualify for this malfunction, we're talking self-gratification here—the act of requesting something from God simply to have a lust fulfilled or asking with the guise of one motive when, really, it's another. According to Dr. Dan McCartney, "James is using [the Greek term *hedone]* broadly, including the desire not just for physical pleasures but also for the headier wine of power and honor."[4]

See the part of that sentence from the words "but also" on? Need an example of a desire for "the headier wine of power"? How about requesting an anointing from God so we can be admired and sought after? And, an example of "the headier wine of ... honor"? Requesting successes for our children so we can live our lives vicariously through them. But, let's be fair. For many of us Christ followers, it's not nearly so blatant. Often our motives are neither completely pure nor impure. They're such a concoction of the two that we don't know where one leaves off and the other begins.

God does, and I'm so glad He does. Nothing has the capacity to keep us out of trouble like the certainty of God's gaze piercing through all our pretense to the heart of our desires. Only He can sort out the blur of our motives. Let's have the guts to ask Him what's in our hearts and, when He reveals it, die to the self-gratification and live for the greater glory. That's when the attic door to the throne room of God will fall open and answered prayers will tumble out like boxed-up treasures.

Day Two

THE WORLD'S BEST FRIEND

FLASH FORWARD

"Whoever wants to be the world's friend becomes God's enemy." James 4:4

Today we're going to talk about friendship. Just staring at that 10-letter word shoots a sudden surge of warmth through my soul. All sorts of faces pop into my mind's eye. As I write to you from the third floor of our ministry building, I picture co-laborers in Christ working hard downstairs to serve women like you. My social life would be null and void without several bouts around the lunch table with them each week. They are my best friends. The word *friendship* also stirs up thoughts of the section in our church sanctuary where I've worshiped for years. From that eighth or ninth row from the front and seven or so seats from the aisle, I've watched children grow up and the rest grow older. I get tight, loving squeezes every Sunday from fellow church members ranging in age from 6 to 75. They are true friends.

What qualifies as friendship, anyway? After all, what concept has morphed more dramatically in recent decades? *Befriending* long since gave way to *friending,* but sometimes they're still the same. Like you, I've developed some bona fide, time-tested friendships floating through the streams of social networking. But an odd thing happens when I let the virtual kind replace the life-to-life variety. A profound sense of loneliness starts creeping up my spine like a vine of poison ivy. I just don't recognize it until I'm itching all over for something I'm missing.

James has his own take on friendship. To grasp it, we have to turn back the clock to an ancient perspective and find it timeless. First, read James 4:4-6 and write the segment in the back of your book.

Within this succinct, straight-to-the-point epistle, we find two diametrically opposed opportunities for friendship. I held out on the last phrase of James 2:23 until now so that we could paint a picture from the canvas of contrast. Compare James 2:23 to 4:4.

Record the two kinds of friendship in these passages on opposite ends of this spectrum.

Wait a minute. Didn't God so love the world that He gave His only Son? You can bet your life on that one, Sister. The "world" denotes different things in different Scriptural contexts. Take John 3:17, for instance. "God did not send

His Son into the world that He might condemn the world, but that the world might be saved through Him." Here and in other places like it, the "world" is the God-created, global harvest field of human hearts in need of the gospel.

On the other hand, "James uses the word *kosmos* ('world') … to refer to the system of evil controlled by Satan. It includes all that is wicked and opposed to God on this earth. James is thinking especially of pleasures that lure men's hearts from God. By its very nature, then, 'friendship with the world is hatred toward God.' To have a warm, familiar attitude toward this evil world is to be on good terms with God's enemy."[5]

How does that last sentence hit you? The thought of being "on good terms with God's enemy" is enough to make the hair stand up on the backs of our necks, isn't it? Then again, try to wrap your mind around the possibility that mortals could carry on a friendship with "the blessed and only Sovereign, the King of kings, and the Lord of lords, the only One who has immortality, dwelling in unapproachable light; … [who] no one has seen or can see" (1 Tim. 6:15-16).

Yet that's exactly what Abraham did. On three separate occasions Scripture testifies to that supernatural fact (see 2 Chron. 20:7; Isa. 41:8; Jas. 2:23). He's not the only one.

Take a glance at Exodus 33:11 and record the parties to and nature of the friendship described.

We have a natural propensity to flip the verse and picture Moses talking to God like a friend. The greater significance is the reverse: "The LORD spoke with Moses face to face, just as a man speaks with his friend." Before we sigh and suppose that divine friendship was limited to those Old Testament figures, let's splash a moment in the new wine of John 15:13-16.

Honestly, does Scripture get any better than that? Jesus not only chooses disciples. He chooses friends. Friendship with Jesus lasts and so does its fruit. The passages we've talked about so far today present what may well be the ultimate relationship a mortal can practice with God.

The key word is *practice* so circle it please.

Yes, Christians comprise the Bride of Christ and, in eternity, no higher honor exists but, in this earthly realm, that glorious identity comes with our salvation and not necessarily with our practice. Because I have received Christ as my Savior, I am part of His Bride whether I act like it or not. Friendship with God, on the other hand, comes only by practicing the elements of that beautiful, almost unfathomable relationship.

No one has greater love than this, that someone would lay down his life for his friends. You are My friends if you do what I command you. I do not call you slaves anymore, because a slave doesn't know what his master is doing. I have called you friends, because I have made known to you everything I have heard from My Father. You did not choose Me, but I chose you. I appointed you that you should go out and produce fruit and that your fruit should remain, so that whatever you ask the Father in My name, He will give you.
JOHN 15:13-16

Let's get a glimpse of how this concept plays out in Scripture and what insight can be gained about friendship from both ends of that spectrum—with God and with the world. Here are some key elements, first: *Faithfulness:* Glance back at James 2:20-23.

What did Abraham's faithfulness to God have to do with being "called God's friend"?

Faithfulness means all the things we think it does: *loyalty, trustworthiness, attentiveness.* Faithful also means *faith to the full.* The enduring message of James is that authentic faith cannot help but act; therefore, Abraham believed God and it was demonstrated in his obedience. Look again at John 15:13-16.

How can we parallel Abraham's faithfulness as we follow Christ?

Now, contrast friendship with the world. You surely didn't miss the way James began the portion of the letter we're considering today: "Adulteresses!"

If perchance your version has the masculine wording, it's not a literal translation of the Greek. True to his Jewish form, James meant to use the word in the Old Testament tradition of an unfaithful wife. From a spiritual perspective, idolatry is adultery. Take a good look at James 4:5. You'd have a hard time pegging a verse in this book with a wider variety of interpretations since James quotes more of a Bible theme here than a word-for-word Scripture in our canon. What does he mean?

The primary question on the table is whether or not the "spirit" God caused to live within us is the human spirit or the Holy Spirit. If it's the Holy Spirit, the verse echoes the Old Testament's references to the Lord as a jealous God. Biblically speaking, He is certainly that (see Ex. 20:5; 34:14).

On the other hand, if the "spirit" in James 4:5 is the human spirit (see Gen. 2:7), it conveys the idea that we were created with the capacity for tremendously strong desire and envy. Biblically speaking, that is also true. In the fullness of their original intent, our hearts are home to a passion for God, His fellowship, and His purposes. In a twist of their intent, our clamoring desires can open us up to unlimited false gods and worldly appetites. This is one of those gorgeous times when either major interpretation works. However, look at the verse that immediately follows: "He gives greater grace."

Think for yourself. Which interpretation of "spirit" in verse 5 do you think fits best with this follow-up in verse 6? Why?

Friendship means *closeness:* One of the most common Hebrew words translated *friend* is *rea.* It bears all the elements we imagine in friendship but can also mean *neighbor.* In fact, when Jesus illustrated loving your neighbor with the story of the good Samaritan, He drew from Leviticus 19:18 where rea is translated "neighbor."

Here we stumble on a big reason why our online and on-phone friendships can't offer the same satisfaction as the less-convenient face-to-face kind. The essence of close friendship is presence. That's one reason skyping met a need that talking by cell or e-mail couldn't touch.

What does all this have to do with befriending an invisible God? Recall Exodus 33:11! "The LORD spoke with Moses face to face, just as a man speaks with his friend." Moses never literally saw that face (see Ex. 33:23), but he came presence-to-presence with Him until his own face grew radiant. You and I are invited to come face-to-face or presence-to-presence with Christ, too, but that kind of intimacy only comes intentionally.

Face-to-face or presence-to-presence intimacy with Christ only comes intentionally.

Friendship with the world is vastly more convenient because we live on the crowded pinhead of its epicenter. It's as close as our nearest billboard and shouts at us from our grocery-store checkout. It holds hands with us in the movies and eats with us in front of the TV. It promises pleasure and often delivers. So, no one who lives in this world is a friend of God accidentally. We make a choice where we want to be most present. A hard choice.

Friendship means *insider knowledge:* Take one more look at the segment from John 15.

What is the distinguishing mark of friendship between Christ and His disciples according to John 15:15?

Close friends know things about one another that aren't common knowledge. One of the signs of deep friendship is that we tell each other secrets. Things that aren't posted on status updates. Things that don't get forwarded to our entire address list. Christ tells secrets to His intimate friends, too: "The secrets of the kingdom of heaven have been given for you to know, but it has not been given to them" (Matt. 13:11). He goes on to say that those who receive the revelation He gives them will end up receiving more and those who don't will lose what little they had.

The Bible is wide open for any eye to read, but the natural mind alone cannot discern it (see 1 Cor. 2:12-14). The Holy Spirit reveals "what eye did not see and ear did not hear, and what never entered the human mind … for those *who love Him*" (1 Cor. 2:9, emphasis added).

The irony of it all? The unspeakably high privilege of friendship with God makes a person humble and friendship with the world makes a person proud. The former He graces. The latter He opposes. Can you think of anything in this world scarier than standing opposite of God? Me neither.

The **NEXT LEVEL** with Melissa

PERFECTION, PART ONE

In my relatively short lifetime, I've participated in more than my fair share of conversations about "favorite verses" or "life verses," and to be honest, I've forgotten a good many of them along the way. You probably have too, especially if you dated, oops, I mean, "courted" during your Bible college years where the "favorite verse" moment is legendary and inevitable on any respectable first date. But, let's not go there, right?

I did however, once have a conversation I will not likely forget. In this memorable exchange a friend told me his *least* favorite verse in the entire Bible, a verse that made him angry and kept him up at night.

Guess what verse he cited? Matthew 5:48. You know that little verse? "Be perfect, therefore, as your heavenly Father is perfect." I know, I know, you were trying to forget about it, weren't you? I was too.

Now, I'm not advocating the practice of championing favorite or least favorite verses, but I do think we can learn a lot about ourselves if we are honest about which Bible verses make us uncomfortable. You know, those verses that just won't fit neatly in our theological systems no matter how hard we try, the disquieting verses that remind us of Mark Twain's legendary quote. "It ain't those parts of the Bible that I can't understand that bother me, it's the parts that I do understand."[1]

Now, you're wondering what this bizarre encounter has to do with James, aren't you? Well, if you're reading the Sermon on the Mount (chaps. 5–7 in the Gospel of Matt.) in a Bible with cross references, when you get to Matthew 5:48, if you are daring enough to glance at the footnote, just guess what you will find. James! James 1:4 to be exact. It just so happens that the attribute commanded in Matthew 5.48, the adjective τέλειος rendered "perfect," is actually one of James' favorites.

Mom mentioned the various meanings of the word τέλειος way back in week 2, but they are worth mentioning again here in a bit greater depth. While the word τέλειος in its most basic understanding means *attaining an end or purpose* or *complete,* it can be divided into two very broad categories with different shades of meaning.

First, τέλειος can refer to a person who is full-grown, mature, adult, complete, or an expert. Second, it can mean *perfect* or *fully developed* in a moral sense. Generally speaking, in the Septuagint, the Greek Old Testament, and various Jewish literature τέλειος tended to fall under the first category meaning something like *complete* while in Greek literature τέλειος tended to take on the moral sense meaning *perfect.*

If you have studied the difference in Hebrew and Greek thought, you may see a profound example here. Hebrew thought tended to be very concrete and practical, so the word τέλειος in the Septuagint meant mature or complete to the Jewish reader. Greek thought, and ours today, tends to be much more idealistic and philosophical. Hence Greek-thinking people would think in terms of some ideal level of perfection.

Some scholars view these meanings as radically different while others think the difference is only slight. For example, some would question whether much difference exists between a Christian who has attained "completeness" or "completion" and a Christian who has attained "perfection," while others would argue with fervor for a profound difference.

Bible translators must face these kinds of subtleties on a daily basis. Aren't you glad it isn't your responsibility?

Me, too.

Here is James 1:4 in several different versions. The words in italics are renderings of the Greek word in question, τέλειος. You can also see the repetition in the Greek text.

HCSB	"Endurance must do its *complete* work, so that you may be *mature* and complete, lacking nothing.
NIV	"Perseverance must *finish* its work so that you may be *mature* and complete, not lacking anything."
NET	"Let endurance have its *perfect* effect, so that you will be *perfect* and complete, not deficient in anything."
ESV	"Let steadfastness have its *full* effect, that you may be *perfect* and complete, lacking in nothing."
GNT	ἡ δὲ ὑπομονὴ ἔργον τέλειον ἐχέτω, ἵνα ἦτε τέλειοι καὶ ὁλόκληροι ἐν μηδενὶ λειπόμενοι

The English versions vary because τέλειος has a wide range of meanings. Though all these versions contain legitimate translations, I like the NET best because it shows the twofold repetition of the word τέλειος. Though a word can mean two different things in the same sentence, I think James intentionally uses τέλειος twice for emphasis. To highlight the wordplay in English helps.

How one translates τέλειος depends on the context. Translators disagree from text to text on precisely how this should be done. The text I mentioned earlier, Matthew 5:48, jars us so because the adjective is not only commanded of Jesus' followers but is also used to describe God Himself. Thus we rarely (if ever) find an English translation that renders the word anything but "perfect" in Matthew 5:48.

It turns out James actually uses the τέλειος word-group seven times (twice in 1:4; 1:17,25; 2:8,22; 3:2). The use of this word-group seven times probably is not accidental, since the number seven is the number of perfection and completeness. Some maintain, and I think they may be right, that James' use of this important word-group and concept is one of the keys to understanding his overall purpose, which is, to motivate his readers toward the goal of perfection. But what does perfection really mean for James? This is the question I hope you'll ruminate over before our next segment where I will seek to unpack the significance of this discussion.

Oh, and just in case you are curious, the reason I chose to discuss this topic in week 5 and not in weeks 1 or 2 is because it takes a working understanding of the gist of the whole book to be able to engage this discussion. At issue are not just the seven usages of the word τέλειος but the entire concept of perfection in the Book of James. We cannot confidently discuss the purpose of an author without first having a good understanding of the content of the book.

Day Three
ONE LIFE UNDER GOD

FLASH FORWARD

"Submit to God." James 4:7

He gives greater grace. Therefore He says: God resists the proud, but gives grace to the humble.
JAMES 4:6

"But He gives greater grace." Don't rush past those five words. Soak them in like rain on parched ground. Submerge yourself in them like a pitcher tipped and sinking to the bottom of the spring, surrendering to the weight of the water.

For the next little while, you don't need to be the pitcher so many people in your sphere of influence look to for filling. Simply receive. Say those five words out loud as if they were written just for you.

Think of all that weighs on you: yesterday's regrets, today's demands, tomorrow's plans. Let the pitcher become the cup, and don't just agree to be filled. Sink yourself in those five words until all your fears of failure, inadequacy, unforgiveness, and insufficiency drown.

Don't come up for air until those fears lay lifeless and cold on the bottom of the sea. Let Jesus lighten your burden until you float to the top, youth renewed, heart restored. He is enough. Let me say that again: He is enough. When you need more, you will have more. When your woes are great, His grace is greater. When our sins are vast, His mercy is deep. We cannot exceed Him. We cannot outrun Him.

Those five words from James 4:6 are life to us. Without them, we would destroy ourselves and destroy one another. The crown of earthy thorns pierced the tender face of grace and by His wounds we were healed. But, why, believer, do we have so much grace yet live in so much lack?

I hate playlike. If it's not going well, let's say so. I don't like philosophies and theologies that are sweet on our tongues but inept in our lives. I don't care how sacred they sound. If greater grace does not mean greater victory, deeper depths, gladder joy, and higher heights with Jesus right here in this land of briers, to quote the consummate James question, "What good is it?"

So, if God has greater grace and we have greater need, what is the hold up? How on earth does His lavish grace flood our canyon space?

James doesn't leave us fumbling in the dark. He takes us firmly by the hand, drops to his camel knees, and tugs on our arm to join him. There on that rug, the practical overtakes the mystical and we find a command we can well understand. James 4:7 begins: "Submit to God."

I hope to prove to you today through the power of Christ and the authority of His Word that there is nothing on this earth we'd really rather do.

Please read James 4:7-10 and write it on the appropriate page.

Go ahead and let the bath of your soul be disturbed over James 4:9, then be sure not to miss our next session. That portion is turbulent enough to warrant class time. Though you are handwriting all four verses, today's lesson will preoccupy us with verses 7 and 8, so let's get started.

In the margin list the five commands in these two verses. I'll supply the first and last. You jot down the three in between.

1. Submit to God.
2.
3.
4.
5. Purify your hearts.

James intentionally set the two commands, "resist the Devil" and "draw near to God," next to one another to display their active and opposing agendas toward us. Scripture by no means presents God and Satan as equal opponents. One is Creator. The other is creature. God could exhale the next breath and blow Satan to oblivion like a million shards of glass. The Father lets Satan exist and exert power and influence until Kingdom purposes are served. Satan is smart, vicious, and sly, but spiritually speaking, he also has a collar on his neck and a leash on his back, held tightly and rightly by the sovereign hand of God. Let's illustrate in a picture what James paints in words.

Draw a diagram toward the bottom of this space with the words "The Devil" on the far left hand side and "God" on the far right. Put your name in the middle. Leave plenty of room between your name and theirs. Next, draw a long arrow on each side of your name, pointing toward each of those forces.

James may well intend a wordplay in 4:6-7 using Greek synonyms. The HCSB makes it easy to spot by repeating the verb. "God resists the proud, but gives grace to the humble. ... Resist the Devil, and he will flee from you."

Note the repeated words. This lesson is about learning to be deliberate in what we resist and what we draw near. Look back at your diagram. As much as we may wish we could stay right there in the middle, we can't. Life is dynamic, full of pushes and pulls. We can't have one foot on God's side of the center and the other foot on Satan's without getting ripped like a zipper right up the middle. That's why James says, "Purify your hearts, double-minded people!" In other words, "Make up your mind and your motive and set your whole heart where you want it. You cannot have it both ways!"

Be deliberate in what you resist and what you draw near.

With that in mind, go back to your diagram and draw a question mark over each arrow to remind you to ask yourself which direction you want to go.

Satan doesn't have to talk us into sprouting horns and a forked tail to draw us his direction. All he has to do is fan our pride. That way, he doesn't have to go to all the trouble of actively opposing us. He has much more to gain if God does His brand of opposition instead. If we wonder how God could possibly oppose His beloved child, let's role-play a moment. Let's say each of us is a really wise parent with a rebellious, arrogant child. Think how we'd want to say something like, "I'm not going to help you destroy yourself. I will oppose you if that's the way I can help you." Of course, we're blind to events in the heavenly realms and seldom realize that God's sudden resistance to our swollen, wounded ego is still an act of love.

Satan hopes that, instead of repenting, we will get defensive with God when He rises up against us in our pride. He hopes we'll think God has suddenly turned on us and we'll grow stiff-necked and hardhearted.

If we're in Christ, the Devil cannot have our souls. ... For us, eternity is settled.

The scariest part of all is that, when we resist God, we draw near to Satan. Now, don't misunderstand what that means. If we're in Christ, the Devil cannot have our souls. To keep that truth ever before you, go back to your diagram and draw a cross right over your name. For us, eternity is settled. Satan can, however, wreak havoc with our indecisive, prideful earthly lives and sift us like shredded wheat.

"So submit to God" (Jas. 4:7, NET). The Greek word *hypotasso* means to "put in order under."[6] I don't know about you, but I'm not a very orderly person naturally. Most of the time I work in what a co-worker calls creative chaos. My desk looks like a grenade has gone off in my office, and I have about three drawers at home that nearly throw me into self-loathing every time I open them. (That is, if I can open them.) And don't get me started on the garage. Or my purse. So, that's why I love this overarching statement we can make, based on the definition at the beginning of this paragraph:

If it's under God, it's in order.

I'm not saying we couldn't all stand to fold our pajamas in that overstuffed drawer, but only one brand of order is necessary to open the door for grace outpoured. Put your sweet self under God. Entirely. No arms and legs kicking out to the sides. Knees to the floor. Eyes to the skies. Hands open wide. Death to your pride. Here we run aground on the reason the Devil flees.

He doesn't flee from us, Beloved. He runs from God who is standing right there over us every time we submit. Take off your shoes. That's holy ground.

Glance back at your diagram for a moment. Pitch philosophies aside and let's talk practicalities. Picture yourself right there in the middle of that drawing in the very situations that loom over you at this time.

Go ahead and write a few key words over your name on the diagram representing some of your present challenges.

Both God and your adversary, Satan, have very distinctive wills concerning what you should do in those situations and where you should stand. (See 2 Tim. 2:26 for a reference to the Devil's will.) You and I have one of two directions we can move. The question? Do we submit to God and draw near to Him because He's the less toxic of the two tyrants? Why can't we just be independent?

What light does Matthew 16:23 shed on Satan's schemes to frustrate our walk with Christ?

Satan doesn't have to convince you and me to do *his* will for our life. He only has to tempt us to demand our own. God has something bigger for each of us than our human minds can hug. Something eternal. Something that will still matter when our bones have turned to heaps of dust.

- God knows everything about you and every matter concerning you. Nothing is hidden from His sight. So submit to God.
- He is always looking out for your ultimate good and takes your hurts personally. So submit to God.
- He is holy and worthy and incapable of abusing His divine authority over you. So submit to God.
- He knows when your motive was right but your mouth messed up. So submit to God.
- He knows exactly how to work terrible into good. So submit to God.
- He loves you completely and unconditionally and will never let you go. So submit to God.
- He knows the well-deliberated plan for your life and how all things must fall into place for you to fulfill your destiny. So submit to God.
- He will never put to shame those who trust in Him. So submit to God.

The Devil is trying to steal from you and destroy you and make it look like it was all your idea. *So, Girlfriend, submit to God.*

Which "submit to God" encouragement most spoke to you? Why? I'd love to hear the girls camp out on this one.

Day Four
ONLY ONE JUDGE

FLASH FORWARD

"There is one lawgiver and judge who is able to save and to destroy. But who are you to judge your neighbor?" James 4:12

A strange phenomenon can happen when man's awareness of his significance stirs into a lofty peak. It's a twisting of sorts that happened first in the garden. Adam and Eve were created in the image of God and, since no other creatures on the face of Eden were like them, they no doubt knew it. They surely cherished such divine esteem, and they should have. God wills that we all would. After all, He dripped enough ink on the ancient scrolls of both testaments to leave no doubt that "God created man in His own image; He created him in the image of God; He created them male and female" (Gen. 1:27).

In this strange phenomenon, the one who marvels at the wonder of his own significance can either feel humbled or so superior that the trip from Imago Dei to Dei seems one small jump. We can go from a blessed awareness of expressing the image of God to playing God and not even feel the shift.

The trip from Imago Dei to Dei seems one small jump.

Nothing muffles conviction as effectively as entitlement. The mind-set morphs something like this: I am created in the image of God. ➤ I represent God. ➤ I am Junior God. ➤ I am like God.

We're on a slippery slope by the first shift to the right.

We must check our hearts and His Word the very moment we feel compelled to represent God. With the second shift—*I am Junior God*—we jump off the cliff but, Heaven help us, we don't even know we're falling. By the third shift, the only remedy is hitting the ground so hard that we break to pieces then the real God gets to show up and put us back together.

For the sake of all those in our sphere of influence, the shorter the period between playing God and breaking to pieces, the better. Again, these mind-sets are not necessarily conscious. Sometimes we're aware they exist only by catching ourselves in an act, thought, or speech that belong to God alone.

Before we turn to James, I'd love to show you something in Psalm 139. Turn there while I issue an extremely important disclaimer. By no means am I suggesting at any point that the psalmist David, the man after God's own heart, spun off into the mentality I highlighted above. He was under the inspiration of the Holy Spirit. Instead, I'd like you to consider a similar scenario from the perspective of someone operating out of the flesh rather than the Spirit.

I am created in the image of God. ➤ I represent God. ➤ I am Junior God. ➤ I am like God.

Glance over the first 18 verses of Psalm 139. What caused the psalmist to marvel?

Is any psalm more beautiful? Is any Old Testament truth more awe-inspiring? Anyone who takes these words personally and speaks them back to his or her Creator with genuine humility will enter into true wonder.

Now, read Psalm 139:19-22, the words following the segment you just considered. What "if only" did David present to God?

Here in Psalm 139, we see a man under the inspiration of the Holy Spirit pose an "if only" from a pure heart. But if it were me instead and I was operating out of my fleshly nature, I might have twisted off right there at the end with this spin: "God, why don't You deal with those awful people? Don't I hate the people who hate You? Why don't You hate them, too?" My fleshly rendition put another way: *Lord, since You're all knowing, You know how terrible people are. Especially Your enemies! Why don't You deal with them? You should hate these people like I do!*

Now, we're ready for James 4:11-12. Read the segment and write it on the appropriate page. Would you admit with me that, among God's titles, "Judge" is one we can feel most entitled to? Thankfully, we don't always give in to the temptation but leaving the judgment to the Judge can be a hard job at times, can't it? Sometimes God just seems late getting to the bench.

Notice that the context in James 4:11-12 is judgment among believers. Our protagonist deals with the issue several times in his letter and each time from the standpoint of astonishment. Slander among siblings in Christ should not be the fare of the day but shocking and appalling.

Slander among siblings in Christ should not be the fare of the day but shocking and appalling.

OK, I'll put myself out there if you will. At times I wonder how this or that person in Christ is getting away with something he or she appears to be doing. The hypocrisy is gross and particularly revolting coming from yours truly. For the life of me, I'm hard-pressed to find many fellow Christians who have sunk as low into sin and bondage as I have. Judgmental thoughts toward other believers put me at greater risk of trouble with God than those old sins did. In the Gospels, nothing curdled Christ's blood more than self-righteousness. (See Luke 18:9-14!)

Now it's your turn to put yourself out there. How are you most prone to play judge?

So maybe we could all use today's lesson, even if we're feeling particularly cheerful toward our fellow siblings. Tomorrow's a new day and a new opportunity to grab a gavel and try to hammer somebody with it. Let's take the pulse of James again because it throbs with life throughout this epistle.

What exactly is "the royal law" stated in James 2:8?

When we studied the phrase several weeks ago, we looked at its original home back in Leviticus 19:18. Wait until you see how steeped James must have been in the entire segment surrounding it.

Read Leviticus 19:15-18. Sound familiar? Which part of it coincides with the verses we're studying in James 4:11-12?

Trying to read James without the Old Testament is like trying to sift the white out of a bag of bleached flour.

James was a man who knew the Scriptures. Trying to read his letter without the Old Testament is like trying to sift the white out of a bag of bleached flour. In our next session together, we will talk more about slander especially in regard to a brother or sister in Christ. Know for now that the Greek term translated "slander" in the NIV also means "criticize" (HCSB) and "speak against" (NASB). The original word doesn't leave us room to excuse ourselves because what we said was simply the truth. To James, if it was said critically or against another person, it was sin.

Dangerous sin at that. Widen the lens again from slander to the broader range of judging. Does Matthew 7:1-2 make you squirm like it does me?

Read Christ's words and jot down why we're much safer exercising mercy toward one another.

James knew what he was talking about. "Mercy triumphs over judgment." Another segment that makes a powerful point about human judgment is Romans 2:1-2. "Any one of you who judges is without excuse. For when you judge another, you condemn yourself, since you, the judge, do the same things. We know that God's judgment on those who do such things is based on the truth."

To make sure we got a major point from Romans 2:2 above, what do "we know" about "God's judgment"?

Spending years engrossed in women's ministry can make you privy to more personal information about people than you ever thought you wanted to know. Occasionally you can get jaded and wish you could take your purse to somebody's husband's head, but then you stumble on the other side of the story and sit bug-eyed. Suddenly, the situation is not nearly so cut and dry.

God bases His judgment on truth. I just stopped and said those words out loud. I wish you would, too. *God bases His judgment on truth.* Thank goodness. He even knows the truth about what motivates people in the inmost places to act out as they do.

God alone knows the origins of our wrecked-up emotions. Our inconsistent actions. He alone knows when we're sincere and when we could win an Oscar®. Girlfriend, He alone even knows if our hatefulness was hormones. He knows if someone needs to get a grip or go to a specialist for medication. He alone knows if a spouse's unrelenting pornography problem warrants a period of separation. He alone knows beyond all doubt if a person's apology was sincere.

We have to bend our knees and go eyes-to-the-skies and say, "God, You alone know. So, You alone please lead."

Humanly speaking, a fine line can squiggle between wise discernment and sinful judging. We need discernment in the worst way and we also need to know when to distance ourselves from spiritually dangerous people. (We should *always* separate ourselves from physically dangerous people.)

Humanly speaking, a fine line can squiggle between wise discernment and sinful judging.

According to Dr. Douglas Moo, "In light of the argument of these verses, therefore, we should note that James is not prohibiting the proper, and necessary, discrimination that every Christian should exercise. Nor is he forbidding the right of the community to exclude from its fellowship those it deems to be in flagrant disobedience to the standards of the faith, or to determine right and wrong among its members (1 Corinthians 5 and 6)."[7]

Then, where on earth is the line? The harder but most biblically appropriate answer is seeking to walk in the Spirit. True discernment breeds wisdom. Sinful judgment breeds a condemning spirit. When I've judged, I feel rotten later if not sooner.

First Corinthians 2:15 can help us put some black ink to the white page: "The spiritual man makes judgments about all things, but he himself is not subject to any man's judgment" (NIV). People who walk in the Spirit judge "things." Not people.

"There is one lawgiver and judge who is able to save and destroy. But who are you to judge your neighbor?" (Jas. 4:12). We hear You, Lord. Please help us. This one can look gray from way down here.

The **NEXT LEVEL** with Melissa

PERFECTION, PART TWO

This morning I happened across the following words from a popular author, "Perfectionism is the voice of the oppressor, the enemy of the people."[1] Nothing surprised me about that quote. In fact, I could have written it myself, just not as beautifully. I mention the quote to show I'm aware that talking about perfection is unpopular and virtually heretical in some circles. I don't enjoy talking about it either, but no doubt our modern discomfort with perfection influences the way we read texts like Matthew 5:48 and James 1:4.

Patrick Hartin says the problem is we uncritically transpose modern understandings and preconceptions about perfection to ancient documents. He reminds us that we must first discover the biblical understanding of perfection before we disregard the idea as unacceptable.[2] Because of this understanding barrier, we need to define our terms.

Hartin, who wrote nearly 200 pages just on the theme of perfection in James, posits that James' understanding of perfection can be captured best by our English term *integrity.*[3] Scholars have also suggested *authenticity, completeness, wholeness,* and *consistency.* My favorite is *wholeness* because I think it best captures James' threefold purpose for enduring trials in 1:4: to be "perfect and complete, lacking in nothing" (NASB). Notice James uses three synonyms for emphasis.

Does James really believe in his heart of hearts that we can be perfect, complete, and lacking in nothing? On one hand, he's pretty honest about the human struggle. In 3:2 he confesses, "We all stumble in many ways." Though James may leave open a hypothetical possibility for perfection ("If anyone does not stumble in what he says, he is a perfect man, able to bridle the whole body as well" [NASB]), that James really believes folks can attain this is doubtful because in 3:8 he says, "No one can tame the tongue; it is a restless evil and full of deadly poison" (NASB).

Even though James is realistic about our inability to tame our tongues, he does not refrain from preaching about the necessity for us to do so. As Moo points out, James presents perfection or completeness as the ultimate goal. Even if he is not claiming that believers will attain the goal, we "should not 'lower the bar' on the expectation James sets for us."[4] His call to perfection is not about achieving an abstract state of moral perfection but about living holistic lives before God.

James packs the theme of perfection in his five chapters, but room allows us to discuss only three ways he integrates it. The most obvious is James' understanding of faith. James gets a bad rap for his concept of faith, but for him faith is necessary. Only people who ask in *faith* for wisdom can expect to receive anything from God (see 1:5-6). Only requests offered in *faith* will restore the sick (see 5:15). Yet no matter how vital and necessary faith is, it remains incomplete without works. Faith is perfected by works; and for James only perfected faith is truly faith.

My favorite example that demonstrates James' concern for wholeness comes when he exclaims: "You believe that there is one God. Good! Even the demons believe that—and shudder. You foolish man, do you want evidence that faith without deeds is useless?" (2:19-20, NIV). Demons affirm the first part of the great commandment; they believe God is one and they fear God. But to affirm only the first part of the Shema is not enough. To affirm the creedal statement without loving God with one's entire being (see Deut. 6:5) is to keep *half* of the Shema. James calls us to obey it all: "Hear, O Israel: The LORD our God, the LORD is one. Love the LORD your God with all your heart and with all your soul and with all your strength" (Deut. 6:4-5 NIV).

Lack of follow-through on this point marks the difference between life and death, light and darkness. Another excellent example of the theme of wholeness is James' twice-used word διψυχος "double-minded" (NIV). Mom mentioned that he may have coined the term.

A double-minded person is halfhearted in his commitment to God; his loyalties are divided, making him unstable, incomplete, and vulnerable to weakness. As Bauckham points out, the double-minded, in attempt to please both God and the world are "attempting a 'both and' which cannot be true unity, but only an impossible compromise."[5] The prophet Elijah once asked the people of Israel gathered on Mount Carmel: "How long will you go limping between two different opinions? If the LORD is God, follow him; but if Baal, then follow him" (1 Kings 18:21, ESV). The loyalty James demands echoes the all or nothing sentiment of the prophet Elijah.

James' concept of Christian wholeness is also firmly rooted in the One God. To live a life of perfection is not to make all A's or to never miss a Sunday at church; rather, it is to live a life true to our identity as children of an utterly untemptable God who never changes, shows no partiality, and has no darkness in Him at all.

To live a life of perfection is not to make all A's or to never miss a Sunday at church; rather, it is to live a life true to our identity.

James may echo Jesus' command to imitate God in Matthew 5:48 ("Be perfect, therefore, as your heavenly Father is perfect") but "only in a way that is consistent with creaturely distinction and difference from God."[6] That last part is crucial to this conversation.

James' stress on wholeness is a countercultural challenge for our postmodern society where "interesting" folks are fraught with contradictions.

> Wholeness cannot be found simply by accepting whatever one is in all one's disordered and distracted existence. Wholeness is a goal towards which one can move only in relation to a centre which is already whole and from which one can gain wholeness. This means moving in one direction rather than others. It means rejecting values and behaviour which are inconsistent with the goal. … The quest for wholeness is important today because it responds to another cultural trend, which accepts and even celebrates the fragmentation of life in the name of openness and diversity.[7]

James questions my alternate desires and motivations while challenging me to forsake the alternate worldviews I unsuccessfully try to combine with my Christianity.

Day Five
WHAT IS YOUR LIFE?

FLASH FORWARD

"Instead, you should say, 'If the Lord wills, we will live and do this or that.' " James 4:15

This is one of those times when I feel a little sheepish about asking you to handwrite the daily Scripture segment. It's a tad long today. No, you're not off the hook but, in case good intentions help, I really would write it for you if I could. But I can't. So, go ahead and read James 4:13-17, then write it.

Why is the attitude that we control our destinies and can enforce the fulfillment of all our plans a little absurd?

Do you think James is saying that making plans of any kind or jotting notes on monthly calendars is wrong? If not, what do you think he's saying? Or, if so, what are his grounds?

When I was in junior high, I could hardly wait to start smoking cigarettes. One of my parents smoked and so did several of my older siblings. It seemed a rite of passage for getting to linger at the dinner table and talk like you had something substantial to say. I come from a clever family, and they were never cleverer than when they were passing around the Pall Malls. I loved how one of them could balance a cigarette in between two fingers and hold her coffee cup, too, all with the same hand. Smoking was just a matter of time for me. I practiced on several occasions with my older sister so I'd be ready to inhale like a professional when the time came for me to go public.

Once when Gay and I stole Mom's old Buick Skylark, we lit up and drove right down Main Street in our small town. It was a bold move since my Dad, the retired Army major, worked on Main. He was a former smoker who, by then, gagged and coughed violently at the smell. Needless to say, he kept his lingering at the dinner table to a minimum. Sure enough on that ill-fated drive down Main Street, we caught a glimpse of the Major. When my sister yelled, "Duck!" she failed to suggest pulling the cigarette out of my mouth first and I was eons from thinking for myself. I bent straight over and burned a hole right through the hem of my navy-blue pleated skirt. Talk about pungent. Dad would have heaved his head off. I only smoked a time or two after that. I meant to get back to it but just never did.

The NET words James 4:14 like this: "What is your life like? For you are a puff of smoke that appears for a short time and then vanishes." The word James used means mist, vapor, or fog. Smoke also works as a sound translation but, admittedly, not the aforementioned variety. Since I memorized the verse out of the NET, however, I've pictured that table setting no few times. Something about all the puffing stuck. Anyway, we're real people here and messier than we wish. Praise God that His Word still applies.

The verses we contemplate today can have a profound effect on the way we view human existence if we're willing to adjust our lens. Let's sit first in the main audience James intended to address. To do so in the most applicable way, lift James 4:13 out of its ancient context and set it squarely in our culture.

In the margin describe what these kinds of people look like in our world, even if they are *us*.

We've come to know James as a man of the sacred text. At this moment in his letter, he might have drawn from any number of teachings found in the Old Testament or from the mouth of his half brother.

Read Psalm 39:4-8 in the margin and underline every similarity in this Old Testament segment to James 4:13-17.

On the other hand, perhaps Proverbs 27:1 was on James' mind: "Don't boast about tomorrow, for you don't know what a day might bring." When was the last time you were reminded that you don't know what a day might bring? Keep in mind that this kind of fresh astonishment can come to us in positive moments as well as negative.

Jesus' teaching shouts over the noise of our consumerism. In your own words, what did Christ say in Luke 12:15?

Consider a few things we can take away from James even if we've tried to guard our hearts against pursuing prosperity over the presence of God.

This life goes fast. A vapor. A mist. Picture someone exhaling warm breath into the freezing cold. There it is. Then it's gone. Dr. Dan McCartney's commentary on James 4:14 raised my eyebrows and caused me to think. He points out that, in answer to the question, "What is your life?" we "would expect the answer 'It is a wisp.' But James does not say, 'It [your life] is a wisp'; he says, 'You are a wisp.' "[8] Whew.

Mind you, the metaphor is not about our value. Never forget that we were significant enough in God's eyes to offer the life of His one and only Son. The metaphor is about our length of time here. When circumstances are really

LORD, reveal to me the end of my life and the number of my days. Let me know how short-lived I am. You, indeed, have made my days short in length, and my life span as nothing in Your sight. Yes, every mortal man is only a vapor. Certainly, man walks about like a mere shadow. Indeed, they frantically rush around in vain, gathering possessions without knowing who will get them. Now, Lord, what do I wait for? My hope is in You. Deliver me from all my transgressions; do not make me the taunt of fools.

PSALM 39:4-8

rough, we can find comfort and courage in the verses about life's brevity. We can think to ourselves, *In the eternal scheme of things, He's only asking you to do this hard thing for a few minutes. You can be faithful. It's not that long!*

Every new day is willed by God. Fix your eyes on the portion of James 4:15 that says, "If the Lord wills, we will live ..." Go no further than that until you absorb the implications of those seven words. Maybe this is too simplistic, but I'll take a chance on it that we might grasp something profound in the practical. Your eyes opened to earthly life this morning because God still wants you here. Mine did, too. If the Lord did not will for us to be alive in these tents of mortal flesh, we would have seen His face by now. We live because the Lord wills.

You see, these verses aren't just polemical. They are strangely beautiful. Ephesians 1:5 adds another layer to the complex will of God. It says that we've been adopted as God's children "through Jesus Christ, in accordance with *his pleasure* and will" (NIV, emphasis added). He not only willed for your eyes to open to earthly life again today, He was pleased.

God is the one with the real plan. "You don't even know what tomorrow will bring" (Jas. 4:14), but He indeed does. We have all sorts of plans jotted on our calendars pertaining to the next year, but they're mostly based on theory. His is the only day-timer based on certainty. That's one reason why spending time with God in His Word in the morning is so vital. He wants to prepare us for the reality of our upcoming day. Not our theory. Here are a few verses that give us insight into His side of the plan. In the margin record your first reaction to each one, even if you're troubled.

Reaction

Psalm 139:16: "Your eyes saw me when I was formless; all my days were written in Your book and planned before a single one of them began."

Reaction

Acts 17:26-28: "From one man He has made every nationality to live over the whole earth and has determined their appointed times and the boundaries of where they live. He did this so they might seek God, and perhaps they might reach out and find Him, though He is not far from each one of us. For in Him we live and move and exist, as even some of your own poets have said, 'For we are also His offspring.' "

Reaction

Ephesians 2:10: "We are God's masterpiece. He has created us anew in Christ Jesus, so we can do the good things he planned for us long ago" (NLT).

Psalm 33:10-12: "The LORD frustrates the counsel of the nations; He thwarts the plans of the peoples. The counsel of the LORD stands forever, the plans of His heart from generation to generation. Happy is the nation whose God is Yahweh— the people He has chosen to be His own possession!"

Reaction

I loved this commentary excerpt. See if it speaks to you, too: "This life cannot be properly understood without considering the spiritual realm, a realm that impinges on and ultimately determines the material realm in which we live day to day."[9] Maybe we've heard this until the holes of our ears have grown over, but God is the only one looking through every layer and at every implication. He also looks upon a situation in context of what *is*, what *was*, and what *is to come*. His deliberations don't just involve immediate impact. He sees our place and our positions amid carefully woven generations.

What difference, if any, might these thoughts make in your present struggle?

Perhaps we get to end with the very best part. Remember the most immediate group of people James singled out in 4:13-17? His words were a serious indictment against those who arrogantly plan and pursue personal prosperity, priding themselves on their successes and risking their souls. Heaven is appalled by such human audacity but watch this irony: " 'I know the plans I have for you,' declares the LORD, 'plans to prosper you and not to harm you, plans to give you hope and a future' " (Jer. 29:11, NIV). You might want to circle the word "prosper."

Are you ever tempted to think that this whole human thing is rigged? That God formed us with souls that seek well-being yet shuns us when we do what comes naturally? What if we understood down to the marrow of our bones that His is the only plan that really does end up prospering us? What if we really believed Jesus when He said that those who insist on finding their own lives will lose them and those who lose them for His sake will find them (see Matt. 16:25)? What if we really believed that, if we seek God's kingdom and His righteousness, everything else of true value would be given to us, too (see Matt. 6:33)? What if we really believed that "He did not even spare His own Son but offered Him up for us all; how will He not also with Him grant us everything" (Rom. 8:32)? What if we really believed that "godliness is profitable for all things, since it holds promise for the present life and also for the life to come" (1 Tim. 4:8, NASB)?

What if?

What if we really believed that God is not only great, He is good?

viewer guide | session six

Part One will center on a troubling verse purposely saved for this session. Part Two will encourage us in our journey with one another.

Part One: James 4:9-10

When is it appropriate to turn our joy into gloom?

- When we've consciously ____________ the _______ of the Lord for the _______ of the ___________. "Whoever ____________ to be the world's friend makes himself God's enemy" (Jas. 4:4, NET).

- When we don't _______ God _______________.

  "Or do you think the scripture ____________ ______________ when it says ..." (Jas. 4:5, NET).

- When we're ______________ in or about ______ ______.

- When _______________ sincere believers is our idea of ______________.

Part Two: James 4:11

Premise: In a religious pop-culture where we hear so much and see so much, ____________ is one of our top risks. Five top reasons not to get ___________:

1. Jesus is still flagrantly ______________ _________.

2. Real _________ are doing the real _________ all over the real _________.

3. The appetite to _________ ________________ is increasingly _______________.

4. Some long-standing _____________ are ______________ ________.

5. God will _________ your _________.

WEEK SIX

POWERFUL EFFECTS

Day One
GETTING & GIVING

Day Two
TO PROVE THE LORD'S BOASTS

Day Three
A YES KIND OF YES

Day Four
SOMETHING WE CAN DO

Day Five
TO PRAY & TO BE PRAYED FOR

Day One
GETTING & GIVING

FLASH FORWARD

"Look! The pay that you withheld from the workers who reaped your fields cries out, and the outcry of the harvesters has reached the ears of the Lord of Hosts." James 5:4

Take a deep breath, Sweet Thing. We've got one more garlic-strong word from the Book of James. You've stayed the course like a champ, and I am so much the better because of your companionship. Even if this lesson is confrontational, I think you'll find yourself intrigued and involved as we navigate our bare feet through a briar patch of conviction.

Today is also the last of the six-verse segments you'll be asked to handwrite in the back of your book. Day 3 only calls for one verse so, if you need to save part of today's writing portion for that time, go right ahead. Just keep track of it. And, by the way, I care about you and pray that God is kindling a fresh fire in your soul through this journey. To squirm while we learn at least means that we're listening.

Read James 5:1-6 and write it on page 223.

Search for two anthropomorphisms, when James gives inanimate objects humanlike attributes. List them here.

Here are other occasions when Scripture does something similar. Look up each and record the anthropomorphism.

Genesis 4:10

Job 31:38-40 (see v. 38)

Mark 4:39-41 (see v. 41)

Fascinating, isn't it? Call it a metaphor if you want, but we have a God before whom "the mountains and the hills will break into singing ... and all the trees of the field will clap their hands" (Isa. 55:12). A God who commanded Ezekiel, "Prophecy concerning these bones and say to them: Dry bones, hear the word of the LORD!" (Ezek. 37:4). In that prophetic vision, they clacked and rattled till they were bone-to-bone, then grew tendons and flesh, and drew breath from four winds.

Before you think all the wild imagery ended with the Old Testament, hail a God who can open the mouths of stones to praise His Son if men remain silent. If humankind fails in compassion and lets oppression prosper, the land itself will tattle and the blood of innocents will wail. God will hear and, in time, He will act. He will also call see-no-evils to serious task.

Look back at today's text from the Book of James. If the instructions were clear, you noted earlier that the first of two anthropomorphisms in James 5:1-6 was the rust or corrosion on the silver and gold. Kurt A. Richardson explains: "The rust is personified. The rich had willfully refused to listen to the voice of justice calling for fair wages; now the rust was given a voice declaring their guilt. Thus, instead of paying wages, the gold and silver would be paid to the rust. The hoarded wealth would help pay for the trial against them. Again, there was hope for repentance because the judgment was not yet here; nevertheless, to borrow a metaphor from the testimony of John the Baptist, 'The ax is already at the root of the trees ...' (cf. Luke 3:9)."[1]

The idea of the hoarded wealth paying for the trial against the hoarder is an unexpected twist.

The idea of the hoarded wealth paying for the trial against the hoarder is an unexpected twist, isn't it? The second anthropomorphism is the pay withheld from the workers who'd earned it. Peter H. Davids calls it "the cry of the wrongfully imprisoned wage."[2] Picture it. When we withhold money that someone else has earned, our wallets become jail cells for wages beating on the bars for release. Remember that portion of Leviticus 19 that James keeps drawing from? Here we go again!

What does Leviticus 19:13 say?

Glance back at James 5 and split hairs between verses 3 and 4 for a moment. Technically, they call out two different indictments against the unrighteous rich. While we pick them apart, I want you to know something. Tears streamed down my cheeks while studying for part of this lesson.

I am terrified at the thought of being counted among those who hoard treasure in these last days. The command not to withhold pay from a worker is clear-cut. Paying people for their work should go without saying and is often a privilege and a joy. I'd give my co-workers every limb on my body if I couldn't scrounge up their wages. It's the hoarding part of this section of James that turns my stomach. Where is the line between saving and hoarding?

I'm blessed to be married to a man who believes in the biblical concept of saving, but how much is enough? According to James, a point can come when we've "gorged [ourselves]" on wealth or goods as in a day of slaughter.[3] What exactly is that point? Here's another question I have: how much spending within his or her means can a person do out of sheer love of family without displeasing God? Where are these lines? While in the throes of self-evaluation, I dropped my head in prayer and asked God if He was unhappy with our household over our relationship to finances or possessions.

Where are the lines?

I don't want to shove conviction where it doesn't fit but, if you're feeling queasy, too, would you be willing to ask Him something similar?

Trudging through the remaining research, blowing my nose, and trying to hold my heart open, I ultimately responded to God in three ways:

1. I repented of sin.
2. I restated a vocal confession that everything we possess is His alone and that He is welcome to do with it anything He pleases. I asked Him again to please make us lavish givers, then I also asked Him (squirming) to take anything that is dishonorable or displeasing to Him.
3. I became awash with an odd sense that my tears were appropriate whether or not I was in grave rebellion regarding these issues.

The first two came with fresh force, but they were not new practices. Let's elaborate on the third response because it may cause the bigger eye-opener.

Follow this stream of thought with me: Sometimes we feel badly and come to tears because the Devil harasses us. Call that spiritual warfare. Sometimes we feel badly and come to tears because we're self-condemning. I could be awarded an honorary doctorate in that sick skill. Neither demonic harassment nor self-condemnation originate with God or bring Him honor. But let's take this path a few more steps that do.

Sometimes we feel badly and come to tears over conviction. That's a gift from God meant to lead us to repentance and relief and, ultimately, to joy and blessing. If that's what we get from today's lesson, so be it! If we've blown it, let's own it. Still other times we may come to tears over the pure fear of sinning against God. For our purposes today, let's label them *fear tears.*

Maybe sometimes they're a gift. After a few hours of wet-faced grappling, I decided that maybe God wanted me to shudder at the thought of falling into sin. Most of us women in this prosperous Western world should quake in our spiked heels at the thought of 1 Timothy 6:10. "The love of money is a root of all kinds of evil, and by craving it, some have wandered away from the faith and pierced themselves with many pains." *Day 1 continues on page 162.*

The **NEXT LEVEL** with Melissa

THE ELEPHANT IN THE ROOM

A question races through my mind as I read James 5:1-6. *Who are these rich people James scathingly rebukes?* Three possible answers fit the question: (1) *any* and *all* rich people who misuse their wealth; (2) rich *Christians* who misuse their wealth and live self-indulgent lifestyles; or (3) rich *non-Christians* who misuse their wealth and oppress the Christian community.

Mom applied the text according to the approach in option 1. In this segment I want to present an alternative reading by arguing that James rebukes rich non-Christians who oppress the Christian community (option 3). Several issues in the text argue for this view.

First, the form of this segment resembles a prophetic oracle, especially one that pronounces judgment on pagan nations guilty of oppressing Israel (see Isa. 34:1-4). The similarity in form adds support to the idea that this segment is written to the rich outside the Christian community. As Douglas Moo says, James "unrelievedly attacks these people, with no hint of exhortation."[1]

Second, in verse 7, with a very noticeable shift in tone, James says, "Brothers, be patient until the Lord's coming. ... Strengthen your hearts, because the Lord's coming is near" (Jas. 5:7-8). The obvious shift in tone and in audience (from "you rich" to "brothers") both supports the argument that James' readers were not among the "rich people" of verse 1.

Third, together verses 1-6 and 7-11 follow a common pattern in biblical literature. Moo gives the example of Psalm 37 where the psalmist encourages the oppressed righteous who are described as humble, afflicted, and needy (v. 11,14) to give up their rage since the wicked will soon be no more and the righteous will enjoy abundant prosperity (v. 11).[2] The flow of thought in our text is similar; James encourages oppressed believers to be patient until the Lord's coming when He will vindicate the righteous.

All of this data, however, leads me to believe that the rich of James 5:1-6 are not Christians but non-Christians. Wealthy landowners who unethically misuse their wealth and take advantage of their needy workers epitomize these rich unbelievers. Naturally, my goal is to discuss the ramifications of such a view. So, I started writing a segment on an alternative reading of James 5:1-6, one that would sort of exonerate Christians from personally absorbing this text.

After hours wrestling with this passage, I'm puzzled because, for the life of me, I can't seem to figure out whether James can even conceive of a *rich Christian*. Do you see the irony that we who are both professing Christians and among the world's richest are grappling with a text in which the author comes so close to equating Christians with the poor? This is the elephant in the room for Western Christians grappling with James' text. The more I read James 5:1-6, the more it reminds me of Matthew 6:19-24.

> Do not lay up for yourselves treasures on earth, where moth and rust destroy and where thieves break in and steal. ... For where your treasure is, there will your heart be also. ... No one can serve two masters; for either he will hate the one and love the other, or else he will be loyal to the one and despise

the other. You cannot serve God and mammon (NKJV).

The vivid moth-eaten clothes and the rusted gold and silver in James' oracle make me wonder: *Is James actually assuming the content in Matthew's text?* Gold and silver don't rust, right? Apparently, in God's economy, even earth's version of imperishable and incorruptible corrodes.

The Matthew text is so key here because it argues that when we store up treasures on earth, we actually demonstrate our allegiance to the world and not to God. No way exists to combine these two ways of life: they are alternative and competing realities.

So what does James' text mean for those of us who are both wealthy in the global economy and professing Christians? At this point even my alternative reading provokes the same question Mom asked: "Is this text speaking *to* me or *about* me?" Wasn't this the question that my clever little alternative reading was supposed to evade? Egads.

Working through this text, I asked myself: *What do contemporary Western Christians have in common with wealthy and unethical landowners of the first century?* I didn't receive a vision from God, and I could totally be wrong, but I think the answer is greed.

The other day a professor I highly respect commented that he could not remember the last time he heard someone give a talk about the pitfalls of avarice. Avarice, in case you wonder, is an immoderate desire for wealth. He mentioned that our entire culture is based on this attribute; wanting more is completely acceptable, if not desirable.

I didn't think about it until later that day when I joined a fun and popular online community where you catalog various things you love. Basically your profile is a virtual pin board where you gather and collect various online images of beautiful and inspiring things: food, people, products, places, interiors, and even words.

Nothing is wrong with this Web site but the insatiable greed in my own heart corrupted the well-meaning experience. After several compulsive days pinning gorgeous images on my virtual pin board, I had to deactivate my account. I couldn't stop thinking about things I don't own or extravagant vacations I've never been on, and I was daydreaming through my next purchase(s).

My experience with this Web site coupled with the professor's insight reminded me that I need to protect myself from avarice. Like the sin of lust, when we know something cultivates immense greed in our hearts, we need to cut ourselves off from the source, whether or not the source is sinful. Even if I pay all my bills and rightly pay every laborer I employ, is not my superfluous spending on myself when others need the basics for survival a contradiction of loving my neighbor as myself?

Excessive desire to possess things is hardly innocent and left unrestrained will result in a harvest of evil. We all know the statistics about global poverty. We simply cannot be obedient disciples of the Lord Jesus and continue to willingly choose self-indulgence, all the while ignoring the desperate needs of others. We need to get serious about guarding our hearts from this ugly sin.

We don't have to have it to crave it. Human pincushions. That's what we'll be if we don't shield ourselves. We pledge allegiance to the hope of prosperity for more than security. We also crave more stuff. My research surfaced an eerie phrase that ancient Latin moralists used: *"amor sceleratus habendi."* It means "the accursed love of getting."[4]

Sit on that a second. How could such a love be "accursed"? Plan to discuss this one with your group.

Yep. Some things are worth fearing. When I talked over the idea of *fear tears* with Melissa, she related the concept to an occurrence not long ago among a circle of friends. One had gotten entangled in an affair and left her husband. Melissa described how a mutual friend in this same circle could hardly pull herself together over the news. "She didn't just cry over their broken marriage, Mom. She cried over the thought that all of us have the potential of doing something that destructive. It scared her half to death." If that fear became a liquid shield against a wave of temptation, could it be appropriate?

Not all fear is unhealthy. Some of it qualifies as reverence.

Not all fear is unhealthy. Some of it qualifies as reverence. Maybe the apostle Paul felt the kind we're discussing in 2 Corinthians 11:3. "I fear that, as the serpent deceived Eve by his cunning, your minds may be seduced from a complete and pure devotion to Christ." Look at it this way: We lock our doors at night to keep out intruders. Fear can be wise.

As God would time it, the writing of this lesson's conclusion fell on the day after my birthday. My buddies at work threw a staff party yesterday and gave me such fun gifts. I didn't feel a hint of disapproval from the Lord. I did something the moment I got home, however, as a direct result of those fear tears two days earlier. I filled a bag with nice things I already owned and gave it straightaway to someone who'd enjoy them. The Book of James has a way of crawling all the way into our closets and drawers, doesn't it?

Here are two things we gorged ones might do to make room in our lives for love and obedience.

Use it or abuse it. Several sources suggested that the sin of hoarding is more than just having. It's having without using. The wickedness accelerates in the waste. In part, hoarding means withholding what we don't even use from others who'd treasure it. All of us are accustomed to the saying "use it or lose it" but, the fact is, we're going to lose it all anyway. We're not taking one ounce of this stuff with us when we die.

If we get something, give something. This one's not for all of us. Some of you doing this study today truthfully aren't engorged with possessions. Your lives are already lean. You get a hall pass on this one unless the Holy Spirit leads you otherwise. The rest of us might consider saying, "I've got all I can stand and possibly use. If I get something new, something else needs to go."

Oh, please don't take these ideas as just two more laws to keep you roped in legalism and sulking in self-loathing. When we close this book of the Bible, may our heads be the wiser, crowned by one royal law: *Love your neighbor as yourself.*

Day Two
TO PROVE THE LORD'S BOASTS

FLASH FORWARD

"You have heard of Job's endurance." James 5:11

I love what we've been doing here for the last five weeks. Even when the words fly into our faces and make us confront our own duplicity and false piety, many of us feel most alive in the thick of learning. I suspect you're one of those since you're still here. Even when we're not as glad about what God says, as long as He's talks and empowers us to hear, our relationships with Him teem with spirit and life. He is so faithful, Sister. I pray we'll wrap up this lesson with that one binding truth wrapped around our ailing hearts.

Please read James 5:7-11 and write the segment on the appropriate page. Glance back at the first sentence in verse 7.

What is the word we love to hate? ______________________

If you wrote "brothers," you might consider counseling. If you wrote "patience," you're in really good company. This segment of Scripture will be our complete preoccupation in session 7 at the end of this week, so if we ignore a portion that seems really rich, that's probably why.

In the meantime, list three reasons why patience might be infinitely more challenging in our current culture?

1.

2.

3.

Yesterday afternoon I got an e-mail from a loved one who has a jaw-dropping testimony. Scores of people need to hear it and, several years out of the pit, she's ripe to tell it. In her letter she shared with me her understandable desire to move on out there in volunteer ministry and leave behind her day job. Mostly, I told her to listen to God and watch for Him to open and close doors, but I also shared with her that, try as you may, you can't rush training.

Really, what I meant was this: you can't rush *God*. You can't push Him. You can't pull Him. You can't tug Him or taunt Him. If He has a mind to linger right where He is, you can't budge Him one inch. You can, however, try to go without Him; but, chances are, you'll come back because, if you really have a heart for God, you'll be miserable beyond His blessing.

If you really have a heart for God, you'll be miserable beyond His blessing.

From a throne's-eye view, the point is not just getting us into our proverbial lands of promise where we bear much fruit. The point is developing the spiritual muscle on our way so once we receive it, we are strong enough to keep it. The hardest part of possessing the land is defending it. A person has hardly begun to have a real fight on her hands until she starts serving in her full-throttle giftedness and effectiveness. She who proves a threat earns an enemy you can bet will do everything he can to make her sorry. Nothing in the visible realm is a greater reality than the unseen battle raging over our heads.

Ask Job. God love him, no one in history has been the bull's-eye for more sulfurous darts. He makes us look like we're whining over someone kicking a little dust on our pedicures. James says in today's segment, "You have heard of Job's endurance." As a matter of fact, we have but, since he thought the man's story was worth revisiting, let's follow suit.

Incidentally, the mention of Job's name in James rises from the page as a refreshing departure from the unrighteous rich who raised the writer's ire. Job was both prosperous and genuinely pious. The irony is that he'd done nothing wrong to provoke such suffering. He became a target precisely because he did so many things right.

Flip to Job 1:8 and record the question the Lord asked Satan:

How did the Lord describe Job in the same verse?

Now, read Job 1:9-12. What claim of Satan became the springboard for the most legendary test in human history?

Day 2 continues on page 166.

The **NEXT LEVEL** with Melissa

THE OLD TESTAMENT & JAMES 5:11B

I'm delighted Mom lacked room to address James 5:11b because it fascinates me. It says: "You have heard of Job's endurance and have seen the outcome from the Lord. The Lord is very compassionate and merciful." Exodus 34:6-7 is the background for the two adjectives πολύσπλαγχνος ("very compassionate") and οἰκτίρμων ("merciful").[1]

In Exodus 34:6-7 God reaffirmed His covenant faithfulness to adulterous Israel after the golden calf incident. He passed before Moses declaring: "Yahweh—Yahweh is a compassionate and gracious God, slow to anger and rich in faithful love and truth, maintaining faithful love to a thousand generations, forgiving wrongdoing. ... But He will not leave the guilty unpunished." God's self-proclamation became a platform that Israel's leaders stood firmly on for years to come.

In Numbers 14, fearful and grumbling Israelites threatened to return to Egypt. God furiously threatened to destroy them but Moses interceded by invoking, word for word, the formula from Exodus (see Num. 14:18).

We see a similar phenomenon in Israel's great prayer in Nehemiah. By this time Israel had all but forsaken the law and intermarried with foreigners. Lamenting, the people appealed to the Lord's description of Himself after the golden calf incident (see Neh. 9:17,31).

In a gorgeous articulation, the psalmist creatively extrapolated on the original formula: "The Lord is merciful and gracious, slow to anger and abounding in steadfast love. ... For as high as the heavens are above the earth, so great is his steadfast love toward those who fear him; as far as the east is from the west, so far does he remove our transgressions from us (Ps. 103:8-12, ESV).

Last but not least, Jonah was reluctant to preach repentance to Nineveh precisely because of Exodus 34:6-7. He knew God's bent toward forgiveness, so he fled to Tarshish to prevent God from pouring mercy on the cruel Assyrians. When God did forgive Nineveh, just as Jonah suspected, the prophet protested, "That is why I made haste to flee to Tarshish; for I knew that you are a gracious God and merciful, slow to anger and abounding in steadfast love" (Jonah 4:2, ESV).

Remarkably, James is one of few New Testament authors to echo this famous theological refrain. He does so to encourage believers to persevere knowing God will both restore the righteous and judge the guilty (see Jas. 5:6).

James also links the outcome or purpose of the Lord in the Book of Job to the core of God's character. Although Job pleaded with God for answers, he never got one. In fact, he got a question: "Where were you when I laid the foundation of the earth?" (Job 38:4, ESV). Ultimately Job's fortune was restored twofold, but we never know why God granted Satan's request to wreak havoc on a righteous man. God never gave Job the backstory; He never told Job he's the subject of a cosmic bet.

Like Job, we endure cycles of suffering and restoration, sometimes without the slightest clue as to God's specific purpose. Being a child of God means accepting God is fully free to do as He sees fit and abiding in His core attributes. Our heritage as God's people is to stand firmly on the platform of God's person, knowing He moves exclusively in ways consistent with His covenant commitment, even if we cannot grasp them with finite minds.

Kurt A. Richardson writes, "Here is the sobering truth about the nature of trials in the life of righteous persons, that God allows them to be tested in order to prove their faith. … In some ways their endurance proves the Lord's boast in them."[5]

Write those last six words in the margin.

Those words keep rolling around in my bleached-blond head. The Lord boasting in any mortal is almost unthinkable. We feel like our feet of clay mainly just leave muddy footprints. Consider the even wilder part: God can't lie (see Num. 23:19), so His boasts are always based on truth. He permits and sometimes even dictates difficulty for those in whom He boasts so that they will prove what He already knows is true. The Lord does not put us to tests that He knows in advance we don't have the wherewithal to pass. He boasts in His faithful followers then lets them prove Him right. Sometimes the person most shocked by the proof is the human put to the test.

How will we ever know what He's accomplished in us if He doesn't show us? And how will Satan otherwise be proved a liar in our eyes?

Oh, I know, I know. This one's always easier on paper than it is on the pavement. We always feel more romantic about suffering when we're not doing it. Still, the thought that God might boast in us puts a shot of iron in our anemic souls, doesn't it? The irony may be that no greater compliment exists in this temporal realm than for God to say, "Have you seen my servant ________________________?" (If you have the courage, fill in your name. Yes, it makes me nervous, too.) Let's jump to the good part of the story.

Read Job 42:1-12 carefully, like a person on pins and needles, biting her nails about how the story might turn out. Check here when you finish: ☐ Job never realized the battle that had taken place over his life in the unseen realm. He did, however, arrive at some conclusions.

Write a one-sentence summation of Job's response in 42:1-6.

Pay extra close attention to the next several instructions. First, please write Job 42:5 in this space:

Now, turn back to James 5:11 and fill in the following blanks accordingly.

"You have ________________________ of Job's endurance and have ________________________ the outcome from the Lord."

Draw an arrow between each of the corresponding words in Job 42:5 and James 5:11.

The repetition of the words "heard" and "seen" in these two texts may be profoundly deliberate. Some scholars believe James' exact wording recalls that of Job himself. James may have even intended to make the dramatic shift from the original first-person statement "I had heard … but now my eyes have seen" (Job 42:5) to second person: "*You* have heard … and have seen" (Jas. 5:11, emphasis added).

That's the thing about the suffering of God's own faithful children. The end He desires to bring about is never just for those involved. It's also for those who *hear.* For those who *see.*

What exactly was the "outcome from the Lord" (Jas. 5:11) according to Job 42:12?

I promise this final hunt for today will be worth the trip. How does Isaiah 61:7 tie to Job in 42:12?

Job won't be the only child of God who receives a double portion instead of his shame. Out of God's great mercy, may this glorious reversal be equally true for those of us who live in the wake of the Incarnation. After all, we are coheirs with Jesus Christ, the only begotten Son of God.

Beloved Sister, God is the only one who knows the end from the beginning (see Isa. 46:10). Maybe we've heard this so many times that it ceases to move us. Oh, that hope would fall afresh on us as we reaffirm this sublime reality: God knows how everything will turn out. And, for every single person who belongs to Him, it turns out *well*. We are not the exceptions. Neither our sins nor our sufferings are big enough to offset the ordered outcome.

God knows how everything will turn out. And, for every single person who belongs to Him, it turns out *well.* We are not the exceptions.

In Job 19:23, a man in cavernous anguish cried out, "I wish that my words were written down, that they were recorded on a scroll." Well, as it turned out, they were. And from his pen came one of the most beautiful confessions to ever erupt from a broken heart in a quake of hope.

> I know that my Redeemer lives, and that in the end he will stand upon the earth. And after my skin has been destroyed, yet in my flesh I will see God; I myself will see him with my own eyes—I, and not another. How my heart yearns within me! (Job 19:25-27, NIV).

Day Three

A YES KIND OF YES

FLASH FORWARD

"Above all, my brothers, do not swear, either by heaven or by earth or with any other oath. Your 'yes' must be 'yes,' and your 'no' must be 'no,' so that you won't fall under judgment." James 5:12

Today we focus on only one verse, so let's get straight to it! Read James 5:12 and write it in the back of your book and, if you saved any of your writing for today, be sure to catch up. Just think. I'll be completely out of your hair in one and a half weeks of study. Considering the source, your hair may not be nearly as big when I'm gone.

The kind of swearing James is talking about in 5:12 doesn't fall under the category of four-letter words that could earn you a mouth washing back in the day. Profanity tumbles easily into the ills of the unbridled tongue in James 3, but the swearing in James 5 is a whole different sort.

What appears to be the issue at hand in James 5:12?

See, I have set the land before you. Enter and take possession of the land the LORD swore to give to your fathers Abraham, Isaac, and Jacob and their future descendants. **DEUTERONOMY 1:8**

Perhaps the most interesting part of our oath-taking concept today is the way it changes from era to era in the Scriptures. The Old Testament makes numerous references to God swearing to take certain actions (see Deut. 1:8, for instance). The Book of Hebrews makes reference to the original oath God made to Abraham and suggests why God is in a league of His own on the subject.

How does Hebrews 6:13 say God is unique regarding oaths?

That verse makes me happy every time I see it. I love that God would have to lie to go second and, since He can't lie, He stands alone, preeminent in all things. Furthermore, He's not only the first. He's also the last. He's not just the beginning. He's also the end. No one is above Him and, below Him, all will bow. Imagine existing for an eternity and never running into a single soul who can outdo you. No one is greater. No higher name by which to swear.

Interestingly, in the Old Testament God's people were not forbidden to take oaths. A section of Scripture in Deuteronomy keeps circling through my thoughts, looking for a place to land. Let's give it a glance together.

Read Deuteronomy 10:17-21. What are the first four words of verse 21?

In the margin list all the reasons residing in that five-verse segment why God is worthy to be our praise.

In terms of our subject matter today, Deuteronomy 10:20 encapsulates the instruction we'll find most intriguing. At the end of the verse, what did Moses tell them to do?

Although oaths and vows differed, don't think they didn't face sobering cautions under the Old Covenant. The common denominator was God as the object. Generally speaking, an oath was swearing by Him and a vow was swearing to Him. Once they named God as their witness, they'd lifted the matter to a very sober level. Deuteronomy 23:21-23 is a powerful Scripture that I don't recall studying with any seriousness before.

Read it and record its basic instructions.

Perhaps Ecclesiastes 5:4-6 in the margin is more familiar to us. That's some serious stuff, isn't it? For the sake of simplicity, you might think of an oath as taking a vow (or swearing) by God. So, how did James, under the inspiration of the same Spirit, go from taking oaths seriously (per the Old Testament) to not taking any at all? Discovering that answer is our task at hand, and I think you'll enjoy the hunt.

The process of attitude change about oaths with James probably began back in (drumroll, please) Leviticus 19. For the rest of our lives, I pray that we'll associate the Book of James, in all its colorful Jewish flair, with chapter 19 of Leviticus. When James lifted the royal heart of the law from that body of Scripture, he seemed to leave every adjoining artery attached. It's like a New Testament heart transplant with all the dangling valves. I never pictured growing such an affection for a portion of Leviticus, did you? This time James' target would have been verse 12: "You must not swear falsely by My name, profaning the name of your God; I am Yahweh."

Keep in mind that much of their oath taking involved future events. They would swear to take this or that action under certain potential conditions. James raised an objection by the end of his fourth chapter: "You don't even know what tomorrow will bring—what your life will be!" Perhaps to him, to swear at all was to take the risk of swearing falsely since when push came to shove a man could not know what his life would be like.

When you make a vow to God, don't delay fulfilling it, because He does not delight in fools. Fulfill what you vow. Better that you do not vow than that you vow and not fulfill it. Do not let your mouth bring guilt on you, and do not say in the presence of the messenger that it was a mistake.
ECCLESIASTES 5:4-6

When was the last time someone asked you to swear not to tell something before you knew what it was? Did your stomach ever sink once you learned the information because you knew it needed to be told? Maybe it was a suicide threat or something unethical at work. Or, maybe you learned that your best friend's husband was having an affair. Suddenly you were thrown into an insufferable quandary: do I break my vow or withhold vital information?

Those would be reasons enough for a leader like James to insist on avoiding oaths, but they pale against the most prominent reason why he took his stand. He caught it like a virus from his own half brother. As you stare at James 5:12, you have before you "the closest thing to a direct quote from the Jesus tradition in any text in James."[6] See for yourself. Below you have Christ's words in Matthew 5:34-37 in the first column and James' words in the second.

Read each carefully. Circle every corresponding portion, then draw a line between them to connect them.

"I tell you, don't take an oath at all: either by heaven, because it is God's throne; or by the earth, because it is His footstool; or by Jerusalem, because it is the city of the great King. Neither should you swear by your head, because you cannot make a single hair white or black. But let your word 'yes' be 'yes,' and your 'no' be 'no.' Anything more than this is from the evil one."
Matthew 5:34-37

"Above all, my brothers, do not swear, either by heaven or by earth or with any other oath. Your 'yes' must be 'yes,' and your 'no' must be 'no,' so that you won't fall under judgment."
James 5:12

We've compared the two texts, so now let's contrast them. Go back to the columns and place a *D* by every difference then list them in this space.

There is no truth in him. When he tells a lie, he speaks from his own nature, because he is a liar and the father of liars.
JOHN 8:44

The final lines of the two segments are probably more in sync than they seem. Jesus said, "Anything more than this is from the evil one" and James said, "So that you won't fall under judgment." Satan couldn't be happier to assist a person to a place of divine judgment or chastisement. Either is icing on devil's food cake. But why would the evil one focus particular activity on the area of swearing or oath taking? John 8:44 answers that question for us.

Satan is ecstatic when we make a vow and don't keep it. Can you think of any reasons why? Think of a few past the obvious.

We've circled back around to the first question in our lesson today: What appears to be the issue at hand in James 5:12? Truthfulness, that's what. Swearing or oath taking suggested the same thing then that it does now: holding ourselves to a truthfulness that otherwise wouldn't be our standard. Oaths say in effect, you can trust me because I'm qualifying it with this oath but, without it, all bets are off.

As bishop over the earliest New Testament church, James' sights were set on building a healthy, functioning community of faith. Relationships, regardless of their appearance, can never be stronger than the bond of trust between them. Their "yes" had to be their guarantee. As James B. Adamson puts it, "swearing is necessary only in a society where the truth is not reverenced."[7] For mortals like us, swearing doesn't indicate our trustworthiness. Ironically, it indicates our lack of it and should flag suspicion in the other party.

Glance back at the columns on page 170 and in the margin note every other thing a person could swear by besides Heaven (another way of saying God).

Here's something I didn't know until studying for this lesson. In James' culture, as in ours, people might shy away from swearing to or by God but, since they still wanted to attest to their trustworthiness, they'd swear by something else sacred but less risky. We hear something like it when a person says, "I swear by my mother's grave."

To "swear by your head" is probably new to us and may be worth a grin since Christ referred to hair color. We might say "never swear by your hair" and for good reason since nothing on our body would be less reliable for some of us. I'll speak for myself. God alone knows my true hair color.

This was the catch: if they were caught in a lie or without follow-through, they'd often cop out by saying that they swore by something less binding and, thereby, claim a loophole. Christ called out this very brand of game playing in Matthew 23:16-22. By Jesus' day, personal oaths were so flagrantly misused that He commanded them to cease altogether. James echoed His sentiments.

Personal oaths were so flagrantly misused that Jesus commanded them to cease altogether.

So we don't leave any confusion, note the qualifier of *personal* oaths. Neither the Gospel of Matthew nor the Book of James forbid the use of oaths in legal proceedings. We are not in sin when we "swear to tell the truth" in a court of law or vow to be faithful for better or for worse at the wedding altar. Furthermore, the apostle Paul, under direct inspiration of the Spirit, several times called God as a witness to the truth of his statements.[8] How his practice differs from the prohibitions in today's lesson is not enormously clear, so we're better off attributing it to the sovereign purpose of God. Anyway, the Scriptures he wrote could qualify as their own form of legal documentation. So, I'm curious to know what stood out to you in today's lesson. Anything?

I've come to a few conclusions. Certainly we should leave "I swear to God" completely out of our vocabulary. Those who have lived by that oath or, terrifyingly, lied by that oath have done so at considerable risk. Now that we know better, we do better. We've also learned today to drop the use of lesser oaths while we're at it and to simply let our word be our bond. It would be just like God to give us the privilege to be tested soon but only so we can pass with flying colors. Let's keep an eye out for a test and, if we're still on our journey together, share it with your small group.

OK. Would you mind ending with a quirky story not meant to be taken too seriously? My best friend Dodie and I were inseparable from the sixth grade through the ninth. We shared a locker, clothes, secrets, burgers, and almost everything else in our young, limited lives, except boyfriends. That was a definite no-no. When we were in the seventh grade we took a vow with one another never—and I do mean never!—to let our toenails go unpolished, except to change colors. We agreed that such a gross oversight would render the offender a complete fashion failure. We reaffirmed our vow with countless shades of polish, talking a hundred miles an hour and fanning our toenails dry.

After dropping by to see me one day, Dodie was killed in a head-on collision. I heard sirens after hugging my twin friend's neck but didn't know until later that one of those ambulances had her in it. I'm not positive my heart ever completely healed because perhaps a friend is never dearer than at age 15. No matter what takes me back to my home state of Arkansas, I make the trip to Dodie's grave and often still cry just as I could now. One thing helps me pull myself together. I always step out of my shoes, stand with my toes on the edge of her grave marker and say, "I'm keeping my promise. Are you?" Then I grin and blow my nose. I've been painting these toenails a long time now. Sometimes I think they could use some air but, then again, girlfriend took an oath.

OK, have you done anything similar? If so, share it here and perhaps with your small group.

Day Four
SOMETHING WE CAN DO

FLASH FORWARD

"Is anyone among you suffering? He should pray. Is anyone cheerful? He should sing praises." James 5:13

I keep thinking about an encounter a few days ago. While a tight layover in a sprawling airport left no time for fooling around, it takes a better woman than me to resist the smell of fresh buttered popcorn. I stepped up to the counter to place an order and the young cashier's face was frozen in the oddest expression. She wasn't smiling or frowning.

"I've seen you before," she said, then hesitated for a moment, flipping through a mental file. "Yeah. On TV." Her reaction was different than the one you and I might have upon meeting. We'd both feel such kinship, like good friends who'd been apart too long. She did not know my name. She did not know what to call the show or the kind of message. She glanced off to the side and her deep brown eyes filled with tears. "I watch sometimes."

I would have hugged her if the counter hadn't been so tall. Instead, I stretched my hand over the top of it to clasp hers. As much as I tried to engage, she did not say another word or look back up at me. When I tried to pay for my popcorn, she just waved her hand to motion a *no.*

I fought unexpected tears all the way to my gate. Something big was going on in that heart. Something painful. The airport was like a stomped-on anthill that day. As all of us bumped shoulders, hurrying to our flights, I wondered how many of us were faking like we weren't dying inside.

How many of us were faking like we weren't dying inside?

A sense of anonymity makes agony insufferable. To hurt that badly and still go unnoticed can leave you feeling swallowed alive in a cold, black hole: *No one knows I'm here. Why should I feel hope when no one around me does? Why would I ever be well when my whole family has gone mad? If a god is really up there, how would he ever find me?* Faceless. Nameless. Then comes the Son of Man, looking for you like no one else exists.

He loves us like that. Please read James 5:13-16 and write it. We are closing in on the last of James' letter even if we don't want to be. Since we only have a few verses remaining, let's sit up straight and pay special attention.

If you're like me, the way you close an important letter is of extra significance because the ending is meant to elicit the emotion or response you want to linger. That's the part we might obsess over most because the close of any personal document carries special weight. God employed a form of benediction common among the Greeks. They'd often put the finishing touches on a letter with a health wish of sorts, not unlike those in several New Testament letters. James is almost certainly emulating that style in his prescription for the sick, but he may intend to include the whole remaining segment in his wish for their wellness. Either way, his benediction is unique and beautiful and we'll begin walking through it together today.

In verses 13-14, James roll-calls people in one of three conditions. What are each of the conditions and the prescriptions that go with them?

1.

2.

3.

One of the hardest things our ears can ever hear is when the doctor says, "There's nothing we can do." Have you ever faced those words? If so, explain when in the margin.

Perhaps you'd agree that helplessness is its own form of demoralization. If we do not guard ourselves, we can inject a victim mentality right into the vein of our relationship with God. We can decide that we're mostly powerless down here on planet Earth and that God is going to do what God is going to do, no matter what. We can default into the mentality of pawns and puppets and resolve that our only real decision is whose victim we're going to be.

God could seem to become the lesser of two evils.

God could seem to become the lesser of two evils. The lesser oppressor, so to speak. We could reason that we're at least better off being God's victim than anyone else's. Better to spend eternal oppression in Heaven than in hell. The repercussions of this kind of mentality are toxic and completely invasive in our lives. Nothing will remain untainted by it.

Listen carefully to James and other inspired writers of Scripture: there is rarely nothing you can do. Being still and knowing He is God is a long shot from nothing. Trusting in a God you cannot see is a long shot from nothing. Holding your tongue is a long shot from nothing. Being patient is a long shot from nothing. Counting it all joy is a long shot from nothing. Submitting is a long shot from nothing. Confessing sin is a long shot from nothing. Resting in Christ is a long shot from nothing, and hear this one really loudly: praying is a long shot from nothing. But let's save that one for tomorrow.

The health wish at the end of the Epistle of James is the furthest thing from an edict of helplessness. According to the half brother of Jesus, there is always something we can do. Think of a to-do list on a poster entitled "How to Have a Healthy Soul," hanging on a wall in a doctor's waiting room. Number 1 might be, *Lose the victim mentality.* Number 2 might be, *When you're feeling powerless, don't let anyone tell you there's nothing you can do.*

Now, take particular note that each element on the to-do list deliberately engages us with God. That, beloved Sister, is our ultimate health measure. Number 3 might be in all caps like this: *LIVE LIFE WITH GOD*.

To stay alive and to thrive, the branch must abide in the Vine. Even the instruction in James 5:14 to summon the elders for prayer when we're sick is a flagrant means of placing us before God. Whatever you do, please don't miss the part of the health wish written specifically to the "cheerful" in verse 13. The Greek can also be translated: "Is anyone feeling good?"[9] "Is any merry?" (KJV). "Is anyone happy?" (NIV). "Is anyone in good spirits?" (NET). The Message poses the question this way: "Do you feel great?" As a matter of fact, sometimes I do. Do you?

Name a few reasons why we can't be healthy believers if we disassociate all of our good feelings or merriment from God.

We can know we're in bondage when we realize that, somewhere inside of us, we're convinced feeling good is a sin. Christianity does not cause us to develop a sudden allergy to happiness, despite what some would argue to be our reputation. Life can be bone hard but a skewed belief system can turn it into granite. Glance back at James 5:13 and fill in the following blank.

"Is anyone cheerful? He should ____________________."

Can you think of any reason for this particular prescription to the glad-hearted? If so, record it.

All of us who don't sing well wish we could. Thank goodness vocal skills are not prerequisites to good health in the benediction of James. Sometimes I've been known to make up songs to God to personalize them. With a wide grin, may I say it always goes better in my mind than it does out of my mouth?

One problem is that I try to make the lines of the song rhyme. Awkward, to say the least, especially if I'm incorporating the names of loved ones. How many words, for instance, rhyme with *Amanda?* The next line is forced to include "demand a" and, invariably, I'm at a loss to think up what. Another problem is that I make numerous, unplanned key changes. Hope as I may to return to the original tune, I've wandered too far. Perhaps no one else is the least amused, but I'm almost too tickled to type.

Let's just say you're better off with someone else leading worship. But I can indeed make a joyful noise and, if you're my kind of singer, so can you. And we must, if we're to thrive here.

We will run our race on one leg if we only engage with God in our suffering or sickness. He is the author of life "From Him and through Him and to Him are all things" (Rom. 11:36). We woefully shortchange our earthly experience if we, with well-meaning hearts, relegate Christ to the top of our list of priorities and demand that He stay put.

We've been taught to live by lists of priorities but, if marriage is second on my list, what will happen without Christ's intervention? If children are third on our list, what will become of them if Jesus sticks to our church category and doesn't invade our parenting? If friendships are fourth on our list, how can we ever hope to break our cycle of broken relationships without Him who is wholeness incarnate? Colossians 3:4 doesn't call Jesus number one in your life. It says He "*is* your life" (emphasis added).

We have an open invitation to a divine invasion.

"All things are open and laid bare to the eyes of Him with whom we have to do" (Heb. 4:13, NASB). If it has to do with us, then it has something to do with Him because it is "Him with whom we have to do." We have an open invitation to a divine invasion. If we're willing, God is our song when we are happy, our escape when we are tempted, our hope when we're despairing, our joy in tribulation, our strength in weakness, and our immortality in dying. Ultimately, He Himself is our health.

"The LORD be exalted. He takes pleasure in His servant's well-being" (Ps. 35:27). May the song of our hearts echo the words of the wonderful old hymn: "It is well, it is well with my soul."[10]

If we're willing, **God is our song** when we are happy, **our escape** when we are tempted, **our hope** when we're despairing, **our joy** in tribulation, **our strength** in weakness, **and our immortality** in dying. Ultimately, He Himself is our health.

Day Five
TO PRAY & TO BE PRAYED FOR

FLASH FORWARD

"The urgent request of a righteous person is very powerful in its effect." James 5:16

Today is our final official day of homework centered in the Book of James. Can you believe it? If you took the level 3 challenge, you're also about to write your final entry in the back of the book. Please also answer the question at the end of the allotted space. If you've left any gaps, perhaps you can catch up over week 7 since we won't have any further writing assignments. Let's get right to it so you hardworking, handwriting women can feel a healthy dose of well-earned satisfaction.

Everybody gets a pat on the back today. Pressing through six full weeks of in-depth study is an accomplishment, Sister. May God gain much glory from transplanting this potent book of the Bible into the marrow of your faith. Please read James 5:17-20 and write the final segment. Heads-up: we will discuss the last few verses in the sessions rather than today.

To set the stage for today's lesson, look carefully at James 5:13-18 in your Bible (a slightly different segment than the one you read earlier). Count how many times you find any form of the word *pray*.

No need to ask James, "What's your point?" I asked a section of women in my Houston group to stand every time they heard a form of the word *pray* as I read this section. They popped up like a massive Jack-in-the-Box a whopping six times. The point was not lost on us. You, either, I hope.

If the Book of James were a strand of pearls, we've come to the place where it would circle back around our necks and clasp. Right here he links the end to the beginning. Remember the opening in James 1? Here at the end of his letter, James loops back around to some of those earliest concepts, specifying several kinds of tribulation: *Is anyone suffering? Anyone sick?* Then he offers the prevailing prescription: *Prayer! And the kind with faith!*

Our James was tagged "camel knees" because he knelt and prayed so long that he developed thick calluses.

Most of us don't mind being told what to do as much if we know that the teller practices what he preaches. Our James was tagged "camel knees" because he knelt and prayed so long that he developed thick calluses.[11] Even if they'd called him that to his face, I doubt he'd gotten his cloak in a knot over it. Our protagonist proved to be one of the most practical teachers in early Christianity and, if he in particular spent that much time in prayer, he was convinced all the way to his knobby knees that it worked.

Could you use the reminder right about now that prayer is never a waste of time? If so, why?

Remember day 4 and that imaginary poster on the waiting room wall entitled "How to Have a Healthy Soul"? Number 4 might be, *Pray and be prayed for.* Let's go through the text and highlight specific places a man with camel knees called believers to prayer.

What is the first condition according to James 5:13?

Since James categorizes sickness later in the segment, "suffering" here encompasses other conditions that cause people hurt or heartbreak. Some Christians avoid praying for themselves out of genuine selflessness. Their faithful prayer lives are almost entirely intercessional. I'm baffled by it, though. What if nobody else prays for us that day? We have heavy responsibilities. We need prayer! Not at the exclusion of intercession, of course, but added to it. We need to pray for ourselves for another vital reason, however. Think about that imaginary poster again. Glance back at yesterday's lesson.

Write number 3 in all caps.

A pair of hands clasped in earnest prayer is the best means we have this side of heaven to hang onto Jesus for dear life.

Our sufferings etch engraved invitations to intimate places with God. A pair of hands clasped in earnest prayer is the best means we have this side of Heaven to hang onto Jesus for dear life. Even our groanings before Him are echoes of intimate prayer. Fellowshipping with Christ in our suffering guards it from purposelessness. While James in no way suggests that we can't call others for prayer when we're in anguish, we need not wait on another soul to seek prescription from God in our urgent need.

Sometimes God answers prayer by alleviating the suffering. Other times He eases the suffering. Still other times He shows His sufficiency in the suffering, but make no mistake. He never abandons us in our suffering. Prayer can prime the well of our souls to a bath of His beautiful presence. It is often the most determining factor in whether, in our anguish, we sink or swim.

Let's open our hearts wide to the next call to prayer.

Reread James 5:14. What are the conditions and instructions?

Ink jets drain dry, ruminating over whether the purpose of the oil was medicinal, spiritual (for consecration, for instance), or symbolic. None of the three would be unbiblical or even unlikely. All had a place in antiquity. Based on 2 Chronicles 16:12 some Christians fear that seeking medical treatment dishonors God.

In the thirty-ninth year of his reign, Asa developed a disease in his feet, and his disease became increasingly severe. Yet even in his disease he didn't seek the LORD but only the physicians.
2 CHRONICLES 16:12

Exactly what did Asa do to displease the Lord?

Several major translations specify that Asa sought doctors instead of the Lord. Scripture cautions us not to place our trust in man but whether or not God can use substances, poultices, or various practices is answered even in the ministry of Christ. At times He healed through words and at times He healed through touch. Other times He even used mud and saliva. We're hard-pressed to find a formula. We simply know that Jesus alone is our Savior and, by His stripes, we are healed. Let's get to the main question hovering over our heads.

In your own words, what does James 5:15 say?

You'd have to run for your life from the Gospels and Acts not to believe that early Christendom saw scores of healings. We might even safely say that healing was more the norm than the exception among those earliest believers. Remember when we learned in session 2 that the Letter of James was probably one of the earliest New Testament documents? He would have witnessed and been aware of multiple healings, signs, and wonders.

"So, why doesn't God still heal?" Oh, Beloved, He does or we wouldn't be sitting here working this Bible study right now. The bigger question is "Why doesn't God *always* heal?" No one in Acts participated in more recorded healings than the apostle Paul, so let's check with him. For crying out loud, Acts 19:11-12 even reports that aprons and handkerchiefs he'd touched were brought to the sick and they were healed. But read 2 Timothy 4:20.

What piece of information is significant in our discussion?

Well, what do we make of that? Perhaps we flip to the end of our New Testaments with this balance: When we're sick, we pray like mad for healing and summon leaders to pray likewise over us and, yes, anoint us with oil. If we remain ill after diligent, enduring, faith-filled prayer, particularly upon the part of our intercessors, what do we do? We entrust ourselves to the hands of our faithful God and His sovereign plan, abiding voraciously in His love.

> During His earthly life, He offered prayers and appeals with loud cries and tears to the One who was able to save Him from death, and He was heard because of His reverence.
> **HEBREWS 5:7**

Hebrews 5:7 offers us the ultimate example. This was God's very Son. He cried out loudly, tears streaming, and God *heard* ... yet He did not save Him from death. An infinitely greater work was accomplished through the cross. When we cry out, our God hears whether or not He heals. Something greater must be at stake. Something we may not know till we see Him.

Others may still be healed in time on this earth but, if God does not raise us up here, He will adamantly raise us up in His glorious presence. Until then, I can tell you what this woman is going to do: I'm going to believe God for healing—for those I'm interceding for and for myself—until He clearly tells me no. I've experienced His healing. I've witnessed His healing. I know He still does it. If I'm going to err, let me err on the side of faith.

What about you? You don't have to agree! Please share your true stand.

Please draw your attention back to the word "elder" in James 5:14. The Greek word *presbyteros* literally means "older one."[12] Note that these older leaders were assumed to possess the most vivacious faith. We battle a reversal in our current climate where many outgrow that out-on-a-limb kind of prayer and leave the outrageous faith to Christians who haven't been beaten up by life yet.

Harsh circumstances make that trend understandable but maybe we're due a little revival. Maybe it's time we remembered Daniel 3:17. "Our God whom we serve is able to deliver us" (ESV). Say that out loud, Sister. But, what if He doesn't? Let it be known to every worldly influence and evil principality that "we will not serve your gods" (Dan. 3:18, ESV). We will believe till we see.

No one can explain to everyone's satisfaction why God doesn't always heal. The mind-set that makes the most sense to me is that His greater priority in this era of the church is manifesting His power in our inner man (see Eph. 2:20) by seeing us walk by faith and not by sight. This I can promise you: we could work our bodies into mint condition but, without prayer, our souls would ail with an aggressive cancer of unbelief. Never stop praying and believing, Sister. OK, think back a final time to that imaginary poster on the waiting room wall because James 5:15-16 offers one last maxim for a healthy soul.

Fill in the blanks:

"If he has ______________________________, he will be forgiven.

Therefore, ______________________________ to one another."

Number 5 could be, *Confess sin! To God, and, when appropriate, to others!* Healing could be at stake! God knows us so well. He is intimately acquainted with our burdens of guilt and our tendencies to associate sickness with sin. The Bible affirms that they can sometimes be connected, but our self-destructive assumptions turn sometimes into always. Here's why: Who on earth hasn't sinned enough to fear that a present ailment is tied to a past failure?

We're like those first disciples who, when they saw a man blind from birth, asked: "Who sinned, this man or his parents?" (John 9:2). To our great relief, Jesus answered "Neither this man nor his parents sinned. … This came about so that God's works might be displayed in him" (v. 3).

Sometimes it takes more faith to feel forgiven than it does to feel healed.

The glorious heath wish of the half brother of our Lord Jesus Christ gives us the simplest prescription of all when we fear that sin is involved with our suffering: confess it and be forgiven. Should we go forward on this fallen soil with bodies still crippled by disease? Confession silences the taunts of our accuser, makes our hearts clean, and makes our souls well.

Come what may, we pray. After all, "The prayer of a righteous person has great effectiveness" (Jas. 5:16, NET). Sometimes, Beloved, it takes more faith to feel forgiven than it does to feel healed.

The **NEXT LEVEL** with Melissa

JAMES 5 & 2009

The year 2009 seemed a year of promise, not least because Mom and I had newly decided to collaborate on James. I was so excited except for the tiny fact that my perfectly normal health suddenly went absolutely bonkers. I found myself battling incapacitating migraines, spasms from a herniated disc, racing heartbeat, labored breathing, and debilitating nausea. With the physical pain came its good friend mental torment.

I don't say this lightly, but some days I truly believed I was dying. Loneliness and despair penetrated my heart in ways I never thought possible. A distracting and bizarre combination of James research, MRIs, physical therapy, blood tests, CAT scans, and ultrasounds filled my days.

After many months, I had an upper GI series to explain the nausea. During X-rays I noticed the technician seemed disquieted, but I tried not to start diagnosing myself. Besides, I could read Web MD later, right?

Before I made it home, the specialist called. "You have a *very large* ulcer. I'm not sure what is going on, but we need to do an endoscopy as soon as possible."

The procedure was to be done the following Monday. That's rapid in medical time, but I still had to wait apprehensively through the weekend. The fear was not the ulcer itself, but why a person my age would have it. The test would biopsy and possibly treat the ulcer. Most important, it was to determine whether cancer was the cause of my problems.

I'll never forget the sound of the doctor's voice on the other end of the line. Chills spread across my body like a cold, sinister wind. I didn't really know what to say to him so I said, "Umm. OK, what am I supposed to do in the meantime?" Didn't he want to keep a close eye on me? Did I mention I lived 800 miles away from my mom? He could have invited me to stay the weekend with his family, you know? I'm kidding. I think.

For me, growing up was not graduating from college or getting married but the jarring awareness how little power the medical world has to alleviate suffering and even less to eliminate it. It was facing my own mortality and realizing that, in this mad world, even my own cells could rebel against me.

Left to fend for myself in these despondent conditions, I resumed researching James. Of course, I reread James 5:14-15. I knew the passage but I read it again, this time with more personally at stake: "Is anyone among you sick? He should call for the elders of the church, and they should pray over him after anointing him with olive oil in the name of the Lord. The prayer of faith will save the sick person, and the Lord will restore him to health; if he has committed sins, he will be forgiven" (Jas. 5:14-15). The passage always made me a wee bit nervous.

These two verses seemed best suited as proof texts for sensational types, not perfectly normal folks like me who had no qualms with modern medicine. Not to mention, Colin and I were still new to Atlanta, so though we were attending a church, we weren't members. I couldn't possibly contact a church I didn't really know to do something so vulnerable.

So I didn't contact them. Mom did.

The elders were gracious enough to meet and intercede for me. They were wonderful. I was greatly moved and humbled as they wholeheartedly prayed for me. I left the church built up in spirit but physically, I still felt terrible.

The next morning I had my procedure. You know things are bad when you look forward to anesthesia just to be without pain for a while. When I awoke, dazed and confused, the doctor came in. He looked puzzled, but I was coming off drugs so things were naturally a little weird.

He said, "Well, Melissa. I guess the good news is we were wrong. There is no ulcer."

I wish I could say at this point that I was clapping my hands, singing an old gospel chorus, and converting the doctor to Christianity. But I wasn't. Initially I was frustrated and dissatisfied. *Back at square one,* I thought.

After a dreadful year, answers seemed as important as a solution. If not an ulcer, what had the entire year been about? I sat silently, completely stunned. Little did I know, this moment would be the beginning of the road back to whatever normalcy means for me.

After recovering from shock and repenting of ingratitude, I pressed into the journey of healing God seemed to have for me. I dared to believe He would not just inflict pain for my good but might heal for my good, too.

Though for the next year and a half I was under the care of a neurologist for migraines and a physical therapist for neck issues, the life-threatening problems ceased and the chronic nausea is still gone. To the great praise of God, the Giver of all good gifts, the season of all-consuming physical pain ended.

If you're wired with a theology like mine, you're a little reluctant to view healing as one of God's good gifts. We readily accept suffering and adversity as a providential gift from God, but we tend to be incredulous that God could heal for His glory, too. James has the power to transform our minds, maybe our lives, if we have the courage to make room for him in our tidy theological systems.

When I think back to 2009, I still shudder. It was dark. The light I saw was mostly by way of migraine auras. If you're lucky enough not to understand that reference, stop and give thanks.

I do not tell this story because I think it scores a 10 on the testimony scale. I'll never be able to prove I had an ulcer or that God healed it that Sunday. But you can bet, in the back of my mind, I'll always have the sense that whatever happened that day had everything to do with a dozen faithful elders circled around me invoking the ancient ritual commanded in James 5:14-15. I'll never read those two verses without feeling compelled to testify of God's healing power.

I should safely end with a disclaimer now, but I really don't want to. I mean, seriously, we all know God doesn't always heal. Some of the most faithful people we know pray for saints who suffer terribly without a healing response from God.

Miracles of healing in response to faith-filled prayers are baffling and temporary exceptions to the way we normally experience the world. *But James challenges us to make room in our theology for them, nonetheless.* And James doesn't feel the need to give a disclaimer. He just leaves us hanging there in the tension. Maybe so we'll risk enough to actually *believe* and *pray.*

Soli Deo Gloria.

viewer guide | session seven

James 5:7-11

Our homework leading up to today's session has centered entirely upon the 5th and final chapter of James. Today we will return to several portions of the chapter that call for extra emphasis.

Let's give this session a specific title drawn from verse 7: ________________ the ________

According to James, what do we do when we find ourselves in this particular season?

1. Accept the _____________ of the _____________.

2. Actively ___________________ God's __________________.

"Every reference to '__________ and __________ __________' in the OT occurs in a context affirming the _______________ of the _______."[1]

Compare Deuteronomy 11:13-14 and Hosea 6:3.

3. Avoid a ____________ ____________________ (vv. 8-9).

The key word *grumble* is especially captured in the "______________ feeling of bitterness or the ______________ resentment that may express itself in a __________ or a _______."[2]

4. __________ fresh resolve through the __________ of __________ (v. 10).

hupodeigma—a ___________

"See, we _________ as ____________ those _______ ______ ___________" (v. 11).

5. Ask of God like _________ is ___ ___________ (vv. 17-18).

In verse 17 "a man _______ _______ _______" (NIV)—

Greek *homoiopathes*—"It means, literally, 'to be of like ______________/______________' but has the sense of 'like _________.' "[3]

Let's conclude with a glance at the original story in 1 Kings 18:41-46.

1. Douglas J. Moo, *The Letter of James* (Grand Rapids, MI: Wm. B. Eerdmans Publishing Co., 2000), 223.
2. *The Expositor's Bible Commentary*, vol. 12, *Hebrews-Revelation* (Grand Rapids, MI: Zondervan Publishing House, 1981), 202.
3. Luke Timothy Johnson, *The Anchor Bible*, vol. 37, *The Letter of James* (New Haven, CT: Yale University Press/Doubleday, 1995), 336.

WEEK SEVEN

ON THE WAY HOME

Day One

SCRIPTURE'S LAST GLIMPSE

FLASH FORWARD

"When we reached Jerusalem, the brothers welcomed us gladly. The following day Paul went in with us to James, and all the elders were present." Acts 21:17-18

Today we begin our final week of study together. With the Book of James mostly behind us, we now turn to the final appearance of our protagonist in the Book of Acts. Let me give you a heads-up over the larger portion of Scripture we'll cover today. We've been blissfully spoiled by smaller segments that allowed much deeper looks. This lesson will take us to a narrative instead and one with significant twists and turns. Now, don't start dreading it. You'll find it interesting. Just don't get sleepy on us here.

Your reading catapults you right into the middle of Acts 21, but first let's throw some paint on the canvas for background. The year is approximately A.D. 58.[1] The Holy Spirit had compelled the apostle Paul to go to Jerusalem but also warned him that chains and afflictions awaited him (see Acts 20:23). The journey took Paul's traveling party through Caesarea where they received a jarring visit from the prophet Agabus. He reaffirmed the previous warning by taking Paul's belt and tying up his own hands and feet. "This is what the Holy Spirit says: 'In this way the Jews in Jerusalem will bind the man who owns this belt and deliver him into Gentile hands' " (Acts 21:11). The prophetic confirmation was so vivid and disturbing that even Luke joined in with the others, begging Paul not to proceed.

What was Paul's response in Acts 21:13-14?

Now, read Acts 21:15-19 where you find our James mentioned. What was the context and James' involvement?

We're not surprised to find James in Jerusalem because he was the bishop of the Jerusalem church. Picture the scene in Acts 21:18-19. Some commentators believe as many as 70 elders could have been present with James when Paul and his companions arrived.[2]

They gathered for a reception of sorts, somewhat like a church might give for missionaries on furlough. Paul had come bearing a financial gift for the church in Jerusalem (see 1 Cor. 16:1-4; Rom. 15:25–27) but, in all likelihood, he was filled with apprehension. Read Dr. Richard Longenecker's explanation carefully because it is key to understanding our lesson. Underline portions that seem most pertinent.

> To understand Paul's fears, we must realize that the Jerusalem church was increasingly being caught between its allegiance to the nation and its fraternal relation to Paul's Gentile mission. To accept the contribution from the Gentile churches was to be identified further with that mission and to drive another wedge between themselves and their compatriots. True, they had accepted such a contribution earlier (cf. 11:27-30) and had declared their fraternity with Paul in previous meetings (cf. Gal. 2:6-10; Acts 15:13-29). But with the rising tide of Jewish nationalism and a growing body of scrupulous believers in the Jerusalem church ... Jewish Christian solidarity with the Gentile mission was becoming more and more difficult to affirm if the Jerusalem church's relations with the nation were to be maintained and opportunities for an outreach to Israel kept open. Undoubtedly Paul recognized the increased tensions at Jerusalem. No wonder he feared that James and the elders, for the sake of their Jewish relations and mission, might feel themselves constrained to reject the contribution, thus severing, in effect, the connection between the Pauline churches and the Jerusalem church—which would have been a disaster in many ways.[3]

See the challenge the Jerusalem church faced to keep open a witness to their nation? In what ways do you feel a struggle between remaining faithful while reaching out in our society?

A wave of relief must have washed over Paul in the first part of Acts 21:20. How did they react?

The relief may, however, have been a tad short-lived. Read the verse and note a vital piece of information that surfaces in the quote attributed to James and the elders in Acts 21:20. They met Paul's good news with some of their own: "Many thousands of Jews ... have believed, and they are all zealous for the law." If we were watching this scene on video, this might be the point where the music grows dramatic and the lens narrows onto a facial expression. The news wasn't bad, but let's just say it was loaded. Mind you, these new believers celebrated by James and the elders were Jews who had come to faith in Christ. The law was unspeakably dear to many of them. Now, narrow your lens upon James. You might find him over there between a rock and a hard place.

Remember, these events fall within the early era of the New Testament church. New Gentile believers didn't have to figure out what to do with their God-given, life-saving holy heritage that Jesus came to complete, not abolish. Gentiles had no such allegiance.

The Messiah these Jewish believers had come to trust had been an adherent of the law in His earthly tenure. We live this side of the completed canon. We live in a culture in which everything seems explainable in 140 characters. Some things are not that simple. The way wasn't cut and dry for them.

Even though Paul preached justification by faith through grace alone, he also felt free to observe Jewish feasts and make occasional vows. You might say that Paul felt free to observe the law and free not to. To him, what was no longer an obligation could still be an expression of devotion. Other times, it was simply the better part of wisdom. Case in point: Acts 16:3, when Paul circumcised Timothy before taking him along on a trip where Jews knew full well that the boy's daddy was Greek.

Some things are not simple enough to fit into 140 characters.

Read Acts 21:20-25 and watch what happened next in the narrative. In the margin briefly record what James and the elders requested from Paul.

Our commentary excerpts are longer today but Dr. Longenecker explains a delicate situation that I'd talk into a lather for pages on end. Take this one in.

> James and the elders responded to Paul's report and the gift from the churches by praising God. Yet they also urged Paul to join with four Jewish Christians who were fulfilling their Nazirite vows and to pay for their required offerings. In effect, they were saying to Paul, "We can accept this gift from the churches and so identify ourselves openly with your Gentile mission, if you will join with these men and identify yourself openly with the nation." Thus they were protecting themselves against Jewish recriminations while at the same time affirming their connection with Paul and his mission. And, as they saw it, they were providing Paul with a way of protecting himself against a slanderous accusation floating about that he was teaching Jews to apostatize from Judaism. In view of his having come earlier to Jerusalem in more placid circumstances to fulfill a Nazirite vow of his own (cf. 18:18-19:22), Paul would not have viewed such a suggestion as particularly onerous. It doubtless seemed to all concerned a particularly happy solution to the vexing problems both Paul and the Jerusalem church were facing.[4]

Paul did as they asked and 1 Corinthians 9:20 best explains why. What was Paul's perspective? Respond in the margin.

Hence, the events in Acts 21. While in the temple complex toward the end of the seven days, doing what James and the elders requested, Paul was seen by Jews from Asia. They seized him and accused him of bringing a Gentile into a strictly prohibited area, a violation punishable by death for the non-Jew.

These same Jews had seen Paul earlier in the city with a Gentile named Trophimus and "they supposed that Paul had brought him into the temple complex" (Acts 21:29). They were wrong but convincing enough that the whole crowd howled with the wolves. Can you handle one more portion?

Read Acts 21:30-36 and record the results in the margin.

A plan intended to protect Paul and keep him from further trouble ironically tumbled him into the fury of it. Fathom the mercy of God to warn Paul earlier. Surely the scene of Agabus's bound hands and feet played again and again in Paul's thoughts. The warnings issued by the Holy Spirit, as dread-inspiring as they were, might have stood as faithful guardians over his human heart.

Second thoughts can be torturous, can't they? Paul may not have been the only one offered to entertain them. We'd have to make James either superhuman or callous-hearted to imagine him with no backlash from these events. If I'd been him, I'd have been nearly ill, considerably confused, and maybe even questioning why God let me make a recommendation that landed Paul in trouble. "Do what we tell you" (Acts 21:23). I'm not saying any of those feelings would have been appropriate or that James even had them. All of this is speculation. I'm suggesting those feelings might be natural. Picture yourself in the situation. What if you'd been James?

How do you think you might have responded with the news? Share your thoughts in the margin.

Maybe I'm completely off base. Maybe James had the maturity not to cave to blame. For many of us, however, the only balm for our self-incrimination would be the desperate hope that God Himself had appointed the event for greater good. And that He did. This stony road led Paul to his own via dolorosa through the very gates of Rome.

God alone could have such faith in His indwelling Spirit to entrust humanity with the torch of the gospel.

I heard a pastor say that real church is messy, and if we were doing the gospel according to the Book of Acts, congregations could be considerably less lovely. I stared off in the distance, wondering if he was right. I have a dear loved one who believes that we are our own gods. Occasionally, I look in the mirror and think, *If I'm as good as God gets, we are in serious woe.* We miscalculate actions and reactions sometimes. Sometimes we mean well and things don't turn out well. And, still, God gets it done. He alone could have such faith in His indwelling Spirit to entrust humanity with the torch of the gospel. Maybe we were never meant to arrive at our destinations unblistered.

Do you want to hear something sad? We don't get a single further glimpse of our beloved James on the pages of Scripture. He served faithfully at his post for several more years and tradition alone can suggest what became of him. Of this we can be certain: The same Savior who led Paul to Rome held on tight to the twelve tribes scattered abroad (see Jas. 1:1) and to a Jew named Jacob.

The **NEXT LEVEL** with Melissa

THEOLOGY OF THE COLLECTION

Today Mom noted that the apostle Paul was likely apprehensive about going to Jerusalem. We see this clearest in Romans 15:22-33.

Paul hoped to go to Rome on his way to Spain, but first he was going to Jerusalem. The apostle wanted the Roman church to pray three things for him: (1) that he be delivered from the unbelieving Jews in Judea; (2) that the Jerusalem church would receive the financial gift from Paul's churches; and (3) that he would make it to Rome to spend time with the believers there.

In Galatians 2 when James, Cephas, and John acknowledged Paul's ministry to the Gentiles, they asked only that he and Barnabas remember the poor. Paul's collection for the Jerusalem saints fulfilled "a key 'clause' in the agreement made with the 'pillars.' "[1]

Mom mentioned this momentous occasion back in week 1. By the way, can you believe we're in week 7? Did I mention I'm not very good at saying good-bye?

Paul never revealed what was at stake for *him* in delivering the collection to Jerusalem. Neither does the Book of Acts mention what was at stake for *the Jerusalem church* in their receiving the collection from Paul. Mom presented what some scholars suspect accounted for the Jerusalem church's possible reluctance to receive Paul's gift. Here I want to consider the *nature* of the collection. While Paul's collection was certainly a financial contribution for the Jerusalem saints, its significance extends much further.

Paul said the collection was about creating greater unity between the churches (see 2 Cor. 8:1-4; 9:11-15). Upon receiving the generous gift, Paul said the Jerusalem saints would glorify God for the Gentile churches' obedience to the confession of the gospel.

The collection was also staunchly theological in nature. In Romans 15:26-27 Paul said he was traveling to Jerusalem to serve the saints. Since the Gentiles shared the Jews' spiritual blessings, they had an obligation to minister to Jews in material needs.

Paul considered the Gentile church indebted to the Jews for their spiritual heritage. Moo aptly states, "Paul understands that the Gentiles' status as members of the people of God is inextricably tied to a salvation history that has an indelible OT/Jewish cast."[2] The collection was a tangible way for Paul's churches to acknowledge Israel's special place in salvation history.

Some scholars even speculate an eschatological background for the Jerusalem collection.[3] The Jewish prophets spoke of a future day when the wealth of the nations would stream into Jerusalem (see Isa. 45:14; 60:5-17; 61:6; Mic. 4:13). Possibly the collection somehow fulfilled prophetic expectations as a kind of Gentile tribute to Jerusalem.

To our great dissatisfaction, we're never told directly in the New Testament whether Paul's collection was rejected or accepted by the Jerusalem church. I can't help but wonder, though, if maybe, just maybe, James accepted the collection and that he, like so many other brothers in the Lord, somehow gained confidence from Paul's imprisonment and dared to speak the message of Christ even more fearlessly (see Phil. 1:14).

Day Two
PRECIOUS IN HIS SIGHT

FLASH FORWARD

"You have condemned—you have murdered—the righteous man; he does not resist you." James 5:6

The grave is the way of sons and daughters of Adam but, for crying out loud, it's still sad.

Have you ever spent intentional time with someone you knew in advance wasn't long for this world? In a strange sort of way, that's what you've done for seven weeks and what I've done for over a year. We knew from the start that this journey would end with James' death. The grave is the way of sons and daughters of Adam but, for crying out loud, it's still sad.

I've gotten so wrapped up in our journey with James that my eyes are blurred with tears as we begin today. It's a little silly, I know, but some of you may feel the same way. We've invested significant energy into his life and message. If you're like me, you hate to see the man go. Of course, what makes our relationship with him a little odd is that he's not feeling it. Still, one of these days after we've gazed at the glorious face of Christ Jesus, we'll run into his earthly half brother and maybe feel like saying, "Hey! I know you!"

You'll recall from yesterday's lesson that no mention of James appears in Scripture but what we've already examined. You and I have scaled his life biographically from his first mention in the Gospels until his last mention in Acts 21. So, at which point did he pen the letter bearing his name? As much as we'd love a tidy time line, the fact is, no one can be certain.

We learned early on that the Book of James may have been among the earliest documents of the New Testament church. Regarding the timing and circumstances of his demise, we'll look to historical and traditional accounts to help fill in the blanks. Nothing is peculiar about a missing account of James' death in Scripture. The Bible only records the deaths of two of the original twelve disciples, Judas Iscariot and John's brother, James, and few of Christ's other devotees. Stephen's death got generous ink by Luke probably because he was the first Christian martyr. We can, however, run to Scripture to meet someone whose death may mark the spot on a loosely knitted time line for James' exit.

Yesterday where did we leave the apostle Paul?
(See Acts 21:31-36.)

Remember that we approximated the time of Paul's arrest in Jerusalem to be around A.D. 58. He was taken into custody, allowed a chance to address the crowd with his testimony (see Acts 22:1-19), placed under Roman protection (see Acts 22:24), freed long enough to stand before the Sanhedrin (see Acts 22:30-23:8), and, because the commander feared that he'd be torn apart, was rescued and taken back into custody (see Acts 23:10). That very night the Lord stood by him and said, "Have courage! For as you have testified about Me in Jerusalem, so you must also testify in Rome" (Acts 23:11). The next day a plot for his assassination was uncovered and he was sent by night to Caesarea where he remained in custody. While there, Paul was allowed to give his defense to the governor named Felix. His successor is the biblical figure who becomes a bold dot on the James time line of tradition.

Read Acts 24:27 carefully. How much time passed?

What governor took Felix's place?

What happened to Paul?

Festus is our bold dot on the time line for what became of James. For reference, both Festus and Felix, his predecessor, held positions similar to Pilate during the trials of Jesus.[5] Festus finally said the words Paul yearned to hear: "You have appealed to Caesar; to Caesar you will go!" (Acts 25:12). Days passed and King Agrippa came through Caesarea and dropped in on Festus as a courtesy. While there, he learned about Paul and asked to hear his defense. As Paul blatantly shared the gospel, Festus became enraged and said something I find priceless. "You're out of your mind, Paul! Too much study is driving you mad!" (Acts 26:24). To Festus's certain relief, the apostle set sail beside other prisoners on a ship bound for Italy. Ultimately, Paul would find himself under house arrest in Rome from around A.D. 60–62 awaiting trial.

Now we circle back to James according to the Jewish historian Josephus. In *Word Biblical Commentary*, Dr. Ralph Martin calls this "the clearest and most historically reliable report."[6] In A.D. 62, Festus died and a three- or four-month interval fell between his death and the arrival of his successor, Albinus. A rash, young man named Ananus (II) was High Priest at the time in Jerusalem where Jewish patriotism was waking like a bear from hibernation. With the Roman administration in brief hiatus, Ananus seized a golden opportunity to get rid of several "popular leaders" who were believed to pose threats to rising patriotism. You guessed it. One of those leaders was "James the brother of Jesus."[7]

Hold on to your hat for the charge: "A formal Sanhedrin trial was called and an indictment brought against James and others for offenses against the law."[8] Offenses against the *what? Our* James? Does that sound a lot like him to you? Some think the charges were trumped up, but note another highly significant theory in terms of yesterday's lesson: "It may be that the memory of James' failure to rebuke Paul openly and publicly to dissociate him and his fellow Jewish believers in Jerusalem from the apostle to the Gentiles still rankled."[9]

Good grief. Life was not only complicated for leaders of the early church. It was risky. No, it was more than that. It was deadly. Don't call it martyrdom till you call it murder. So, in the 62nd year of our Lord, James the Just, a man with the knees of a camel from time spent in prayer, was seized by treacherous men and tried for crimes punishable by death. The arrest had no other point.

Had James been less popular, he would have been less vulnerable. "In the esteem of the people, the charismatic quality and personal magnetism of these prophets would have commanded a widespread following."[10] James also preached with abandon that "the Lord's coming is near" (Jas. 5:8). Even the slow-witted could put two and two together: the followers of the Lord's brother believed in the imminent displacement of every competing power. The trial was over before it started.

While you're picturing James' arrest, please hear the echo of the words he penned with every thundering footfall to his death: "Love your neighbor as yourself. … Do not murder. … Speak and act as those who will be judged by the law of freedom. For judgment is without mercy to the one who hasn't shown mercy. ... Who is wise and has understanding among you? He should show his works by good conduct with wisdom's gentleness. ... But the wisdom from above is first pure, then peace-loving. … What is the source of wars and fights among you? ... You murder and covet and cannot attain. You fight and war. … God resists the proud, but gives grace to the humble. … There is one lawgiver and judge who is able to save and to destroy. But who are you to judge your neighbor? ... So it is a sin for the person who knows to do what is good and doesn't do it. … Mercy triumphs over judgment."

Mercy triumphs.

The irony would not be wasted on many. The Jewish High Priest sought to silence the man who'd held a megaphone of peace to his mouth, reining in his own people time and again. The plan of Ananus would backfire … but not in time for James. Some say he was found guilty and stoned to death.[11] Don't move past that quickly. Pause long enough to imagine the first few pelts. Recent descriptions of the stoning of women on the other side of the world put fresh chills up our spines. It is not a quick way to die and the hands are bound—if not buried—to keep the victim from protecting herself. James was surely bound as well.

Eusebius, one of the early church fathers, shared a different but no less chilling report: "They brought him into the midst and demanded a denial of the faith in Christ before all the people."[12] I found two different quotes referring to James in a public lynching. The first one: " 'With a loud voice and with more courage than they had expected, [he] confessed before all the people that our Lord and Savior Jesus Christ is the son of God.' … The Jewish mob was enraged: 'They could no longer endure his testimony, since he was by all men believed to be most righteous ... because of the height which he had reached in a life of philosophy and religion.' ... So they killed him at an opportune moment."[13]

The second quote is from James' own lips: "Why are you asking me about the Son of Man? He is seated in heaven at the right hand of great power, and will come again on the clouds of heaven."[14] For that "James was hurled from the temple pinnacle and clubbed to death for his audacity."[15] One eerie account took a different perspective on the beating: "James was thrown down into the Kidron ravine from the top of the Temple area wall, and mercifully 'clubbed' out of his misery by a fuller from Siloam, in the valley below."[16]

When Melissa and I were in Jerusalem last year, our research for this project was already well underway. You could have knocked me over with a feather when the Jewish tour guide took several of us over to an ancient corner in the holy city and said, "This is where James, the brother of Jesus was cast to his death."

"Precious in the sight of the Lord is the death of His saints" (Ps. 116:15, KJV). I don't know what was happening in Heaven when such rancor and violence befell James. This I do know: the last beat of his heart was precious in the sight of the Lord. When Stephen proclaimed the Lordship of Jesus Christ and the part of evil men in His crucifixion, "They [who heard him] were enraged in their hearts and gnashed their teeth at him. But Stephen, filled by the Holy Spirit, gazed into heaven. He saw God's glory, with Jesus standing at the right hand of God" (Acts 7:54-55).

Would you look up Acts 7:56 and record what Stephen said?

"They screamed at the top of their voices, covered their ears, and together rushed against him ... and began to stone him" (Acts 7:57-58). Scripture repeatedly depicts Jesus "seated" at the right hand of God. The thought of Him "standing" on behalf of His faithful follower Stephen moves me every time. One might also wonder if Jesus had to restrain Himself.

Though we have no way of knowing if James saw any such sight in his final moments, we can be sure that the gaze of Jesus of Nazareth was fixed with rapt attention upon the breaking body of one so loved. Whether or not James saw a glimpse of Jesus before he died, he most assuredly caught one after. Body made whole and pain made gain, James was back once again in the home of Jesus.

What would you most like to ask James, should you meet him in Heaven?

Day Three

NOT ONE STONE

FLASH FORWARD

"As Jesus left and was going out of the temple complex, ... He replied to them, 'Don't you see all these things? I assure you: Not one stone will be left here on another that will not be thrown down!' " Matthew 24:1-2

So, what happened next?

What happened historically in the wake of James' death? That's what today is all about. In fact, both today's lesson and tomorrow's will center around the question, *So, what happened next?* We must look again to sources outside of Scripture for some of those answers.

The Jewish historian, Josephus, makes the best offer to fill in the blanks and, though some of his details are unverifiable, the overall account is widely quoted by scholars. For those of us who love a time line, we're going to build one today that diagrams eight highly strategic years following James' arrest. Several of our dates will be approximations but they're close to the target and I think you'll find the process immensely helpful. You'll get to freestyle somewhat on the time line. You can document as many details as you'd like over the course of our lesson but you will be urged to include certain very significant events. Under the bold dot on the left hand side where our time line begins, please write A.D. 62. Under the dot at the end of the time line, please write A.D. 70. Now, place a dot at every 2-year point and mark them as 64, 66, and 68. You'll write the events on top.

You will recall that in the year 62, while Paul was probably still under house arrest in Rome, James was apprehended in Jerusalem. Remember Ananus, the High Priest in Jerusalem who took advantage of the interim between governors? He "assembled the Sanhedrin of judges, and brought before them the brother of Jesus, who was called Christ, whose name was James" and had him and several others put to death.[17]

Label James' death at the beginning of the time line.

According to Josephus, a number of citizens infuriated by the injustice urged King Agrippa to deal with Ananus. Some also went to meet Albinus, the new governor, on the road to his new post and told him that Ananus had assembled a Sanhedrin without his consent and, therefore, had acted unlawfully. Enraged, Albinus penned a threatening letter to Ananus and King Agrippa snatched the priesthood from him.[18] We're relieved for the shred of justice, but James was no less dead.

With James went the Jewish Christianity of the early days in Jerusalem. Behold the profound significance of the ministry and message of James. Without him, imagine the missing link between the ascension of Christ and the development of such a predominately Gentile church.

The loss of James radically transformed early Christianity. Paul ministered vigorously for another five years, "so that the proclamation might be fully made … and all the Gentiles might hear" (2 Tim. 4:17). The Book of Hebrews, however, would be written later. You see, the Jewish tie has never been severed. Indeed, it cannot be. We have a Jewish Messiah, and His earthly heritage is our spiritual birthright.

We have a Jewish Messiah, and His earthly heritage is our spiritual birthright.

What does Galatians 3:29 mean to you about your identity?

Christ is the unbreakable bond between the two Covenants, Old and New. The divine knot, so to speak. The Jewish tie holds fast but the Jewish flair of the early church shot to its peak during the tenure of James and dropped in prominence with his death. Tuck that important piece of information into your church history.

Back to our time line. While under house arrest in Rome, Paul wrote Ephesians, Philippians, and Colossians. He was released in A.D. 63 or 64. Then something cataclysmic happened: the Great Fire of Rome in A.D. 64.

Definitely add that event to your time line.

Nero was the emperor of Rome and, at 27, had held the position for 10 years. The fire ravaged much of the city, leaving even Nero's palace in ashes. Legend has it that Nero fiddled while Rome burned. His plan to build himself a grander palace was common knowledge, so many believed that he set the fire himself to clear the land.

Though Nero made attempts to bring relief to those victimized by the fire, he could not shake the rumor that he'd struck the proverbial match. "Nero felt the need to divert suspicion to another group. He selected the Christians as his scapegoats. He claimed that they had set the fire. A systematic persecution of the Christians followed. Because of his lifestyle and the persecution, many Christians viewed him as the antichrist."[19]

During this season of horrific persecution toward Christians, the apostle Paul was seized and thrown back in prison. His second letter to Timothy was most likely written during this incarceration. It would be the last inspired word to fall from his pen. In A.D. 67 or very close to that time, Paul was condemned by the Emperor Nero and his neck given to the sword.[20] Peter, the Rock, is believed to have met his death during the same wave of persecution and under the same emperor's order. The only account we have is that of Hegesippus, the early Christian writer. *Foxe's Book of Martyrs* paraphrased Hegesippus as follows: "After being captured and taken to his place of martyrdom, [Peter] requested that he be crucified in an upside down position because he did not consider himself worthy to be crucified in the same position as his Lord."[21]

Add Peter's martyrdom on your time line near Paul's.

The very next year, Nero lost favor with his army, his support in Rome dwindled, and the Senate handed him a death sentence.[22] "Realizing that the end was inevitable and near, he committed suicide by stabbing himself in A.D. 68."[23]

Add that episode to your time line as well.

Keep in mind that all the events in the last several paragraphs occurred in Rome. But something of tremendous significance happened in the meantime back in Jerusalem, and it will necessitate you rewinding your time line to the year 66. In that year, the Jews instigated a rebellion against Roman rule.

As we saw, Jewish nationalism had awakened with a vengeance and zeal to shake off decades of Roman tyranny spiked. Then an incident provided opportunity: Florus, the Roman procurator who followed Albinus, confiscated riches from the Jerusalem Temple treasure, and the Jews rose up riotously.

"In June A.D. 66, the daily sacrifices offered in Jerusalem on behalf of the emperor and the Roman people ceased by order of Eleazar, captain of the temple. This action signaled open rebellion against Rome."[24] Consider it a declaration of war and one that would not end for four years. Though the Jews won some battles, the casualties were ultimately catastrophic. The Roman army thundered across the land and sought to regain control from the outside in. Vespasian became emperor of Rome in A.D. 69 and charged his son, Titus, with the task of quashing the Jewish revolt at its very core, Jerusalem.

The result was a siege that lasted 143 days. The coup de grace was a siege wall erected by the Romans to prevent Jews from escaping the city. "Starvation and factional infighting took a deadly toll upon the besieged Jews. The Antonia Fortress fell, and on August 6 sacrifice ceased in the temple. On the ninth of [Av] (August 28, A.D. 70) Roman troops torched the temple."[25] According to tradition, both the "First Temple" and the "Second Temple" were "destroyed on the ninth of the month of Av." The former destruction was by the Babylonians in 586 B.C. and the latter in A.D. 70.[26] The destruction of the Second Temple had been foretold by the Messiah Himself. Please read Luke 19:28-44.

What was the occasion described in Luke 19:28-40?

What was Jesus described as doing in Luke 19:41?

According to Luke 19:42, why?

What did Jesus specifically prophesy in Luke 19:43-44?

Though thousands of Jews had come to faith in Christ, the nation as a whole had not recognized the time of its visitation. In A.D. 70, eight tumultuous years after the violent death of James, the stones of the Temple came tumbling down. "By late September the siege of Jerusalem ended in a complete Roman victory. Titus took captive the Jewish survivors and later paraded them along with vessels taken from the temple in an official triumph before the people of Rome. Jewish prisoners were put to death in public spectacles celebrating the Roman victory. Engraved on the Arch of Titus standing in the Roman Forum today are the spoils of war carried from Jerusalem by Roman soldiers, including the Menorah and table of Showbread looted from the temple."[27]

Detail from Arch of Titus
Holman Bible Atlas, page 262

Remember week 1 and those three "pillars" in Galatians 2:9? Who gave Paul and Barnabas "the right hand of fellowship"?

By A.D. 70, two of those pillars had toppled as if Satan himself stood like Samson between them. Only one remained, and he'd find himself banished to the Island of Patmos. By then, all the other apostles had been counted worthy to die. There in exile, John could not have imagined the revelation he'd been spared to receive. Not long before his pen ran dry, he wrote these words:

> One of the seven angels ... came and spoke with me: "Come, I will show you the bride, the wife of the Lamb." He then carried me away in the Spirit to a great and high mountain and showed me the holy city, Jerusalem, coming down out of heaven from God, arrayed with God's glory. Her radiance was like a very precious stone, like a jasper stone, bright as crystal. The city had a massive high wall, with 12 gates. Twelve angels were at the gates; the names of the 12 tribes of Israel's sons were inscribed on the gates. There were three gates on the east, three gates on the north, three gates on the south, and three gates on the west. The city wall had 12 foundations, and the 12 names of the Lamb's 12 apostles were on the foundations (Rev. 21:9-14).

As the Lamb declared, "I will build My church, and the forces of Hades will not overpower it" (Matt. 16:18).

The **NEXT LEVEL** with Melissa

SO, WHO TOOK THE REINS?

With Paul's arrest, James' premature death, and the impending destruction of Jerusalem, we might naturally forget the church James left behind. Who would shepherd and advocate for these saints (many who were poor) in the wake of James' death?

Just as we have no record of James' death, we have no New Testament record of succession in the Jerusalem church. But church historian Eusebius passed down a list of Jerusalem bishops, a list he apparently retrieved himself from the Jerusalem church's records.[1]

I want to make mention of the second name on the list, directly after our James: Συμεὼν (Simeon or Symeon). Apparently he was the son of Clopas, brother of Joseph (our James' father). If you're tracking with me, this means that the Simeon who took leadership of the Jerusalem church after James was his *first cousin.* That's right, several ancient writers contend that another relative of Jesus led the Jerusalem church after James.

We don't know a lot about Simeon, and that which we do know comes from Hegesippus, writing in the second century. His information is not completely reliable. At times he can be quite sensational, but Hegesippus somehow had access to Palestinian Jewish Christian tradition, and even Eusebius relies on him for his history of ancient Jewish Christianity.[2]

Historian Richard Bauckham, says, "the reliable information about Symeon's death is probably that he was arrested on a charge of political subversion, as a Davidide supporter and relative of Jesus the alleged Davidic king, and was tortured and crucified in the reign of Trajan and under a governor called Atticus."[3] Bauckham suggests that he may have presided over the church shortly after James' death in 62 A.D. until his martyrdom roughly 40 years later.[4]

We hear nothing of Simeon in the New Testament, but if this piece of historical information is reliable, it suggests an impulse among the Jerusalem church to bestow leadership on Jesus' relatives. That is pretty cool if you ask me. If I'd lived then, I'd have done just about anything to meet Jesus' cousin. I'd want to hear every detail about him, especially the stories passed down in the family. Those are always the best stories, after all.

The involvement of Jesus' relatives in the earliest church testifies to the power of His life, death, and resurrection. No doubt Jesus sometimes baffled and disquieted His family. But when all was said and done, they were out on the front lines, in Jerusalem no less.

Many of us have been in the household of God for a really long time. Life in Christ has become too domesticated. Maybe what we need to know is that members of Jesus' own family eventually found Him so irresistible that they gave their lives to and for His mission.

No one is like Jesus, no one so compelling. In the stunning words of Jude, brother of our James and half brother of our glorious Lord Jesus Christ: "To those who are called, wrapped in the love of God the Father and kept for Jesus Christ. May mercy, peace, and love be lavished on you! To the only God our Savior through Jesus Christ our Lord, be glory, majesty, power, and authority, before all time, and now, and for all eternity. Amen" (Jude 1-2,25, NET).

Day Four

LIVING STONES

FLASH FORWARD

"You yourselves, as living stones, are being built into a spiritual house for a holy priesthood to offer spiritual sacrifices acceptable to God through Jesus Christ." 1 Peter 2:5

Our time is going so fast that I can hardly bear it! Only two more days until we say good-bye. Let's make the most of them, Sister. We are currently seeking historical, chronological answers to the question, *So, what happened next?* Let's get our minds refocused and back in the context we established in our previous lesson. Yesterday's time line ushered us to A.D. 70 when something of tremendous significance happened.

What was it?

Jesus predicted this dramatic event around A.D. 30, and the documentation to prove it resides in all three Synoptic Gospels. Mark 13:1-2 contains the most vivid wording for visual learners, so let's set our gaze on those two verses. Bubbling over with fervor, one of the disciples called Jesus to look at several specific objects.

What were they?

To be sure we draw the most obvious link to our previous lesson, how did Jesus respond in Mark 13:2?

To fully appreciate the odds against any such fulfillment, absorb these dimensions: "The temple was constructed of blocks of white limestone that measured 37.5 feet long, 12 feet high, and 18 feet wide. Some of the remaining blocks weigh nearly 400 tons."[28] Add the daunting majesty of Herod's temple, heightening the horror of Christ's prediction. Maybe this rabbinic saying from that time period captures it best: "Whoever has not beheld Herod's building … has not seen anything beautiful in his life."[29] The gleaming eyeful took 46 years to complete and, even up until A.D. 66, embellishments were added to it.[30]

Lock in on the very next verse, Mark 13:3, where Jesus had made His way over to the Mount of Olives. Even today the panoramic view of the old city is never more breathtaking than from that exact spot, perched 300 feet above it.[31] Today, if you and I could huddle on that steep hill together, we'd

The panoramic view of the old city is never more breathtaking than from the exact spot where Jesus made His way to the Mount of Olives.

look upon the Islamic Dome of the Rock where Herod's temple once loomed. We can only imagine how spectacular the sight must have been, wrapped around a luminous wonder of the ancient world.

Which disciples approached Jesus privately?
(See Mark 13:3-4.)

Keep in mind that this "James" is the brother of the apostle John and not our protagonist. At this point in history, our James remained an unbeliever.

Tell us, when will these things happen? And what will be the sign when all these things are about to take place?
MARK 13:4

What two questions did the disciples ask Jesus in Mark 13:4?

1.

2.

The next many verses project Christ's focus on the second question but, for a while, the first one hangs in the air like a thick, ominous cloud. Over those intensifying moments, His prophecies were so disturbing, His disciples might have all but forgotten the first question without Mark 13:14.

What did Jesus say to do "when you see the abomination that causes desolation standing where it should not"?

Hold onto that slice of instruction because we'll circle back to it in just a few moments. Matthew's version (24:15) identifies the location of this abomination as the "holy place," so that's how we know that this prediction ties to the Temple. As is masterfully true regarding numerous prophecies, the reference to abominations in the Temple would find some measure of fulfillment both sooner and later. Its zenith would be much later in the time of great tribulation, a time still to come. The very Temple Jesus and His four disciples looked upon that day from the Mount of Olives would be desolate much sooner, however. We tacked it onto the end of our time line yesterday at A.D. 70.

Stay alert because this is the point where we'll start putting these pieces together. Reflect carefully on our time line and fasten your attention to A.D. 66.

Did you document what happened that year? What was it?

As you glance back at the event in A.D. 66, recall my earlier statement about ornamentation being added to the Temple even up to that very year. It increases the painful irony.

The Jewish revolt placed them squarely on the battlefield against the goliath Rome. Once the emperor set his sights on Jerusalem, and no doubt the Temple itself, many believers recalled Christ's prophesy in Mark 13:14, "Those in Judea must flee to the mountains!" They took Christ's words as a direct order and, according to the early Christian historian Eusebius, many Jerusalem Christians fled to the Decapolis city of Pella.[32]

Some of those fleeing would have come from James' congregation since he was martyred only four short years before the revolt. Among those would have been leaders faced with taking the reins James once held. They likely would have seen themselves as bishops over a people in exile. Remember the question before us in both yesterday's lesson and today's: *After James' death, what happened next? After the destruction of the Temple, what happened next?* The piece of information regarding the escape to Pella is vital to us because it offers one of our only hints toward relocating that early band of Jewish Christians from Jerusalem.

Remember that Peter was one of the four disciples who asked Christ when the events regarding the Temple would occur. We can assume Peter lived long enough to experience the Jewish revolt in A.D. 66 because it almost certainly contributed to his martyrdom. We approximated his death on yesterday's time line at A.D. 67. Peter did not live long enough to see the Temple destroyed or to agonize over the news celebrated in Rome. Yet read this carefully: No one on earth received more divine insight than he regarding the rebuilding plan of a dwelling place for God's presence, a place where stone would once again be stacked upon stone. The very thought of it could put tears in my eyes.

No one on earth received more divine insight than Peter regarding the rebuilding plan of a dwelling place for God's presence, a place where stone would be once again stacked upon stone.

Peter most likely wrote his first letter somewhere between A.D. 62–64.[33] With all the background we've gathered in today's lesson, please read and relish 1 Peter 2:4-10.

How is Christ depicted in verse 6?

What two-word term did Peter give to believers in Christ in verse 5? "You yourselves, as ...

What exactly were they (and are we!) being "built into"?

What insight or inspiration does 1 Peter 2:5,9 bring to your faith walk?

Oh, Sister, do you see it? You and I opened our seven-week journey talking about Christ's ministry as the God-man here on earth, about how His own brothers didn't believe Him, how He was arrested and crucified and, then, how He was raised from the dead. Then we learned that it was there in the shadow of an empty tomb that James, the half brother of Jesus, encountered the glorious, resurrected Lord and was forever changed.

After Christ ascended from the Mount of Olives, we saw James gathered in the upper room along with the disciples, his other brothers, and his mother. Then, we beheld the birth of the New Testament church in the Book of Acts and saw thousands added to their numbers.

The winds of persecution scattered the seeds of Christianity all over Judea and Samaria. The words Tertullian would write almost two centuries later had already proven true: "The oftener we are mown down by you, the more in number we grow; *the blood of Christians is seed.*"[34]

James remained behind and sprang to life as the most prominent leader in the Jerusalem church. He, Peter, and John gave Paul and Barnabas the right hand of fellowship and sent them forth to proclaim the gospel to the Gentiles. Handshake would turn to arm wrestling and arm wrestling back to handshake as Jew and Gentile struggled to find five feet of common ground between the outstretched palms of Christ. This was nascent Christianity.

Within the splintering walls of that infant crib, James lived piously, faithfully, prayerfully, ... and dangerously. Planted in the soil of a city set on a hill, he felt the underground rumblings of a resentful nation, raring to cast off a Roman yoke. He saw the oppression of the poor, felt the pangs of famine, and knew those scorched by the fires of persecution. *And he said so.* He walked a threadbare tightrope between those who lived by the law and those who died by the law. He heard brother speak against brother and vengeance threatened between neighbors. *And he said so.* He called the church to order in a city sick of order. He was loved and revered and, therefore, reviled and feared.

James' presence in Jerusalem would ultimately be the death of him but not the death of his message. It, too, would later seem to experience an odd sort of resurrection. Four years after James was martyred, the revolt would begin and Rome would respond with a vengeance.

One by one those earliest followers of Christ would die, either by the hand of their own countrymen or by the long, winding whip of Rome. The events of A.D. 70 leave you and me in our imaginations huddled up together on the Mount of Olives, looking over what was left of the holy city.

Here at the tail end of the time line from the era in which James lived, Jerusalem is left in shambles, and the Temple bearing the footprints of Messiah Jesus is in ashes.

Yet before a single stone was thrown to the ground, a cornerstone was set in place. Upon it rolled one living stone after another so that, by the time the sanctuary built by human hands was destroyed, another constructed by God's hand was under way. But, this time, no forbidding wall would wrap around it. The gospel would reverberate to the corners of the earth and, at its quake, rocks of every sort would roll uphill to find their home upon the Chief Cornerstone.

You are no longer foreigners and strangers, but **fellow citizens with the saints,** and **members of God's household,** built on the foundation of the apostles and prophets, **with Christ Jesus Himself as the cornerstone.** The whole building, being put together by Him, grows into a holy sanctuary in the Lord. You also are being built together for God's dwelling in the Spirit.

Ephesians 2:19-22

Look really closely with your mind's eye, Sister, and gaze further and further up that heap until you make it to the stack where the 21st century sets in place. See us? You and me?

There we are, two living stones.

The **NEXT LEVEL** with Melissa

THE LEGACY OF JAMES

Today Mom shared historical information about what may have happened to the Jerusalem congregation after the destruction of the Temple. Sadly, the ancient writers don't tell us nearly all we'd like about what became of the Jerusalem church. We don't know what shape the congregation ended up taking nor do we know if, or for how long, it maintained its distinctly Jewish character.

We do know that the Jerusalem church, in exile, no longer carried the same kind of clout in the worldwide Christian movement that it did in James' day. As John Painter suggests, Simeon probably could not fill James' shoes.[1] The Jerusalem church undoubtedly lost influence also due to physical distance from Jerusalem.

Residing in the holy city, in spite of its risks, had been an advantage for the Jewish Christian community, allowing it to maintain relationship with the Jewish community there and to rub shoulders with the Jews from the Diaspora on pilgrimage to the Temple. The bishops of Jerusalem in exile could never exercise the same kind of influence that James had in the wider Jesus movement.[2]

That the Jerusalem church markedly changed without James' leadership doesn't surprise me. For crying out loud, I'm even anxious about what my own world will look like without the daily challenge of his voice. I find myself dragging out this final segment because I'm not ready to let him go.

When we began this study we noticed that James, with just one epistle and relatively few mentions in the New Testament, is often wrongly assumed to have been a marginal figure in the early church. We've learned along the way, that, in his own day, James was arguably as prominent as both Peter and Paul. In spite of our initial underestimate of James' importance in the earliest church, it turns out that the figure of James quickly became legendary in early Christian literature and tradition. For example, Painter explains: "Apart from God, who is righteous, and Jesus Christ the righteous, righteousness is associated more with James than with any other early Christian figure; in fact 'Righteous' became his defining title or characteristic."[3]

This famous title for James can be accurately translated into English as either *just* or *righteous* and points to both his faithfulness and his unjust suffering as a martyr. James' popularity in early Christianity is obvious from the sizable amount of literature devoted to his character. Although much of this literature is legendary rather than historical, the vastness of it certainly attests to his extensive reputation in the church especially up through the fifth century.[4]

James' legacy doesn't end in the fifth century, however, it continues with and in us. As we end our journey together, I'd like to share two final things I'm left reflecting on.

First, James challenges me to think more theologically about salvation history, especially the implications of Jesus' mission for ethnic Israel. Wherever we find him, whether James is speaking before a council in Jerusalem or writing saints dispersed abroad, he is reconciling God's Word through the people and prophets of old with the fresh new thing God has done through Jesus.

James courageously faces the present and although his feet are in step with God's Spirit, they are also firmly grounded in the past. Something is so compelling about rootedness, especially when it is driven by faith and conviction instead of fear and nostalgia. Over 100 years ago F.J.A. Hort made the colorful assessment about the Epistle of James.

> Again and again the wild dream of a "Christianity without Judaism" has risen up with attractive power. But the Epistle of St. James marks in the most decisive way the continuity of the two Testaments. In some obvious aspects it is like a piece of the O.T. appearing in the midst of the N.T.; and yet not out of place, or out of date, for it is most truly of the N.T. too.[5]

James' religion is one that achieves a daunting task. It effortlessly combines themes in the Old and New Covenants, with a remarkable amount of ease and grace. Simply put, the faith James works out is Judaism perfected and fulfilled by the life and wisdom of Jesus. This leads to my second and final point.

James illustrates what it means to embody the life and wisdom of Jesus. My former teacher made a habit of saying something I've never forgotten. He said, "You know that you've successfully understood an author when you're able to express his ideas using your own language." This is so true in the case of James and his relationship to the sayings of Jesus.

While we could identify some 20 or more possible parallels and allusions to traditions in Matthew's Gospel in James, curiously he never quotes Jesus directly. Most of the time James simply echoes images or themes from these teachings. James isn't spitting out a quick proof text or recording sayings of Jesus for historical record; he has absorbed Jesus' traditions into his very being.

The words of Jesus are so deeply implanted in James that he effuses them creatively in his own unique circumstances. This word embedded in James is a catalyst for him to create his own sayings but in the same tenor and tone of Jesus' voice.

This is the bottom line for me. If you asked me what I want to take with me from James, it's this. I want the life and wisdom of Jesus to so transform me that even when I'm not deliberately referencing a Bible verse, I remind someone of Jesus.

Well, here we are, sisters and friends. The journey has been one crazy ride and an unfathomable privilege. I do hope you've had some great discussions, and maybe even a few "spirited" debates along the way. After all, isn't working out the hard stuff in context of community what this thing is all about?

Thank you from the bottom of my heart for graciously hearing me out over these past seven weeks. I've never done this before, so I'm grateful you generously extended your time, patience, and mercy. As I type these few remaining words I recall the final sentence in the first book I ever read on James. I bawled my head off, which isn't my typical emotional state when I finish an academic book. It's usually more like a huge sigh of relief. I knew then I would be hooked on James for life.

That book was written by John Painter and he closed by saying: "The last word then is James the Just, James the faithful, James the righteous."[6]

I can't help but echo his sentiment. So too, my tiny little place in this story ends here with just James.

Day Five

WHAT HAPPENS NEXT?

FLASH FORWARD

"As for you, continue in what you have learned and firmly believed." 2 Timothy 3:14

Oh, Sister, glare with me at what day it is: *week 7, day 5.* We've reached the finish line. Don't you wish we were together right now? Man, I do! Celebrating would be so appropriate. A seven-week, in-depth Bible study journey is no small accomplishment for people like us, fastidiously trained by our culture to have a severe allergy to delayed gratification and the attention span of a fruit fly.

I think God might be proud of us today. He delights in any joy springing from the well of His Spirit. As long as we kick it up with grateful and humble hearts, I think He'd tell us to throw a feast in His honor and have a blast.

To Christ's great credit, we did not quit.

All that said, I'm sitting here in tears. I hate to admit to that if you've done any of the other studies because I am almost positive that this is the 14th time I've confessed to crying on the last day. I planned not to this time, but I will miss the intensity with God so much. And I will miss you. We put ourselves out there and let our minds, hearts, actions, and doctrines be challenged. *Messed with* might be more like it. To Christ's great credit, we did not quit. As we reach our final day, James might say that we let "endurance … do its complete work" (1:4).

You get to have your own reactions to reaching this wrap-up. Feeling a tad melancholy does not make any of us an iota more spiritual than the others who want to clap their hands and high-five over the finished work. By all means, feel whatever you feel, but share those feelings here as a healthy means of debriefing.

How would you describe your finishing feelings?

Perhaps you've heard the old saying that impression without expression causes depression. Let's make sure you get ample time today to express what God has impressed upon you through our journey. Let's look back and, then, at the end we'll look forward.

Early this morning, I spoke the words of the Epistle of James to God as I have many times over previous months. This time, however, I said it slowly so that principles, concepts, and images of many things we've learned together would float to the surface of my conscious mind. It was such a rich way to wrap up the experience that I wonder if you'd do something similar. If you have 15–20 extra minutes, stop right here and read all 5 chapters of the Book of James to God and out loud if at all possible.

If you worked at a level 3, turn to the back of your book and read it from your own handwriting. If you're working toward level 5, say as much of it as possible from memory and read the remainder. If you don't have the extra time today, then just glance back over the epistle and let your eyes scan the page, asking the Holy Spirit to remind you of what Christ has taught you (see John 14:26). Each of the larger rectangles below represents a chapter of the Book of James.

Write the Scripture reference and the concept that stood out to you most and, as much as space allows, why it resonated.

Now, focus your attention on the long, narrow rectangle beneath the others. It represents the impact of James, the person. Flip through week 1 and week 7 of our study and glance at your viewer guides for sessions 1 and 2. What about James' life impacted you most as you reflect on our journey and why?

Write your answers in the rectangle.

After devoting so much of his life work to James and his message, Dr. James B. Adamson wrote a synopsis of the epistle that nearly moved me to my feet.

> The real rub is that this brusque but bracing book "finds us," drives us from the balcony to the road, and hounds us out of intellectualism, mysticism, and dogmatism into a real, living, existential world where, with a hand on our throats, we are hurled into the moment of decision. Why is this? The answer must be the closeness of Jesus to each one of us, in our sorrow, pain, loneliness, darkness and tempest, temptation, hunger and thirst, disappointment, sin and rejection. James parcels up for us the vitals of our earthy existence with Jesus Christ.[35]

Ah, yes. We are hurled into the moment of decision. The last few days of our study have focused on a time line from A.D. 62–70 as we history nuts sought to answer the ongoing question, *So what happened next?*

We looked at what happened next, once James was out of the picture. We then looked at what happened next, once the Jews rebelled against Rome and the Temple was destroyed. Now we move from the historical to the personal and from past tense to present. We marvel at all God accomplished through James and his contemporaries but, glance over your shoulder. They're nowhere to be found. Neither are those who followed closely on their heels.

So, fellow sojourner, what happens next ... with you?

We and our generations of believers are on the top of the heap of living stones right now. We are the building blocks of Christ's church in this era. The next stack is meant to stand on our shoulders. After my track record, the thought haunts me over and over that God either has endless grace or odd taste. Whether or not we would have chosen us, He did. The question we've asked of history now spins the sundial straight toward us: *So, fellow sojourner, what happens next . . . with you?*

With all we've learned and as our series concludes, what now? Will we simply have another study under our belts or will we have Scripture in our bones? What happens next with us? I can tell you a few things I hope happen next with me. I hope to refuse myself the luxury of ever again having a fait talk that exceeds my faith walk. What I live is what I really believe. Period.

I hope to have a heart filled with faith and expectancy when I ask God for wisdom, knowing that He delights to give it. I hope to resist the magnetic pull of this temporal world to shrink my life into a wilting wildflower in a dying meadow. I want to live for what endures. I want to live for Jesus.

And, Lord, help me, I want to persevere in trials, sufferings, and persecutions, and not whine myself into a pathetic lather. For once in my life, I want to know what it's like to count it all joy when I fall into all sorts of difficulty. When deformed desires surface in this flawed heart of mine, I want to rush them to Jesus and request His swift healing. I want to watch my mouth, for crying out loud. Don't you? Our religion is utterly futile if we don't.

I want to keep the poor on my radar at all times and stop protecting myself from the pain and plight of others. Don't you? I want to love my neighbor as myself. I want to live in full expectancy of the glorious return of our Savior Jesus Christ. I want to pray more for the sick. Don't you? OK, I'll catch my breath and let you take this one over for a little while.

What do *you* want to do in light of what you've learned?

Oh, Jesus, help us. Indwelling Holy Spirit, make us who, without You, we are not. Abba Father, do not let us get away with meaningless living. Rescue us from mirroring the image of this grotesquely disfigured world. Do not let up on us until we've done Your will. As James himself said, help us to "think of how we regard as blessed those who have endured" (5:11, NET). This moment we sit before you dying to live differently. Help our unbelief. Do this through us, Jesus.

Why don't you go back to that diagram and write your full name over the top rectangle as a reminder of all God has invested in you? As I say goodbye, please permit me the space to say thank you to two very special people. Melissa, Darling, I'm scrambling for words big enough to thank you enough for your vision for this project and your titanic investment. Our Sister would not be holding this book in her sweet hands without you. What a journey we've had! What learning, wrestling, wrangling, debating, laughing, nodding, and rejoicing we've experienced. I'll never forget it. I respect and love you and Amanda so much.

The second person I wish so much to thank is you, Sister. My heart is so moved, it hurts. Bless you for the gift of your companionship. Without picturing you on the other side of it, I wonder if I'd ever have finished it. Stay in the Word, Sister. Knees to the floor, eyes to the skies. OK, then. Let's go out with one last quote.

> Who is this tremendous personality who speaks to the whole Church with a voice that expects no challenge or dispute? Who appeals to no authority but that of God, knows no superior but the Lord Himself, quotes examples only from the great ones of the Old Dispensation, instructs, chides, encourages, denounces with a depth, an energy, a fire, second to none in the whole range of sacred literature?[36]

That's our James.

viewer guide | session eight

James 5:19-20

Today we close our journey together through the life and Book of James. As a tribute to his message and ministry, we'll return to the last sentence that dripped from his passionate pen.

Note 5:19 in the ESV: "My brothers, if anyone among you wanders from the truth and someone brings him back …"

1. **Anyone ______ ____________.**

wander—Greek *planethe*

2. **God watches for ______________ willing to __________ him or her __________.**

Caution: Our narcissistic culture makes it easy to _________ the concept of ________________ into a practice Jesus didn't teach.

Consider the following:

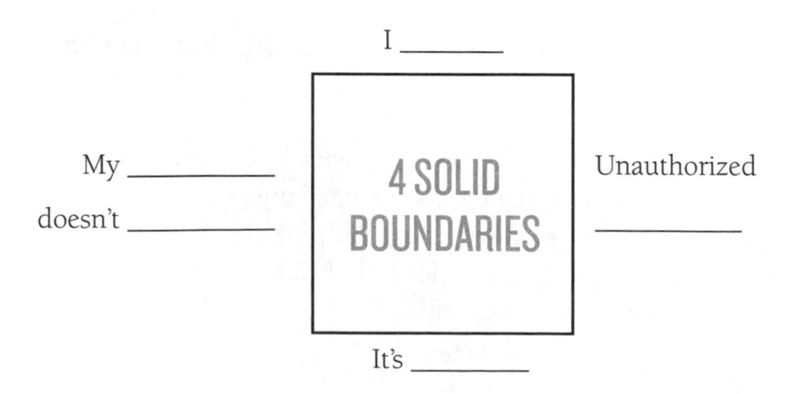

Nehemiah 9:20-22 (Message) concludes with a beautiful guideline:

"You gave them your good Spirit to teach them to live wisely. You never stinted with your manna, gave them plenty of water to drink. You supported them forty years in the desert; they had everything they needed; their clothes didn't wear out and their feet never blistered. You gave them kingdoms and peoples, establishing ____________ ____________."

3. ______one + ______one = A ______ for ___________one

Series conclusion ...

Handwrite the Book of James

JAMES 1

JAMES 2

JAMES 3

JAMES 4

Has God used this handwriting process in your personal life in any notable or surprising way? If so, please share it and be as specific as possible.

ENDNOTES

WEEK 1

1. Scott Korb, *Life in One Year* (New York: Riverhead Books, 2010), 64.
2. Ibid., 22.
3. Ibid., 71.
4. Ibid., 74.
5. Ibid., 83.
6. Ibid.
7. Adapted from John Donne, *Devotions Upon Emergent Occasions* (New York: Oxford University Press, 1987), 87.
8. Scot McKnight, *The NIV Application Commentary: Galatians* (Grand Rapids, MI: Zondervan, 1995), 75–6.
9. F. F. Bruce, *The New International Greek Testament Commentary: The Epistle to the Galatians* (Grand Rapids, MI: Wm. B. Eerdmans Publishing Co., 1982), 89.
10. Richard Longnecker, *Word Biblical Commentary*, vol. 41, *Galatians* (Colombia: Nelson Reference & Electronic, 1990), 57.
11. F. F. Bruce, *The Book of the Acts* (Grand Rapids, MI: Wm. B. Eerdmans Publishing Co., 1988), 239.
12. Ibid., 293.
13. Ajith Fernando, *The NIV Application Commentary: Acts* (Grand Rapids, MI: Zondervan, 1998), 418.
14. Ibid., 419.
15. Bruce, *Book of the Acts*, 297.
16. John Polhill, *The New American Commentary*, vol. 26, *Acts* (Nashville, TN: Broadman & Holman Publishers, 2001), 336.

WEEK 2

1. Ralph P. Martin, *Word Biblical Commentary*, vol. 48, *James* (Nashville, TN: Thomas Nelson Publishers, 1988), 11.
2. Patrick J. Hartin, *Sacra Pagina Series*, vol. 14, *James* (Collegeville, MN: Liturgical Press, 2009), 57.
3. Martin, *Word Biblical Commentary*, vol. 48, 14.
4. *The Expositor's Bible Commentary*, vol. 12, *Hebrews-Revelation* (Grand Rapids, MI: Zondervan, 1981), 168.
5. David P. Nystrom, *The NIV Application Commentary: James* (Grand Rapids, MI: Zondervan, 1997), 47.
6. James B. Adamson, *James: The Man and His Message* (Grand Rapids, MI: Wm. B. Eerdmans Publishing Co., 1989), 318.
7. Peter H. Davids, *The Epistle of James* (Grand Rapids, MI: Wm. B. Eerdmans Publishing Co., 1982), 68.
8. *Hebrew-Greek Key Word Study Bible: New International Version* (Chattanooga, TN: AMG Publishers, 1996), 1677–78.
9. Wendell Berry, *Hannah Coulter* (Washington, D.C.: Shoemaker & Hoard, 2004), 21–22.
10. *Expositor's Bible Commentary*, vol. 12, 169.
11. Ibid.
12. Craig L. Blomberg and Mariam J. Kamell, *Exegetical Commentary on the New Testament: James* (Grand Rapids, MI: Zondervan, 2008), 53.
13. Kurt A. Richardson, *The New American Commentary*, vol. 36, *James* (Nashville, TN: Broadman & Holman Publishers, 1997), 68.
14. Ibid., emphasis added.
15. Blomberg and Kamell, *Exegetical Commentary*, 55.
16. Richardson, *New American Commentary*, vol. 36, 80–81.
17. Thomas à Kempis, *The Imitation of Christ* quoted in James B. Adamson, *The New International Commentary on the New Testament: The Epistle of James* (Grand Rapids, MI: Wm. B. Eerdmans Publishing Co., 1976), 72.
18. Adamson, *New International Commentary*, 73.
19. *Hebrew-Greek Key Word*, 1677.

WEEK 3

1. Sharon Jayson, "2010: The year technology replaced talking," USA Today [online], 30 December 2010 [cited 9 August 2011]. Available from the Internet: *www.usatoday.com.*
2. Adamson, *New International Commentary*, 79.
3. Ibid., 78.
4. Nystrom, *NIV Application Commentary*, 91.
5. Ibid., 92.
6. *Hebrew-Greek Key Word*, 1676.
7. Dan G. McCartney, *Baker Exegetical Commentary on the New Testament: James* (Grand Rapids, MI: Baker Academic, 2009), 118.
8. Blomberg and Kamell, *Exegetical Commentary*, 91.
9. For more information on *genesis*, see Martin, *Word Biblical Commentary*, vol. 48, 11; Adamson, *New International Commentary*, 82–83; and McCartney, *Baker Exegetical Commentary*, 121.
10. Davids, *The Epistle of James*, 99–100.
11. Nystrom, *NIV Application Commentary*, 95.
12. Ibid.
13. McCartney, *Baker Exegetical Commentary*, 123.
14. Mark Twain, *Letters From the Earth* (New York: Crest Books, 1963), 179–80.
15. *Merriam-Webster's Collegiate® Dictionary*, 10th ed. (Springfield, MA: Merriam-Webster, Incorporated, 1997), 988.
16. Adapted from Douglas J. Moo, *The Letter of James* (Grand Rapids, MI: Wm. B. Eerdmans Publishing Co., 2000), 96.
17. Peter Rhea Jones, "Approaches to the Study of the Book of James," quoted in Adamson, *James*, viii.
18. Anne Lamott, *Bird by Bird* (New York: Anchor Books, 1995), 22.
19. Adapted from Martin, *Word Biblical Commentary*, vol. 48, 57.
20. Blomberg and Kamell, *Exegetical Commentary*, 107.
21. Nystrom, *NIV Application Commentary*, 116.
22. Davids, *The Epistle of James*, 112.
23. Adamson, *New International Commentary*, 115.
24. Blomberg and Kamell, *Exegetical Commentary*, 117.

WEEK 4

1. Martin, *Word Biblical Commentary,* vol. 48, 80.
2. Adamson, *New International Commentary,* 126.
3. Ibid.
4. Nystrom, *NIV Application Commentary*, 153.
5. *Expositor's Bible Commentary,* vol. 12, 169.
6. Moo, *The Letter of James,* 144.
7. Ibid.
8. Ibid., 165.
9. *The Expositor's Bible Commentary,* vol. 2, *Genesis-Numbers* (Grand Rapids, MI: Zondervan Publishing House, 1990), 398.
10. Ibid., 399.

WEEK 5

1. Richardson, *New American Commentary,* vol. 36, 173.
2. Moo, *The Letter of James,* 171.
3. Martin, *Word Biblical Commentary,* vol. 48, 146.
4. McCartney, *Baker Exegetical Commentary,* 207.
5. *Expositor's Bible Commentary,* vol. 12, 193.
6. Moo, *The Letter of James,* 192.
7. Ibid., 199.
8. McCartney, *Baker Exegetical Commentary,* 226.
9. Moo, *The Letter of James,* 205.

WEEK 6

1. Richardson, *New American Commentary,* vol. 36, 207.
2. Davids, *The Epistle of James,* 177.
3. Martin, *Word Biblical Commentary,* vol. 48, 180.
4. Ibid., 182.
5. Richardson, *New American Commentary,* vol. 36, 226.
6. Blomberg and Kamell, *Exegetical Commentary,* 236.
7. Adamson, *New International Commentary,* 195.
8. *Expositor's Bible Commentary,* vol. 12, 203.
9. Luke Timothy Johnson, *The Anchor Bible,* vol. 37, *The Letter of James* (New Haven, CT: Yale University Press/Doubleday, 1995), 325.
10. Horatio G Spafford, "It Is Well with My Soul."
11. Isidore Singer, ed., *The Jewish Encyclopedia,* vol. 7, *Italy-Leon* (London: Funk & Wagnalls Company, 1904), 68.
12. Johnson, *The Anchor Bible*, 330.

WEEK 7

1. Ronald Brownrigg, *Who's Who in the Bible?* (New York: Bonanza Books, 1980), 150.
2. *The Expositor's Bible Commentary,* vol. 9, *John-Acts* (Grand Rapids, MI: Zondervan Publishing House, 1981), 519.
3. Ibid.
4. Ibid., 519–20.
5. "Procurator," *Holman Illustrated Bible Dictionary* (Nashville, TN: Holman Bible Publishers, 2003), 1131.
6. Martin, *Word Biblical Commentary,* vol. 48, lxii.
7. Ibid., lxiii.
8. Ibid.
9. Ibid.
10. Ibid., lxv.
11. Adamson, *James,* 42.
12. Scot McKnight, *The New International Commentary on the New Testament: James* (Grand Rapids, MI: Wm. B. Eerdmans Publishing Co., 2011), 21.
13. Ibid.
14. Martin, *Word Biblical Commentary,* vol. 48, lxiii.
15. Ibid.
16. Brownrigg, *Who's Who,* 153.
17. William Whitson, trans., *The Complete Works of Josephus* (Grand Rapids, MI: Kregel Publications, 1999), 656.
18. Ibid.
19. Gary Poulton, "Nero," *Holman Illustrated Bible Dictionary* (Nashville, TN: Holman Bible Publishers, 2003), 1186–87.
20. Charles L. Quarles, "Paul," *Holman Illustrated Bible Dictionary* (Nashville, TN: Holman Bible Publishers, 2003), 1259–60.
21. John Foxe, *The New Foxe's Book of Martyrs* (North Brunswick, NJ: Bridge-Logos Publishers, 1997), 7.
22. Thomas V. Brisco, *Holman Bible Atlas* (Nashville, TN: Broadman & Holman Publishers, 1998), 260.
23. Poulton, "Nero," 1187.
24. Bricso, *Holman Bible Atlas,* 258.
25. Ibid., 261.
26. "Destruction of Temple," *The Encyclopedia of Jewish Life and Thought* (Israel: Carta Jerusalem, 1996), 473.
27. Bricso, *Holman Bible Atlas,* 261–62.
28. *HCSB Study Bible* (Nashville, TN: Holman Bible Publishers, 2010), 1659.
29. Clinton E. Arnold, ed., *Zondervan Illustrated Bible Backgrounds Commentary,* vol. 1, *Matthew, Mark, Luke* (Grand Rapids, MI: Zondervan, 2002), 146–47.
30. Ibid., 147.
31. *HCSB Study Bible,* 1710.
32. Paul L. Maier, trans., *Eusebius: The Church History* (Grand Rapids, MI: Kregel Publications, 2007), 82.
33. *HCSB Study Bible,* 2147.
34. Alexander Roberts, James Donaldson, and Arthur Cleveland Coxe, eds., *The Ante-Nicene Fathers* (New York: Cosimo, 2007), 55.
35. Adamson, *James,* 486.
36. John Parry, *A Discussion of the General Epistle of St. James* (London: Cambridge University Press, 1903), 73.

ENDNOTES FROM MELISSA'S ARTICLES

WEEK 1

"James & The Nazirite Vow"

1. Bruce D. Chilton, "The Nazirite Vow and the Brother of Jesus," in *Torah Revealed, Torah Fulfilled* (New York: T&T Clark, 2008), 63.
2. Baruch A. Levine, "The Nazirite," in *Torah Revealed, Torah Fulfilled* (New York: T&T Clark, 2008), 45.
3. David E. Green, trans., *Theological Dictionary of the Old Testament,* vol. 9, *marad-naqa* (Grand Rapids, MI: Wm. B. Eerdmans Publishing Co., 1998), 307.

"Jerusalem Council, Part Two"

1. Richard Bauckham, *The Book of Acts in Its First Century Setting,* vol. 4, *Palestinian Setting* (Grand Rapids, MI: Wm. B. Eerdmans Publishing Co., 1995), 475.

WEEK 2

"The Epistle of Jacob"

1. Andreas J. Köstenberger, L. Scott Kellum, and Charles L. Quarles, *The Cradle, the Cross, and the Crown* (Nashville, TN: B&H Academic, 2009), 703.
2. John Painter, "Who Was James?" in *The Brother of Jesus* (Louisville, KY: Westminister John Knox Press, 2001), 11.
3. Hershel Shanks and Ben Witherington III, *The Brother of Jesus* (New York: HarperCollins, 2003), 97.

"The Genre of James"

1. E.D. Hirsch Jr., *Validity in Interpretation* (London: Yale University Press, 1967), 76.
2. Martin Dibelius, *James* (Philadelphia: Fortress Press, 1976), 1–11.
3. Luke Leuk Cheung, *The Genre, Composition and Hermeneutics of the Epistle of James* (Eugene, OR: Wipf & Stock Publishers, 2003).
4. Douglas J. Moo, *The Letter of James* (Grand Rapids, MI: Wm. B. Eerdmans Publishing Co., 2000), 1.
5. Cheung, *Genre, Composition and Hermeneutics,* 274.

WEEK 3

"Hearers, Not Just Readers"

1. Meir Bar-Ilan, "Illiteracy in the Land of Israel in the first centuries C.E.," [online], 27 May 1997 [cited 15 April 2011]. Available from the Internet: *http://faculty.biu.ac.il/~barilm/illitera.html*
2. Bruce M. Metzger and Bart D. Ehrman, *The Text of the New Testament,* 4th ed. (New York: Oxford University Press, 2005), 42–53.
3. L. Michael White, *Scripting Jesus* (New York: HarperCollins, 2010), 96.

"Implanted Word"

1. Frederick William Danker, ed., *A Greek-English Lexicon of the New Testament and Other Early Christian Literature,* 3rd ed. (Chicago: University of Chicago Press, 2000), 326.
2. Bart D. Ehrman, *After the New Testament* (New York: Oxford University Press, 1999), 103.
3. Danker, *Greek-English Lexicon,* 326.

"Perfect Law of Liberty"

1. Mariam Kamell, "The Word/Law in James as the Promised New Covenant" (paper presentation, Society of Biblical Literature Annual Meeting, Washington, D.C., November 19, 2006).

WEEK 4

"Unity & Diversity Dance"

1. Timothy George, " 'A Right Strawy Epistle': Reformation Perspectives on James," *Review and Expositor* 83 (1986): 373.
2. Ibid., 372–73.
3. Frank Thielman, *Theology of the New Testament* (Grand Rapids, MI: Zondervan, 2005), 41.
4. Ibid., 38.
5. Ibid., 40.

"Luther, Law & Gospel"

1. Carter Lindberg, *The European Reformations* (Malden, MA: Blackwell Publishing, 1996), 72–73.
2. Ibid.
3. Ibid.
4. Thomas M. McDonough, *The Law and the Gospel in Luther* (London: Oxford University Press, 1963), 1.
5. Markus Wriedt, "Luther's theology," trans. Katharina Gustavs in *The Cambridge Companion to Martin Luther* (New York: Cambridge University Press, 2003), 107.
6. Martin Luther, *Commentary on the Epistle to the Galatians,* trans. Theodore Graebner, 28.

"Gentleness & Wisdom"

1. Danker, *Greek-English Lexicon,* 861.
2. Moo, *The Letter of James,* 170.
3. Cheung, *Genre, Composition and Hermeneutics,* 158.

WEEK 5

"Perfection, Part One"

1. Mark Littleton and Jeanette Gardner Littleton, *What's in the Bible for Teens,* ed. Larry Richards (Minneapolis: Bethany House, 2007), 6.
2. Richard Bauckham, *James* (New York: Routledge, 1999), 73.

"Perfection, Part Two"

1. Anne Lamott, *Bird by Bird* (New York: Anchor Books, 1995), 28.
2. Patrick J. Hartin, *A Spirituality of Perfection* (Collegeville, MN: The Liturgical Press, 1999), 14–15.
3. Ibid., 15.
4. Moo, *The Letter of James,* 56.
5. Bauckham, *James,* 179.
6. Ibid., 182.
7. Ibid., 183–84.

WEEK 6

"The Elephant in the Room"

1. Moo, *The Letter of James,* 210.
2. Ibid., 221.

"The Old Testament & James 5:11b"

1. We know James invokes this formula because of his two attributes. The first πολύσπλαγχνος is a rare but close synonym of the adjective used in the LXX of Exodus 34:6 (πολυέλεος). The second, also rare in the GNT, is the exact word οἰκτίρμων (the only other usage in the GNT is in Luke 6:36).

WEEK 7

"Theology of the Collection"

1. Brendan Byrne, *Sacra Pagina Series,* vol. 6, *Romans* (Collegeville, MN: Liturgical Press, 1996), 441.
2. Douglas J. Moo, *The Epistle to the Romans* (Grand Rapids, MI: Wm. B. Eerdmans Publishing Co., 1996), 905.
3. James D.G. Dunn, *Word Biblical Commentary,* vol. 38A, *Romans 9-16* (Dallas: Word Books, 1988), 874–75.

"So, Who Took the Reins?"

1. Richard Bauckham, *Jude and the Relatives of Jesus in the Early Church* (New York: T&T Clark, 2004), 71–72.
2. Ibid., 79–80.
3. Ibid., 92.
4. Richard Bauckham, "James and the Jerusalem Community" in *Jewish Believers in Jesus* (Peabody, MA: Hendrickson Publishers, 2007), 91.

"The Legacy of James"

1. John Painter, *Just James* (Minneapolis: Fortress Press, 1999), 147.
2. Bauckham, "James," *Jewish Believers,* 80.
3. Painter, *Just James,* 276.
4. Ibid., 167.
5. Fenton John Anthony Hort, "Introduction" in *The Epistle of St. James.* Available from the Internet: *www.ccel.org*
6. Painter, *Just James,* 276.